Computing and Change on Campus

Computing and Change on Campus

Edited by

SARA KIESLER AND LEE SPROULL

Department of Social and Decision Sciences
Carnegie Mellon University

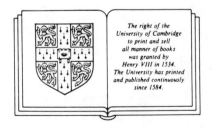

The right of the
University of Cambridge
to print and sell
all manner of books
was granted by
Henry VIII in 1534.
The University has printed
and published continuously
since 1584.

CAMBRIDGE UNIVERSITY PRESS

Cambridge
New York   New Rochelle   Melbourne   Sydney

Published by the Press Syndicate of the University of Cambridge
The Pitt Building, Trumpington Street, Cambridge CB2 1RP
32 East 57th Street, New York, NY 10022, USA
10 Stamford Road, Oakleigh, Melbourne 3166, Australia

© Cambridge University Press 1987

First published 1987

Printed in the United States of America

Library of Congress Cataloging-in-Publication Data
Computing and change on campus.
Includes index.
1. Computer-assisted instruction–United States–
Case studies.   2. Computer managed instruction–United
States–Case studies.   3. Education, Higher–United
States–Data processing–Case studies.   4. Computers–
Social aspects–United States–Case studies.
I. Kiesler, Sara B., 1940–   .   II. Sproull, Lee.
LB1028.5.C5747   1987   371.3'9445   87-12491
ISBN 0 521 34431 X

British Library Cataloguing in Publication applied for

Contents

v

Preface

In 1981 a university provost sketched for the readers of the *New York Times* what life in a dormitory room will be in 1989 (Van Horn, 1981).

Susan awoke to see her television tube staring back at her. Her tube displays not soap operas but output from the personal computer that Susan and all other Computer U freshmen had received upon enrolling three years ago. She keeps it next to her bed in her dorm room. Now, after three years, Susan still finds her computer exciting. It is more than essential; it is even a kind of "old friend" with whom she has shared moments of triumph after days of hard work.

As she has started most mornings, Susan returns from the shower in her bathrobe and turns on her computer to check the day's events. She types "MAIL," instructing her personal computer to collect via the cable any recent messages sent to her and to display a list of sender's names and topics. She saves for later two messages from her boyfriend and one from her mother (who has a terminal at home in New York) but decides she must read now the one from her English professor titled "URGENT." The professor's message reminds her: "The final version of your paper on Chaucer is overdue." Susan yawns, still not entirely awake, and types "REPLY" along with a message that she will submit the paper later that day. As she dries her hair, she quickly scans a display of the university calendar for the day, deciding to watch the women's soccer match that afternoon if she has time…

…After a heated debate over breakfast on woman's equality, she returns to her room to rewrite her Chaucer "paper" before 10 o'clock class. (The term "paper" is an anachronism since papers seldom are written on paper in 1989. Instead, they are composed on the personal computer using a text editor, and when completed, are sent electronically to the professor who reads them on a computer screen.) Susan asks the computer to display her draft, which had been returned yesterday with suggestions from her professor typed along the margins.

The administrator's vision of Susan and the personal computer she can't live without is widespread at colleges across the country. But it is not the only vision. In response to "Susan," this is how one student depicted computing in a dormitory room in 1989 (Novak, 1982):

Ralph looked blearily over toward the alarm clock. Nine A.M. He sat down at one of the four personal computer terminals across from the four beds in his 4 by 7 meter dorm room and attempted a log on. The terminal replied, "SYSTEM CRASH."

…The computer was up again when Ralph got back to his room. So were Bob and Andrew and Fred. Andrew had used his operator's clearance and was perusing other people's mail. Bob was begging core space from Fred to store a new game.

Fred shrugged his shoulders. "Do what you want. I'm going over to the Student Union to see what's happening."

"Why don't you just check the activities update file?" Andrew asked.

"It's too nice a day to just check the activities update file."

"The activities update file doesn't smell like Karen," Bob snickered.

Many people have strong feelings about computers. For some, they symbolize progress, productivity, and innovation. For others, they symbolize isolation and depersonalization of human relations. Often missing in discussions and arguments about the effects of computers are factual data. This book is meant to improve our understanding of what computers mean for organizations by presenting a collection of systematic research studies of the computerization of one university. It does not contain much speculation about the effects of advanced computer systems just now being developed. Nor does it contain retrospective analyses of the long-term social impact of past computer introductions. It offers some close descriptions of the social changes surrounding the introduction and expansion of computer technologies in one organization during the first half of the 1980s.

One benefit of a case study such as this one is that we can observe examples of technological and social changes in detail, which is an improvement over unsupported generalities such as "Computers isolate people," or "Computers are deskilling." One risk is that what we learn about a single institution is so specific as to time, place, and particular technology that we cannot generalize to other organizations. We have tried to reduce this risk by concentrating on social aspects of computerization that transcend particular technologies and organizational milieus.

The site of our research is Carnegie Mellon University (CMU), a small university with extensive computing. The concept of a "computer-intensive" campus was born at CMU in 1980. In 1982 CMU and IBM negotiated a joint-venture agreement to develop powerful computing workstations and network them together across the entire campus. Since that time a number of major events related to computing have occurred at CMU. By 1985, even before the joint-venture technology was deployed, CMU owned 2,800 computers; faculty and students owned hundreds of additional machines that they had purchased personally.

The joint venture with IBM was undertaken with the realization that, as a producer of knowledge, CMU should try to learn about the social, educational, and organizational changes surrounding the influx of new technology. The university established a committee that would conduct and support research on the social aspects of computing technology – the Committee on Social Science Research in Computing, the CSSRC. The committee decided not to conduct one large study of the planned network of powerful computers, but rather to investigate social aspects of computing generally on campus. Our reasoning: Unintended social and technological adaptations that surround the introduction of a new technology can be as important as the intended technology itself. If we had studied only the developments envisioned in the joint venture with IBM, we would have missed other significant changes such as the applications of computation to music and art, the automating of the library, the enormous popularity of personal computers to write papers, the student-built information systems — all uncharted changes that took place well before the joint-venture technology and network were completed. We used social science theory and research to help identify likely places to look for changes. This book reports many of our studies of computers on campus through 1985.

All of the research projects in this book reflect three premises. The first is that computing is a cultural and social phenomenon as well as a technical one. The second is that computers have much in common with other technical innovations that have had major social effects, such as tractors, typewriters, and telephones. We can, and should, learn from the histories of these other innovations. The third is that the social effects of technology are likely to be unanticipated, indirect, and difficult to predict. Therefore, diverse research on the many ways technology might change social interdependencies and interactions is likely to be more fruitful than would any large, preplanned evaluation study.

Our hoped-for audience is educators, business managers, and social scientists. One might wonder what useful information educators would get out of a book about a pioneering university. How could it possibly generalize to other schools? One contribution might be to suggest the advantages and costs of experimenting with new technology, and especially the scope of resources necessary to build an electronic community. CMU represents a prototype of possibility, along with what might be needed to do something like it. For business managers, we offer some examples of what life is like in a highly technological environment. We describe some ways people interact using computers, how new people learn what is going on, what pitfalls need to be avoided. For social scientists, the book is a multi-method case study of technological change in an organization, and to our knowledge, the only one of its kind. We do not present any of our experimental research in this volume, but the book illustrates a variety of other techniques and designs that can be employed in investigating the social consequences of technological change.

This book takes you on a tour of Carnegie Mellon University. Like most tours, this one isn't comprehensive and doesn't go everywhere; it goes to places that enlighten our theme, the social processes of computing and technological change. The tour spans four years, to offer a taste of change during a period of intensive computerization. And it visits many people, to show how different kinds of people use computers to do different things. Part I offers several perspectives on how to think about the social processes of computing and technological change, and a theoretical orientation to the tour. Part II describes three fundamental components of technological change: resources, behaviors, and attitudes, and how they changed over the period from 1981 to 1985. Part III is about effects on workers and managers. Part IV looks at students. Our tour of CMU ends with some reflections by the tour guides: a chapter that reviews some of what we have learned and how our observations contribute to a more general analysis of technological change. In that chapter we set our findings within the context of theories of organizational change. We also offer policy suggestions for those involved in creating and managing computer-intensive environments.

Acknowledgments

The research reported in this volume was sponsored by the Carnegie Mellon University Committee on Social Science Research in Computing, whose members are Sara Kiesler, Allen Newell, Herbert Simon, Lee Sproull, and Braden Walter. Financial support and intellectual encouragement for the research were provided by grants from IBM and the System Development Foundation to the CSSRC, from the CMU Robotics Institute, the National Science Foundation, and the National Institutes of Mental Health to Sara Kiesler, and from the Mellon Foundation and the System Development Foundation to Lee Sproull. The CMU Information Technology Center has supported part of the costs of writing this book. Arlene Simon typed the entire manuscript. Mike Blackwell produced camera ready copy from manuscript text files. The authors of the individual chapters have received expert advice and financial support from additional sources, which we acknowledge separately.

Chapter 1. An earlier version of this chapter was presented as a lecture in the Presidents' Distinguished Lecture Series, CMU, September 18, 1984. The photograph is by Bill Redic.

Chapter 2. This research was supported by grants from the Spencer Foundation, the Stanford Graduate School of Business, and the Hoover Institution. The author would like to thank Stanley Pogrow for comments on the manuscript. The photograph is courtesy of Carnegie Mellon University.

Chapter 3. The cartoon is from A MUCH, MUCH BETTER WORLD. Reprinted by Permission of Microsoft Press. Copyright © 1985 by Eldon Dedini. All Rights Reserved.

Chapter 4. The advice and help of the following persons were essential in gathering data for this chapter: Charles Augustine, Susan Herrod, Patrick Keating, Robert Macy, Robert Rudski, William Sholar, Jane Siegel, Arlene Simon, Lisa Wiedman. Diane Burton and Scott Obrosky served as undergraduate research assistants on this project. Kevin Kiesler designed the figures. In addition to the people listed above, we took suggestions from the following sources: *Preliminary Report on the Future of Computing at Carnegie Mellon University*, Report of the Task Force for the Future of Computing, Allen Newell

(Chair), February 28, 1982; *Research on Social Aspects of Computing at Carnegie Mellon University*, Report of the Committee on Social Science Research in Computing, January 1985; discussions held during meetings of the research group of the Committee on Social Science Research in Computing. The photograph is courtesy of Carnegie Mellon University.

Chapter 5. The author thanks Vince Fuller for technical help, Sara Kiesler and Lee Sproull for their guidance and patience, the rest of the CSSRC for their support, and the CMU Computer Science Department and Robotics Institute for the use of their facilities.

Chapter 6. The data from this survey were collected by classes in social science research methods taught by the author. The CMU Center for Design of Educational Computing, the University Computer Policy Advisory Committee, and the Information Technology Center provided advice on the design of the questionnaire and helped support the execution and analysis of the survey. Jodi Mersay, Andrew Waegel, and Diane Watson carried out many of the analyses.

Chapter 7. The authors wish to thank Mary Catherine Johnsen, Special Collections Librarian, for providing the archived information, and Diane Burton, Anita Gupta, and Scott Obrosky for their assistance in collecting the data. The cartoons by Michael A. Sussman, which appeared November 1, 1983, and October 26, 1982, were reprinted by permission of *The Tartan Newspaper*, Carnegie Mellon University. Copyrights © 1982 and 1983 by *The Tartan Newspaper*.

Chapter 8. The research reported in this chapter was supported by a grant to Lee Sproull and to the author from the CMU Program in Technology and Society, funded by the Mellon Foundation. The author wishes to thank Rick Lau for comments on the manuscript and Karen Ostrow and Diane Burton for their assistance in transcribing the interviews.

Chapter 9. This research was jointly supported by the Committee on Social Science Research in Computing and the Carnegie Mellon University Libraries, with a grant from the Mellon Foundation. The authors thank Thomas J. Michalak, Director of University Libraries, Mark Kibbey, Assistant Director for Automation and Planning, Nancy Evans, Reference Librarian, and the library staff for their help in conducting this research. Annette Giovengo, David Pratto, and Elise Yoder helped in the design of the research.

Chapter 10. This research was supported by the System Development Foundation. The interview schedule was designed by Lee Sproull, Sara Kiesler, and Jane Siegel. Ruth Carroll and Elise Yoder collected the data. David Zubrow and Angela Mucci participated in the analyses. The author thanks Robert Rich for comments on the manuscript. The photograph is courtesy of Carnegie Mellon University.

Chapter 11. The research reported in this chapter was supported by a grant to Lee Sproull from the CMU Program in Technology and Society, funded by the Mellon Foundation, and by grants to Sara Kiesler from the Robotics Institute and the National Science Foundation. We are grateful to Tony O'Dea, Ginny Connolly-Manhardt, Kay Hofmeister, Susan Elster, Herb Sendek, Keith Block, Monica Cellio, Jeff Kaminski, and Jeff Jury, all of whom participated in the collection and analysis of the data. An abridged version of this chapter was published in *Journal of Social Issues, 40,* No. 3, 1984. The photograph is courtesy of Carnegie Mellon University. The cartoon by Mark H. Levine, which appeared February 16, 1982, is reprinted by permission of *The Tartan Newspaper,* Carnegie Mellon University. Copyright © 1982 by *The Tartan Newspaper.*

Chapter 12. The author thanks Sheldon Cohen, Margaret Clark, and Dru Sherrod for providing the data for this research. Scott Obrosky helped carry out the analyses. A speech based on these findings was presented at the IBM University AEP Conference, Alexandria, Va., June 25, 1985.

Chapter 13. Financial support for the research reported in this chapter was provided by the Office of the Senior Vice President, CMU.

Chapter 14. A portion of this chapter draws on an article by Sara Kiesler, "The hidden messages in computer networks," published in the *Harvard Business Review,* No. 86110, January–February 1986. The chapter also draws on a "white paper" produced by the CSSRC on computer policies at CMU, February 1986.

Part I

Thinking About the Social Process of Technological Change

Theories about how new technology affects people and leads to social change can be categorized by: the degree to which they emphasize planned or intentional change in contrast with unintended change, the degree to which they focus on positive effects in contrast with negative ones, and the degree to which they focus on individuals, organizations, or societies – their level of analysis. The intentional theories typically view the computer as a tool. One class of intentional theories, produced by those we might call "technology optimists," emphasizes managerial intentions and positive consequences in organizations (e.g., McFarlan & McKenney, 1983). In these views, astute managers who understand the benefits of new technology install that technology in their organizations with ensuing organizational benefits. A contrasting class of intentional theories, produced by those we might call "technology pessimists," emphasizes managerial intentions and the negative consequences of computing (e.g., Burnham, 1983). In these views managers impose technology deliberately in order to exploit workers and to reap productivity gains at the expense of human dignity. These theories emphasize the potency and prescience of managers or leaders in bringing about change.

Other theories deemphasize managerial initiative and focus instead on the unintended, unanticipated, and emergent consequences of technology. One such class of views focuses on computers as symbol or social object (e.g., Bareff & Galbraith, 1978). In these views acquiring or using new technology has symbolic consequences and is valued for those consequences, independent of any productivity effects. In organizations, computing can become a symbol of status and importance. Therefore one of the consequences of deploying computing can be reinforcing or altering the status hierarchy. Another can be modifying peoples' conceptions of their own status and importance in the organization or in their occupation. In other such views new technology offers a new occasion for fundamental social processes. The processes – such as socializing the young, having fun, explaining anxiety, establishing a sense of competence, negotiating

1

resources, debating fundamental institutional values – occur throughout organizations and throughout time. Computing simply affords a new context and
occasion for playing them out.

All three chapters in this part discuss computing as tool, symbol, and occasion.
Chapter 1, which was written by Herbert Simon, whose own research was
changed profoundly by computers, incorporates the longest time perspective, is
the most optimistic, and illustrates the widest range of levels of analysis. We
have begun this book with Professor Simon's essay in order to set the proper
context for our research, one that emphasizes social stability across time. Because examples of organizational disruption and social change from new technology vividly stand out from the routine, it is easy to concentrate overly on
them. History shows, Professor Simon argues, that stability is a fundamental
principle of society and human behavior. The social effects of technology we
study may seem to have enormous implications, but in the context of the world
social order they are relatively modest. Professor Simon is most interested in a
kind of attentional effect that may derive from research on artificial intelligence
– a change in our self-important view of humans as uniquely intelligent.

Chapter 2, by James G. March, distinguishes among kinds of technology effects: technical, transient, and social effects. Technical effects are intended
ones. Transient and social effects are emergent ones. Some emergent effects,
which may be quite striking, are likely to be transient. More enduring social
effects can be hard to detect at first and may arise only as a secondary consequence of other effects. These distinctions have provided a framework for our
thinking about the social effects of computing in organizations. To illustrate one
long-range potential social effect of computers in universities, Professor March
discusses deskilling. Naturally, today's empirical research cannot address deskilling in the long run, but several of the projects described in this book investigate the immediate impact of computers on deskilling. Whether, in the long
run, these effects are judged to have been transient or enduring is not something
we can predict.

Chapters 1 and 2 primarily discuss the social consequences of new technology.
Chapter 3 describes social consequences as well, but it also describes organizational conditions and processes that lead to them. It proposes our theoretical
perspective on the social process of technological change in organizations. In
our view, certain combinations of organizational attributes, including attributes
of an organization's leaders, are conducive to introducing new technology (or
any social change) in organizations. Organizational processes determine how
this change takes place. We emphasize organizational routines such as resource
allocation and decision making and organizational roles such as secretary,
librarian, and administrator. Because we think the emergent consequences of
computing are at least as important as the intended or technical ones, we also

emphasize the symbolic importance of computing and how computing serves as an occasion for fundamental social processes. Chapter 3 concludes with an organizational description of Carnegie Mellon University to set the context for the remainder of the book.

1   Computers and Society

Herbert A. Simon

This chapter is organized in three sections. The first says something about effects of computers on the economy as a whole on the level of economic activity and what happens to the economy and to people in it. The second discusses effects in the workplace, the home, and school. The third says something about what computers are doing to our view of the world and of ourselves.

The Economy as a Whole

Sometimes, the best way to go about predicting the future is to look at the past. One hundred and fifty years ago in our society (and today still in societies like the Chinese and most of the third world countries on this earth) it took about 85% of the population working on the land to feed the whole population. Over time, we found out how to grow things more rapidly, more productively, and more intensively. We learned how to apply modern technology to the process of agriculture. As a result, today it takes about 3% of the population to feed the whole population. If we take that as a rough yardstick, we should say that there has been a 25 to 1, or 30 to 1 increase in productivity in our society over the past 150 years. Three percent of the population is doing today what 85% was doing before. The interesting question is, "What are the other 82% doing, if they are not needed any more to do what they did in the economy 150 years ago?" The answer is obvious. Those people that we no longer need in agriculture are, except for the 10% who are unemployed, making things in factories or employed in service occupations or white collar occupations. Almost all of those 82% of people are gainfully employed and there is no fundamental reason, or at least no reason coming out of technology, why the rest cannot also be employed.

From that simple historical fact, we can set forth the hypothesis that there is no necessary relation between the level of technology and productivity on the one hand and the level of employment on the other. You can have full employment in a high-tech society. You can have, as we have too much of right now, unemployment in a high-tech society. You can have full employment in a primitive society. And you can have unemployment – as for example China or India does today – on a substantial scale in a third-world economy. There is no

4

logical or necessary connection between the level of employment in a society and the level of productivity in a society. That proposition, if true, is very important, because the first and foremost effect of computers and the reason people want them in factories and offices is that they may increase society's productivity. As my historical example shows, a steady increase in productivity is not new. The first phase of the Industrial Revolution was concerned with supplementing human muscle with machine muscle and this second or computer phase of the Industrial Revolution is concerned with supplementing the human brain with machine intelligence.

The rate of supplementing is determined by the availability of capital, which is required in very large amounts to introduce computer operations, and the return on that capital, which is a function of how good the technology is. Perhaps the limiting factor in what we do with computers today is what we are smart enough to do with computers today. There are still, of course, enormous numbers of human tasks that people do every day that computers cannot do. That boundary is a moving boundary, however. Each year we discover how to do some things effectively and economically with computers that we did not know before, just as the boundary between what was done with human muscle and machine muscle was a moving boundary during the first phase of the Industrial Revolution.

If the basic meaning of these changes is that we are going to continue to increase productivity, and if we are concerned with whether the population can be employed under those circumstances, then we should ask, "Can we consume more output than we do now ?" All of us can occasionally ask, "Why do we need all of these gadgets?" Certainly large numbers of people manage to live in dignity and even in a certain amount of comfort without our kind of high-tech civilization. On the other hand, it would be very hard to argue that our society today produces at a level that meets the needs of a society that everyone agrees are important. No one argues that we have more medical care than we need. On the contrary, many people argue that we cannot afford the medical care that we ought to have. No one argues that we are so productive and so wealthy that we can provide adequate programs for the aging. On the contrary, people warn that our social security system, which has been our society's primary provision for people beyond employment years, is about to be insolvent or that it will be difficult to maintain its solvency at present levels of benefits. No one says that our primary and secondary educational system is so well financed that we can acquire and maintain all of the talent and facilities that we need to do a good educational job. On the contrary, our primary and secondary educational system is in a state of crisis partly because it does not have the kind of funding that it needs to reach high levels of excellence. Given the problems that still beset our society no one can say that it is now unimportant, trivial, or undesirable to continue to increase productivity to the point where we can take care – in the manner in which we would like to become accustomed – of our medical needs, an aging population, and the education of our children.

Of course, there are a lot of questions about technological progress in general; notice that this issue has nothing especially to do with computers. It has to do with anything we do to continue to increase the productivity of our country. But one can talk about it in general and one can also talk about it in terms of who receives these benefits. Again, when we look back at that 150-year history, we see a very interesting fact. We talk about industrialization as being labor saving and so it is. It is labor saving in the sense that the amount of output per man year of labor constantly increases; that is where the 25 to 1 or 30 to 1 increase in productivity comes from. Sometimes, we also talk about technological advance as being capital intensive, meaning that in order to produce goods with less labor per unit of output, we must have much more capital input per unit of output. That statement is historically false. The historical fact is that the ratio of total capital investment – investment in facilities, machinery, and whatever else people invest in – to output during the period of industrialization has been virtually a constant. Look for example at air travel. The amount of capital invested per passenger mile is probably substantially less on an airline today than it was in the late thirties when commercial air travel became reasonably common. This is partly because today's larger planes are more efficient of space, but primarily because they go three times as fast. So the actual capital investment per passenger mile has probably actually declined in that period. You can assess one technology after another and find that we are not using more capital per unit of output even if we are using much less labor per unit of output.

If you thought that the continued industrialization and computerization of our society were making labor a fairly common commodity and making capital rather scarce, then you would predict that wages would decline and all of the productivity benefits would accrue to the owners of the system rather than to the workers. Again, historically that just has not been so, because continuing industrialization has not required increasing amounts of capital per unit of output. Real interest rates over the long haul have not moved very much either up or down. Consequently, labor's share in the total American product has increased from something like roughly 70% toward the beginning of the century or maybe even less than that, to something close to 80% in the last couple of decades. So there is reason to suppose that productivity increases lead to a higher level of goods and services and provide a larger and larger share of those goods and services to wages and to salary.

I have been talking as though anyone who looks at technological change in computers should predict what the future must be. Really, that is not our job at all. The future we are talking about is our future and the only purpose of making predictions is to see whether there are things we do not like about the future and would like to change. Predictions serve as a sort of level-zero plan that we can use as a basis for determining what kinds of interventions we want to undertake in order for that future to come out more favorably.

One point of view says that technology sets the rules of the game; if you have a technology you will use it. I think there is some truth to that. Certainly if you have a technology, there will be a temptation to use it. Remember the famous mountain climber Mallory who, when asked why he climbed a particular mountain, replied, "Because it's there." If there are electric pencil sharpeners, we are tempted to use electric pencil sharpeners whether we need them or not. Nevertheless, we have begun to learn that technology need not be used just because it is there and that technology can be used with concern for the particular effects that it has. One of our first exercises in this kind of self-discipline was the American decision not to build a supersonic aircraft. That decision was made on grounds of both economics and environmental effects. The decision may not have been completely technically correct; that is, some of the relevant predictions have had to be subsequently revised. But the American people and the American government were able to decide not to use a particular technology just because it was there, because it was thought to have deleterious consequences. We have made a number of other decisions of the same sort since that time. We have made decisions, for example, about the conditions under which we would use insecticides. I do not mean to imply that we are always making right decisions, that we are always properly restrained. Every year in our land political struggles determine what technology we will use and to what extent. For example, consider the struggle over the extent to which we can, want to, and can afford to use nuclear energy. But we have clearly demonstrated to ourselves that we can make those decisions. Not everybody will always agree about the decisions; we will not always make the right decisions. But the future is not something just to be forecasted. The future is something to be thought about, it is something to be planned for, it is something that we have to make choices and decisions about.

Let me return to computers. In the short run, any technical device or machine that is supposed to increase productivity will presumably reduce the number of workers that are needed to turn out the product in question. So at least in the short run and at least in the particular place where that technology is introduced, there is reason to be concerned about unemployment. That unemployment may be dealt with in a variety of ways. Under the happiest circumstances, the demand for the product will increase so rapidly that it will absorb the surplus employment generated by the new technology. Some years ago the telephone company thought it faced a serious manpower problem. When it projected the number of operators it would need, it discovered that within a few years it would need the entire national population. Automation, a succession of automations, came along just in time to save the telephone system from that dire fate. So during the entire period in which the system underwent automation, there was no question of people losing jobs. There were periods when people were not hired for new jobs, but people were not losing jobs.

Certainly if we think of the future as something to be planned for and not something just to be accepted, we will worry about shifting from individuals to society the economic burden of these short-term adjustments. Some people will need to change occupations and some people will need to move from one part of the country to another. We do worry about that in connection with technological change and we should. But there is an enormous amount of geographical mobility in this country quite independent of computerization and other high tech developments. A large part of this movement is undertaken by people voluntarily and even gladly and with a spirit of adventure in their hearts. This movement mostly depends on whether people think they're going to have better jobs or a better life at the end of the journey. Many human beings much of the time are not averse to new things, including new places to live and new kinds of jobs. They are averse, of course, to losing a comfortable home, to losing their means of support, to having to move somewhere else without any assurance that when they move they will be any better off. Those things human beings are not very happy about. But in a society that can maintain its employment at a high level, a tremendous amount of social change, a tremendous amount of relocation of jobs, can occur without imposing a heavy burden on people. Consider for a moment, what technological advance – what piece of high or low technology – has caused the largest geographical displacement of people over the past thirty years? The answer is very simple – the air conditioner. The air conditioner was the basis for most of the movement of American population to the Sun Belt. That has affected 10 or 20% of our population, an enormous number of people who have moved and usually have alleged at least that they're pleased to move. Now I do not recall that air conditioners have ever been regarded as a major social problem. So this example shows that you can have a great deal of social change provided that it comes to people as an opportunity and not as a threat. That is the point of view we must adopt when we introduce new technology into the workplace.

To what extent can we accommodate new technology without displacing people by reshuffling jobs or holding off on hiring? If it's necessary to help people move from one kind of occupation to another, what provisions is society prepared to make so that people can do that readily and gracefully? I cannot claim that we have done that very well. I cannot claim that as a society we have been very willing to shift that burden from individuals to the society. Having been most of the time a society that has maintained a pretty high level of employment, those problems have tended to work themselves out. I do not think we can be very happy about our recent history in that respect.

In thinking about these matters we must not focus our attention solely, or even mostly, on the place where the technological change has its initial impact. A society and economy is a system in which one thing affects another thing. A pool table is a system if you are good at shooting pool; if you're good at the game, one thing leads to another. In an economy a ripple started in one part of the pond ripples out to other parts of the pond. For example, what are the most important technological innovations that have been introduced into the medical profession in this century? The earliest one is the Model T Ford, which was the first automobile that most country physicians could afford to drive. The automobile probably reduced the country physician's time load by at least a factor of two or three. The skill that the country physician used most before the automobile was the skill of driving a horse. So when you think of the introduction of something like the automobile you should not be thinking about its impact on an automobile industry or its impact on garages. You need to think of the indirect impacts that trickle through the population. Another technological change that affected the medical profession was antibiotics. Consider the number of doctor hours per pneumonia case or per any other kind of bacterial case before and after antibiotics and you see that this was a great labor-saving device. Now the question is, "Why isn't there an oversupply of doctors?" Since automobiles and antibiotics must have increased the productivity of physicians by at least five times, why aren't 80% of the doctors unemployed? I think in this case we have become more sophisticated in our demands on the medical system than our parents and our grandparents were.

What will the new jobs be like as computers begin to penetrate more and more of the work place, as they begin to do a wider and wider range of jobs? The answer really doesn't have anything to do specifically with computers. We have already seen in our society a gradual decrease in the proportion of our work force that's engaged in manufacturing. That decrease will surely continue whether or not we have computers, so long as we have some source of continuing increase in productivity. The main reason is that our demands for services are increasing more rapidly than our demands for factory-made goods. And so, what kinds of occupations are going to be increasing? The service occupations. Service occupations means a whole range of things: routine occupations, rather unskilled occupations, clerical occupations, elementary and secondary teachers, hospital attendants. The people who provide the things we use in this society besides manufactured goods – the clerks, the attendants, people whose occupations involve a heavy interaction with other people, are probably going to be an increasing proportion of our total employee population quite independently of the computer. Estimates suggest that the largest absolute increase in occupations over the next 25 years is going to be in custodial employees including people who provide security, cleaning, and maintenance to buildings.

The computer does not greatly change the mix of occupations in our society because it is such a general purpose device. Let's just for a moment romantically think of computers as additional brains in our society. Where would we use those brains? Well, brains are usable almost everywhere: brains are usable in factories, behind airline counters, even in universities. A technology that provides more thinking power will penetrate almost everywhere in society and it is going to be very hard to predict where it will make its largest impact. In the past 25 years the computer has had a much larger impact on clerical operations in banks, insurance companies, and offices than it has had in the factory. There are some good technical reasons for that. Robotics is technically more difficult than is running accounting and financial statements on a computer. But the basic message is that computers are spreading everywhere.

Effects in the Workplace, Home, and School

What is life like in a workplace that has a high level of computerization? We can find workplaces that already have a very high level of computerization – for example, insurance offices or CMU. People in those workplaces will tell you what life is like. I'll give you a hint of what I think they will say. I have lived in a computer-intensive environment for about 12 years now, and the thing that impresses me most about it is how similar it is to the environment that I lived in before computers. Obviously, some things are very different. It is very different to use a word processor and have almost painless manuscript revisions instead of retyping every time you thought something was terribly wrong with it. There are all sorts of ways in which productivity is increased. But what is really important about a workplace are the skills you use in it and the interactions you have with other human beings. There are some workplaces where introducing computing or automatic devices does change interaction among human beings. For example, automation is making the traditional assembly line obsolete, particularly the hand assembly line where somebody stands all day and does one thing. It is becoming obsolete because those tasks can be efficiently automated in the workplace. If you look at the workplace in general, however, you find no dramatic changes in the average skill levels in the working population. Some studies record slight increases in skill demands and some studies report that jobs have been a little bit routinized. Nothing very dramatic. And you find that there are not dramatic changes in the kinds of human interaction in the workplace in spite of fancy things like mail systems and electronic communication of all sorts. The number of hours people spend interacting with other people in something like our computer science department or a clerical office that's highly automated is probably not very different from that number before computers.

Many of us have seen Charlie Chaplin's famous film *Modern Times*, in which a poor little man runs around trying to escape from the machinery in a factory. That image has become a symbol of some of the attitudes or anxieties we have about machines and industrialization. But in most of the computerized workplaces that I look at, the machines are well in hand; they're well under human control. And again we should not just predict whether it is going to continue to be this way; we should arrange our affairs and how we go about automating and computerizing so that it will continue to be that way. There are still a lot of people around; we still outnumber computers a little bit. Maybe we can keep that true for quite a long while.

One might argue that much of the change in the office or the workplace is changes in the mind. Any new technology or other change can be treated either as a threat or as a challenge. A secretary can look at the new word processor and say, "Gee, how am I ever going to deal with all these terribly abstruse things I have to learn?" Or the secretary can say, "Gee, that looks like a lot of fun; there's not going to be as much straight typing on this job as there was on the previous job." A lot of the reaction to technology is a matter of how we view it. And how we view it is considerably a matter of whether we think we are in charge of the technology or the technology is in charge of us. In thinking about this we have to ask, who is in charge? We have to ask, how can we organize our society so that we will be in charge? So that we will feel that this is an adventure we're having and not something that is being done to us.

A lot of recent attention has focused on the effects of computers in the home and at leisure. Of course, the most visible aspect has been the great boom in personal computers in the home and in all kinds of fun and games. Almost everybody probably has some basis for interpreting and understanding what kind of an impact this is going to have on our homes. How important will it be that in a few years your computer can deliver to you information that is equivalent to the old Sears Roebuck catalog? How fundamental a difference will it make in your life if you have access to the Sears catalog or access to the World Almanac or access to other data banks? How often do you use data banks? How often do you go to a library in order to get some information other than the information you need for school and education? Schools are rather special places in the demands they make on information. So I think it's an open question of whether the American home becomes a very different place when it is saturated with computers.

Now mind, there will be some computer addicts. Any society has a certain amount of anxiety and certain people have more than their quota of it. It is well known to psychiatrists that if people have a little bit of floating anxiety, one of the soothing things to do with it is to find some kind of task with a fairly quick feedback or knowledge of results. There are all sorts of good therapies we can have in our homes. At one time people were soothed by playing the piano; you can do it by playing chess, you can do it by playing on your home computer. There are all sorts of hobbies useful for that purpose that you can become addicted to. And so we have in our society today some computer addicts. A clinical psychologist at CMU some years ago told me that yes, there were computer addicts, but the population of chess addicts had dropped off. One assumes that there was a certain amount of substitution.

My own guess is that the impact of the home computer on the nature and quality of life is going to be an order of magnitude less significant than that of the telephone, the radio, the TV, and hi-fi. Those are the other lively things around the house with which the computer is going to have to compete and is competing. And two things are not clear: Who's going to win the competition? And what does it matter after all? Radio, television, and hi-fi are completely passive devices. Other people do things and, if it amuses you, you sit and watch them or listen to them. Maybe it is just snobbishness, but it is hard to believe that passivity is all good in more than moderate amounts. The home computer has the virtue at least of being a potentially active device. Of course, you can find all sorts of mindless things to do with it, but it is a potentially active device. Maybe it has some of the same beneficial advantages that playing a round of golf has instead of sitting home and watching whatever you watch. On the other hand, I think it is very rash to suppose that the home computer is going to take over as a recreational and leisure-time device or, for that matter, as a source of information, because it is not clear how many hours of our lives we want to spend in that active posture. Many of us have pretty strenuous and active work, and some people find it great to just sit around for a couple of hours and drink beer with or without pictures flickering in front of them. So I think that after its first novelty value wears off, the home computer is in for very tough competition as a device to occupy our time and our thoughts.

The most important things in almost any person's environment are other people. That was true before we had high technology and that is true as we gain a high technology. People have also always been a little bit in love with their artifacts. People fall in love with sailboats, they fall in love with motorcycles, and I'm sure at one time they fell in love with stone axes. People have always gotten pleasure out of using artifacts well. They have gotten pleasure out of making artifacts. But the real love affair of human beings tends to be with other human beings and I do not see that a high-tech society is any different in that respect from a low-tech society.

Now consider education. There is an experiment, which many of us find very exciting, going on on this campus. This is an experiment in saturating the campus with computers – offering ourselves up, as it were, as experimental subjects to see what those computers do to our lives. Or, more constructively, to see how

The real love affair of human beings tends to be with other human beings.

imaginative we can be in using those computers to make our lives and our education more productive, more enjoyable, and more worthwhile in every respect. Now when one thinks of computers in relation to education, one thinks of computer-aided instruction. And of course, if computers are to pay their way on this campus, if the whole experiment is to be worthwhile, it will only be because we do some of our mental exercising in interaction with this device. So computer-aided instruction is terribly important. But if this experiment is to succeed, we're going to have to mean something by computer-aided instruction very different from what it has meant over the past 30 years. For the past 30 years, computer-aided instruction – there are notable exceptions to this but let me talk about the mainstream – has largely meant computerizing drill and practice exercises that could just as well be done with paper and pencil. Most computer-aided instruction does not, in fact, make any deep use of the superior capabilities that computers have to interact with the user and to engage in genuine problem-solving behavior with the user.

We will move beyond the kind of humdrum use of the computer that has characterized most computer-aided instruction in the past only by producing sophisticated software that uses the computer in more intelligent ways. And in order to do that we are going to have to understand a great deal more than we have understood in the past about how human beings learn, about how they interact with each other in a learning situation, and about how they might interact with devices like computers if those computers were programmed to respond in more or less intelligent ways. That is really what the experiment is all about here, whether we can develop that kind of intelligence on the computer end of this system. Our enrollment policies take care of the intelligence on the human end of the system. I am worried about whether we are going to be clever enough and bright enough to make those computers work as a part of the educational experience here. If we succeed, it will be because we put a considerable effort into research on cognitive science, on understanding the human learning processes.

Over the past 25 years we have made enormous progress in understanding what goes on in the human head in terms of information processing, what goes on in the human head when human beings are solving problems, discovering concepts, thinking, and using language. The task now is to further develop that understanding and to apply it to creating software that we on this campus and other campuses are going to want to use. That is a valuable goal. It is a valuable goal because we do not have any right to be satisfied with the way in which we carry on educational processes, not only here but anywhere in this world. Educating a new generation, which is society's continuing responsibility, takes 10% of our gross national product. And so, making that more effective, increasing the quality of what we are doing with those enormous resources, is certainly a very important goal for us. In engaging in this exciting experiment, CMU can make a very substantial contribution toward that goal.

Our View of Ourselves

In the course of studying human thinking and problem solving, we are learning about the human mind. We're learning to describe the human mind as an information-processing system. We are learning to describe the human mind as a kind of computer made out of neurons that is able to input information, output information, store information, manipulate information. I earlier referred to the computer as a brain and to the fact that some people find that unsettling. Why unsettling? Darwin persuaded a lot of us, apparently not everybody in this country yet but a lot of us, that we are simply wrong in thinking that our species was created in any different way than other species were created. So we lost that sense of uniqueness. I think that some people's anxiety about the computer is that it will relieve us of another source of our uniqueness as the only kind of system in this universe that can think. To say that computers can do what we do when we think and use language and discover is to challenge another area of human uniqueness. But there are responses other than denying that computers can in fact do that, other than denying that it is a good thing for computers to do that. Another response is to say, "Why do we put so much stake on being unique anyway?" We are on this spinning planet – some of us have seen pictures of it from space. Why don't we ask not how are we unique, but what is our relation to that planet? Why don't we try to get our sense of worth in this world, not in uniqueness, not in being apart from the rest of nature, but in being a general and integral part of nature.

2   Old Colleges, New Technology

The Coming of Computers

As popular magazines have proclaimed with tedious glee for over ten years, Western society is experiencing a significant change in information technology; and higher education is a part of it.   The symptoms are conspicuous on American campuses. I am writing these words at a terminal that can communicate via various networks to almost any major university in the United States, as well as to many in western Europe. Computer-based information systems have proliferated around the world. The number of users, their sophistication, and the level of their use are all increasing.   Several colleges and universities have announced that individual terminals or personal computers are, or will be, available for all students.   The familiar trappings of information technology are spreading through universities almost as fast as did photocopying of text material, pass/fail grading, and the Split-T formation.

This diffusion of modern information technology may have consequences for education, but its acceptance in higher education is only partly tied to its practical educational usefulness. Things spread through societies and institutions for many reasons, only some of them connected with their instrumental contribution. We imitate one another and produce fads without assuring their social or personal value. For example, the rock music industry, the fashion industry, and the armaments industry all thrive on non-utilitarian considerations in the spread of their products. Just as the success of a revolution does not certify its intelligence, the sensibility of an innovation is not certified by the market.

Much of the adoption of a new technology depends on the symbolism it evokes. And whatever else it may be or become, the computer and the terminal work station are symbols of a modern university. University administrators and faculties advertise their commitments to computer technology with as much vigor as they do their commitments to progress and social welfare, and the advertisements are believed to augment individual and institutional esteem. Since higher education has a long tradition of counter-snobbery toward shiny technologies and flashy clothes, it is possible that the long-run symbolic significance of computers will become negative in higher education.   At the moment, however, computers are symbols of virtue, intelligence, modernity, and good scholarship.

16

Old colleges, new technology.

Symbolism is important in educational institutions, and we should be neither surprised nor depressed by it. The university library has long, and appropriately, been at least as much a symbol of academic commitment to learning and knowledge and an advertisement of educational quality as it has been a depository of books; and the shelves of unread books in a university professor's office make important symbolic statements about the nature of a life of scholarship. Although the symbolic component of information technology and its diffusion through higher education are obvious and fully adequate to explain contemporary enthusiasms, the practical educational consequences of computers may also be significant, just as it is possible that the educational consequences of a library may be significant.

In any event, important or not, it is the practical consequences to which this essay is addressed. I want to consider how an institution as old and essentially conservative as a university might be expected to adapt to a technology as new and potentially radical as modern information technology. There are some unfortunate pitfalls in such a topic. The most obvious problem is that there are few other domains of modern social science with quite such a large number of unsubstantiated speculations and quite such a small number of serious research studies. I apologize for adding to the speculations; it is a disease of the young and innocent, I guess. I hope by noting it at the start to secure some of the pleasures of speculation without incurring all of its embarrassments.

An excess of speculation is not the only problem. A writer who speculates about the future of social institutions or technology faces a dilemma. On the one hand, we know that most interesting speculations about the future involve surprises, things that are forecasted to change our lives dramatically and unexpectedly. On the other hand, we know that most of the surprising things we might predict about the future are almost certainly wrong. Some surprising things will certainly happen next year, but the likelihood that any particular surprising thing will happen is close to zero. As a result, the most reliable forecast we can make of the future is that it will demonstrate the inaccuracy of most forecasts about it. So a writer has to choose between either saying that most other people's forecasts are wrong, which is certainly true but not very interesting; or saying that the world tomorrow will be like today, which will be true in most respects but also wrong in some important ones and in any event is unquestionably dull; or saying that the future will bring a specific set of surprises, which will almost certainly be wrong but might be interesting; or hedging his bets and saying that forecasting is best left to the astrologers. For the most part, I am inclined to leave crystal ball gazing to crystal ball gazers; but I think there may be some ways of thinking about old universities and new technologies that might help us interpret the future as it unfolds in the present.

Understanding the impact of information technology on American universities over the coming years probably requires distinguishing among intended effects, transient effects, and secondary effects. By an intended effect, I mean something that most people would identify as the rationale for the technology. One example might be the improvements in educational methods. By a transient effect, I mean something that may be very important in the early stages of a new technology but disappears fairly quickly. One example might be the "alien culture" effects that will be described in Chapter 8. By a secondary effect, I mean something that is an unintended and mostly unexpected consequence. One example might be the effects of electronic communication on individual participation rates in group decision making (Kiesler, Siegel, & McGuire, 1984). It seems likely that there are systematic biases in our estimates of these three effects. In the early stages of a new technology, including computer-based information systems in higher education, we probably exaggerate the impact of intended effects, exaggerate the long term significance of transient effects, and underestimate the impact of secondary effects.

To explore intended, transient, and secondary effects of information technology on universities in any depth or with great confidence would require more competence than I would want to claim. They are complicated and uncertain, and I am wary of claims of omniscience. As an alternative, this essay gives one person's cloudy view of four different ways in which we might expect contemporary universities to be affected: First, information technology might affect the ways universities do their housekeeping. Second, information technology might affect the demand for university education. Third, information technology might affect the ways universities teach their students. Fourth, information technology might affect the structure of knowledge itself. I suspect it is reasonable to forecast that some effects of each kind will be observed over the next decade or two, even though their precise character may be difficult to anticipate.

Effects on Housekeeping

The ways universities do their housekeeping are already substantially affected by information technology. A university has a lot of plumbing, that is, activities, investments, equipment, and people that are vital to the university as we know it. Universities maintain records; they prepare and follow budgets; they mow lawns; they deliver mail; they defend themselves against legal, community, and political assaults; they prepare and market food, lodging, medical services, and parking; they maintain equipment; they prepare and distribute newspapers and reports; they advertise; they schedule rooms; they manage performances in the arts; and they keep the toilets working.

Although there are differences between the management of such things in an academic setting and their management elsewhere, the differences are not great. The technologies used to perform basic organizational services in other kinds of institutions will generally be found also in universities. Academic administration uses telephones, photocopying machines, automobiles, and electric light bulbs. Universities are recognizable as modern organizations with the technologies familiar to the times, but their housekeeping tends to be somewhat backward technologically. On average, they have adopted new technologies a little more slowly than other institutions. The slowness in adoption is undoubtedly connected to the traditions of genteel poverty of academe, the reality of scarce resources, and the difficulty of measuring the ultimate contribution of improvements to some widely accepted index of educational effectiveness.

Whatever the reasons for the relative slowness of the introduction of new organizational technologies in academe, however, the historical pattern makes one kind of prediction fairly easy. The administrative and service parts of academic institutions will adopt the paraphernalia of information technology more slowly than most businesses and many governmental agencies; but they will adopt them. Most university administrations now use computers to process various records, reports, and payrolls. Many now have remote terminals for dealing with files and inter-departmental communication. Word processing equipment is becoming as common as the electric typewriter.

In 1979 it was estimated that the average factory worker in the United States had about $31,000 in equipment support, and the average farm worker had

$53,000 in equipment support. This compared with $2,300 in equipment support for the average office worker. There is no reason to assume that the latter figure will necessarily increase ten- or twenty-fold over the next decade; but it seems safe to guess that it will increase. The increase may well be slower and less in universities than in other organizations, but it will be substantial. The university office, like the business office and the governmental office, is becoming automated.

Office automation will produce changes. We are likely to see a sharper division of labor between people who type and people who do other clerical tasks. We are likely to see a gradual shift from file cases to computer files. We are likely to see reduced use of telephones and answering machines and increased use of electronic mail. We are likely to see an increase in the amount of information received each day by a person in the organization. The changes will be important. Their implementation will require talented managers, staff members, and consultants; and some patience. They will affect the allocation of activities to people and the way work is organized and controlled. They may affect the efficiency of the administrative and service activities of a university, though if past history is a guide, such gains are more likely to be used to improve the "quality" of the services than reduce the costs of the function involved.

Despite their importance and the demands they will make on university personnel, the effects of information technology on the housekeeping activities of an academic institution are likely to be relatively easily comprehended and managed. The problems will have been experienced elsewhere already; the technology will have been somewhat tested elsewhere; a cadre of people with expertise on the consequences will exist. In this area, universities will be adopting technologies and procedures that have had enough testing to make them tolerable. University managers and employees will have heard of the technologies and will have grown accustomed to the idea that they are standard. Manufacturers will have experienced the problems of their clients and will know a bit more about how to cope with them. All of these comfortable manifestations of maturity do not, of course, make it possible for everyone simply to relax. It is possible to remove a foot accidentally with an axe, even though axe technology is relatively mature. But if anything in life is likely to be comparatively smooth, the introduction of office automation in the university is a candidate.

Effects on the Demand for Education

A second potential effect of information technology with which we might be concerned is its impact on the demand for education. Society has begun to demand that university graduates exhibit "computer literacy." Although this demand is conspicuous now, its effects on universities are likely to be transient. In the long run, as the computer and its consequences diffuse, particularly into ordinary households, two things seem likely to happen. First, computers are likely to become less and less products designed by and for engineers and adolescent boys. Second, more and more people will accumulate experience with computers. As a result, computer literacy and individual comfort with information technology will be neither a major long-run problem for higher education nor a responsibility.

Beyond literacy, of course, the technology may change the demand for the "products" of education. At present, the major "products" of American higher education are legitimately certified individuals – human capital – and new knowledge. The market prices paid for those products presumably reflect some sense of the way in which the screening and educating functions of universities match the needs of certain social institutions, specifically those institutions having resources enough to enter the market and bid successfully for individuals to fill their requirements. It is clear that one of the things that induce change in educational institutions is change in the employment market for graduates. It is equally clear that the employment market is affected by changes in technology. When computers become important to industrial and commercial activities, the demand for computer scientists increases. And when the demand for computer scientists increases, students flock to computer science departments, and universities encourage their growth.

Surges in demand create well-known problems for academic institutions, particularly when there is some reason to suspect the surge may be temporary; but the problems are familiar ones. In the short run, universities typically find ways to allow student enrollments in a program to vary considerably more than the variation in permanent faculty. In the long run, they follow major non-transient shifts, but with a lag. The adaptation to changing markets is rarely smooth and often the source of considerable internal conflict; but it is hard to see that the rise of information technology poses remarkably new kinds of problems. The transition from the dominance of mechanical engineering to the dominance of electrical engineering has been managed with fair success, and the information technology transition seems roughly comparable. Some universities will, of course, be more favorably positioned than others to exploit new demands, just as some universities were better positioned than others to exploit the recent demand for business education. So some universities will prosper a bit more and others will prosper a bit less.

Effects on Teaching

A third set of possible effects of information technology is the effects on the ways universities transmit knowledge. Recent discussions of computers in education emphasize these effects. Modern information technology is sometimes portrayed as a source for major productivity gains in education. This view is manifested in expectations that computers will make it possible to "produce" a university-educated person with considerably fewer faculty, or in shorter time than we now find necessary. History suggests that a certain skepticism about such speculations may not be entirely inappropriate. University education changes. It is different now from what it was 100 years ago. And university education varies from one country to another, as well as from one institution to another within a country. But the thing that seems to have changed rather little over time, and to vary rather little from country to country, despite considerable pressure to change and frequent announcements of impending drama, is the technology of higher education.

Universities are carriers of central cultural traditions. They adapt new technologies; they bend; but they do not exhibit much inclination to change a basic technology based on reading, talking, listening, writing, and thinking. In recent years, neither audio-visual technology, nor television, nor the teaching machine has made an appreciable impact on the core technology of university teaching. It is arguable that photocopying, by changing the technology of taking notes and producing books, has had an important impact; but the capability of higher education to maintain its basic form in the face of technocratic virtuosity is a primary lesson of academic history. If technology alone were likely to transform the way in which students in universities attend lectures and function essentially as scribes in most of them, the system would have been transformed by the introduction of the mimeograph machine.

For all practical purposes, the technology of higher education consists of five things: (1) A reading list, including the libraries, book stores, and copying machines necessary to such a list. (2) A set of laboratories in which phenomena not routinely observable in ordinary life can be observed and managed. (3) A student body, including the arrangements of life necessary to produce interaction among the individuals involved. (4) A faculty, including the classrooms necessary to make them available to each other and to students. (5) Some cultural norms about leisure and tolerance – a social acceptance of slack, and the temporary suspension of normal social expectations about the behavior and attitudes of adult citizens. It is possible to imagine a university without any one of these, but they are the standard technologies. And they have been standard in something like their present form throughout a long period of technological change in our society.

When we look at universities that have pioneered the introduction of information technology into education, the effect that has been observed most generally and seems likely to affect the greatest number of students and faculty most quickly is hardly a fundamental change in educational conception or technology. Word processors are replacing typewriters, scissors, and paste for the generation of written materials. Faculty members are replacing their own secretaries, where they had them. The general experience with open access to computing is quite decisive on this point. Students and faculty members happily and quickly use computer-based text editors to prepare reports and papers, and any computer system that offers access both to text editing and to computation will find the demand for the former far exceeding the demand for the latter.

A second observed effect, more notable in more mature systems, is the use of electronic mail. As many people have commented, electronic mail has an advantage over telephone communication in not requiring the simultaneous presence of sender and receiver; and it has an advantage over regular mail in offering (almost) instantaneous delivery. It can be best described perhaps as an inoffensive answering service, apparently somewhat more tolerable to many people than its approximate functional equivalent, the automatic telephone-answering machine. It combines this characteristic with the additional advantage (to the sender but not obviously to the receiver) of making easy the sending of identical messages to numerous addresses; thus it is also a screen-based xerox machine, an electronic junk mail generator. Electronic mail linking networks of faculty, students, and colleagues around the country has already become fairly common. Although it could be significant in extending contact within a university, or among universities, it appears to be a relatively modest modification of traditional technology.

As a way of illustrating how computer-based information systems are used in universities, I interrupted the typing (on a word processor) of this text to take a small snapshot of utilization in three different, currently operating university systems that make no user charge to authorized users. I signed onto two computers available to students, faculty, and staff at Carnegie Mellon University and checked current users (at 5:45 P.M.), and onto a computer available to doctoral students, faculty, and staff at the Stanford University Graduate School of Business. Looking only at faculty and students (as nearly as possible; there may have been some misclassification), the results are clear. There were no appreciable differences among the three systems. Overall (if we exclude terminals that were not doing anything), 81% of the users were doing text editing, 15% were reading messages (either electronic mail or system messages), and 4% were computing.

The substitution of word processors for typewriters, scissors, and paste is an incremental change in education (and general office) technology. It has some consequences. For example, it allows and encourages many more revisions of a text; it allows substituting an automatic spelling check for learning how to spell (much as a calculator substitutes a multiplication command for learning the multiplication tables); it may before too long be able to make other modest corrections in natural language text. It may reduce face-to-face contact among colleagues, although that would be hard to do at some universities; and various efforts have been made to attribute ailments of the eyes, back, and liver to extended hours of peering at a CRT. But these effects, however interesting they may be, do not really raise a serious challenge to the basic educational technology of a university.

The only modern technological innovations that have been unambiguously fundamental to higher education are the invention of the printing press and the development of books as depositories of information, knowledge, beauty, and speculation. Everything else has made, at most, small incremental refinements in a basic educational technology that consists of a group of teachers and students sitting on rocks and talking about books they have read.

Effects on the Organization of Knowledge

It is conceivable that computers and information technology will have an impact comparable to that of books. If they do, however, it will not be because they are particularly efficient systems for teaching what we now teach, but because they change the way we organize knowledge and our relation to knowledge. That is, the most far-reaching potential effect of new information technology is not its impact on housekeeping, the demand for education, or the ways in which we deliver knowledge to students, but its effect on the organization and utilization of knowledge, and thus on the nature of knowledge itself.

All knowledge is a form of deskilling. What we do when we generate new knowledge is to take some appreciation, calculation, or inference that previously required extraordinary talent and make it accessible to ordinary talent. Thus, the calculations of the calculus that originally required the genius of a Newton or Leibnitz have now been reduced to the routine comprehension of a high school student of average intelligence. The invention of the printing press and the printing of books significantly augmented our capability to deskill major activities of human life. It made artistic taste accessible to individuals who did not themselves have extraordinary sensitivity or artistic genius; it made becoming an expert navigator possible without ever being on a ship, and without having exceptional computational abilities; it gave any child who could read the authority of expertise to challenge parental authority of age, position, and experience.

Just as books provided a quantum leap in our ability to alienate skill from the talented individual and put it into a form easily accessed and used by persons with only a small fraction of the ability possessed by those who originally developed and exhibited it, information technology could transform our view of knowledge and how we use it. When I first studied statistics, a good deal of talk was devoted to the art of drawing a properly random sample. Some individuals were very good at thinking of possible random devices, most of which seemed to involve shutting your eyes and sticking a pencil at something. Shortly thereafter, all of that skill was eliminated by the introduction of tables of random numbers printed in the back of every statistics text. Now most of us don't use tables of random numbers any more, but simply generate any random number we need by using a standard computer routine. More generally, the use of tables is disappearing from large domains of science. The reduction in the costs of computation has made it more efficient to recalculate numbers whenever they are needed, rather than calculate them once, file them or print them, and retrieve them when needed. Tables of square roots have joined skills at the longhand extraction of square roots as curiosities exhibited by older people to the young, along with other improbable stories of the way life used to be, like the time you used to spell your own words.

Another example: Recently I read a series of electronic messages transmitted in a major American business firm's research division. The series began with a broadside request from a scientist to his colleagues. He was seeking a copy of a book that he had found unavailable in the library. Shortly, several people responded indicating where he could find a copy of the book. One reply was different, however. It came from a librarian who complained that the original request was badly formulated. What was sought was not a specific book but some information that was known to be contained in the book. Had the scientist asked the librarian (information retrieval specialist) for the information, he would have been directed to several other sources, available in the library, that contained the specific information he desired. A trivial exchange, to be sure, but a reminder that our search for information is heavily influenced by our views of the structure of information; and several centuries of a book-based information system have influenced our ways of thinking about knowledge, and obtaining access to it.

It is possible to think of information retrieval systems as glorified card catalogs, as some of them are. It is possible to imagine a world in which books are published by placing them on an electronic system accessible from any terminal properly connected to it. Neither of these concepts changes the university very much, though the second probably redefines the size and geographical accessibility of the university library. But it is also possible to imagine a world in which books as we know them play a much less central role in the organization of knowledge. We are not remotely close to such a state now. It is not at all clear that we will ever be. But it is imaginable. There are some beginnings in the form of accessible data bases. In some areas of research, we are nearing a situation in which, just as we now calculate random numbers rather than look them up, we will prefer to reanalyze data rather than consult a previous analysis, not because we doubt the previous work but simply because it is easier to do it over. In a grander sense, of course, it can be argued that just as books deskilled experience and discovery, modern information technology will deskill problem solving, thinking, and analysis. Books made the ability to use books, to combine them, extract from them, and apply the knowledge in them a primary skill in our society. If some visions of artificial intelligence are fulfilled, not only will important functions of books be superseded but so also will other skills that depend on a book-based organization of knowledge.

Speculations, Visions, and Hoopla

Some of these wilder speculations are, of course, just that. The only kind of credence they warrant is the kind of credence we give to other forms of science fiction. But they suggest the possibility of something rather profound for our conceptions of human distinctiveness, and thus for higher education in its classic role as a temple of belief in human intelligence. Many features of our perspectives on intelligence are specific to the book-based technology with which we are familiar. As increasing numbers of complex analyses are done within computers, using architectures of intelligence particularly appropriate to that technology, some precious axioms of academe may become suspect. For example, we all know that a Shakespearean play will never be produced by a large number of monkeys typing random symbols. Nevertheless, the costs of computation and search, of trying lots of things without choosing too carefully among them in advance, are decreasing at such a rapid rate that it would be remarkable if we did not see a significant change in the relative value of delicate thought on the one hand and exhaustive search on the other. But if we can imagine challenging such a sacred belief, perhaps we can also imagine that other axioms of knowledge implicit in higher education will face significant challenge within a new information technology. And this even though that technology, in its present manifestations, is hardly more than a fancy typewriter, an inoffensive answering service, and a screen-based Xerox machine.

Unless and until the technology changes our conceptions of knowledge, however, the other impacts on universities – on the housekeeping, the demand for education, and on teaching – will be notable, even exciting, but not revolutionary. Computers, like telephones, photocopying machines, and television equipment, will find a place in universities; and we will come to love them and know them. But the university will probably continue to look a lot like the universities we observe today. Contemporary talk of radical change is partly based on a vision of the possibility that we may change the structure of knowledge; and universities need to be aware of such visions, both because they should honor visionaries even when they are wrong and because, sometimes, they are right. But contemporary talk is also partly hoopla to justify spending the substantial sums required to buy and operate this generation's favorite toy and symbol. And if we sometimes should shake our heads at that, we should also recall that much of life is hoopla and much of the glory of the university is its symbolic representation of an arbitrary commitment to discovering whatever there is to be discovered.

3   The Social Process of Technological Change in Organizations

Sara Kiesler and Lee Sproull

Social Change and Computing

Computerization in any organization is a process of making technological innovations and improvements. It is also a process of making social changes such as asking people to change their work habits, changing the kinds of people who are considered experts, creating new organizational units, and distributing important resources differently. In order to understand what computers mean for organizations we have to see what social changes are taking place, not just what the technological changes are. Introducing more or different computers into an organization is equivalent to introducing new ways to do things. It means choosing to be first or choosing to imitate others. It means confidence that change is not foolish. It means somebody has to pay attention or nothing happens. It means energy, chaos, and complaints. All organizations experience a social process of technological change no matter how advanced and friendly the computer system to be introduced. In Figure 3.1 we have outlined the aspects of this social process that we discuss in this chapter.

Conditions for Change

Significant organizational change can emerge out of adversity or prosperity, desperation or enthusiasm, but it more usually arises from relatively benign circumstances. Three conditions conducive to change under relatively benign circumstances are slack, competence, and zeal. Slack means an organization has people with discretionary time and discretionary resources to devote to something new. R & D and marketing departments in some firms and educational institutions are near one end of the continuum of slack. People in universities, especially, have much more discretionary time and a looser definition of their jobs than people do in other kinds of organizations. They also have an attitude of experimentation about resource expenditures – that resources are well spent if they produce knowledge and symbols of knowledge. A second key condition is competence – people with expertise in the new technology and procedures for sharing or propagating that expertise. Where computing is concerned, universities are likely to be near one end of the expertise continuum. A third key

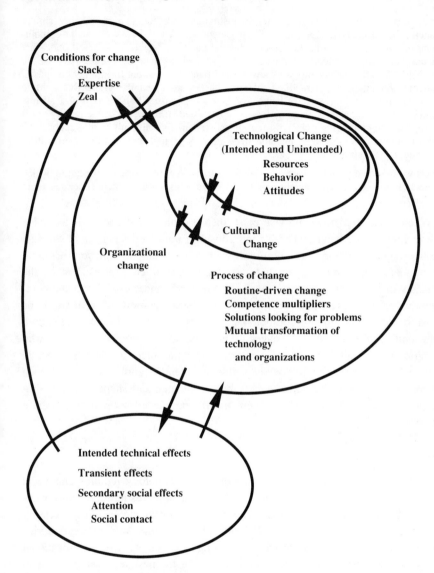

Figure 3.1. The social process of technological change in organizations.

condition is zeal or extreme enthusiasm for the innovation and commitment to it on the part of partisans who can spread their enthusiasm throughout the organization. To be first – to innovate – means a campaign, even a crusade. A recent report of a study of colleges and universities pioneering in computing says of this (Updegrove, 1986: 13–14):

Thus, despite the differences in the six institutions, we found a remarkably similar pattern: the visionary(ies) persuaded the president and faculty to make a major commitment to computing in order to garner industrial partners, foundation support and – not inconsequentially – national attention.... On each campus, there is a sense that "we are special." Clearly, part of this is "Hawthorne Effect," as visitors from other campuses, national and international media (and researchers) are given the grand tour. More important is a common sense of being "on board," of suspending the typical academic criticism, perhaps even suspending disbelief. (At Reed, 100 percent of the faculty voted to support the computing plan!) In fact, it was remarkably difficult to find skeptics on these campuses; faculty, staff, and students were very excited about making their institution better, different, unique, a leader.

What we observed is enthusiasm of a visionary, translated into resource allocation, which generates activity, which (ideally) produces more enthusiasm, which generates more activity.

When slack, expertise, and zeal exist, then organizational energy is available for technological change. These conditions also nourish the culture of the new technology. Computing is a cultural as well as technical phenomenon. Cultural components of computing include generally shared cultural beliefs in the efficacy of computing, cultural roles like "hacker" and "user," and the computer argot used in computer science and engineering communities. It would be hard to imagine any major computerization project uninfluenced by the culture surrounding computing. Managers who purchase computers, experts who program and install them, and novices who encounter them for the first time, all will be interacting with hardware, software, intended applications, and even operational policies, that have already been evaluated and shaped by the computer culture. Their experience of new or different technology will be, in part, a cultural experience.

Processes of Change

To introduce new technology or to modify old technology requires change in three areas: resources, behavior, and attitudes. Changing resources means changing the built technology and creating its necessary infrastructure. The necessary infrastructure of computing includes allocations of time and money, service people, teachers, physical space, computing procedures, and organizational units. Changing behavior means learning to use the new technology. It also means supporting and fostering new technology and acting to introduce it in specific areas. Changing attitudes means coming to believe that the new technology is instrumental to one's work and life. It also means holding symbolic beliefs in the legitimacy and value of computing, regardless of whether computers are actually used.

Changes in resources, behavior, and attitudes do not take place in isolation. They take place as part of the ongoing social interactions of ordinary organiza-

"Someday all these people will have personal computers, and it will be a much, much better world."

A key condition for change is zeal.

tional life. Obtaining computer equipment resources, for example, is both a cause and an outcome of the interactions which produce the capital budget. These ordinary organizational interactions show definite patterns that help us predict or anticipate the social process of technological change. That is, social interaction in organizations is regulated by standard procedures, or routines, and by people's organizational roles. Routines and roles determine how problems, solutions, and people act upon one another (e.g., Cohen, March, & Olsen, .1972). In effect, routines and roles regulate and channel technological change.

Four key social processes for technological change within the organizational context are: routine-driven change, competence multipliers, solutions looking for problems, and the mutual transformation of innovation and organization (March, 1981). The idea of routine-driven change assumes that very few major organizational changes happen all at once. Although the rhetoric of change may imply revolution or dramatic overnight changes, change usually is driven by the same stable procedures for doing things that determines most of organizational action. Thus most of what people do on any given day at work or school looks quite like what they did the day before. Routines for allocating resources, purchasing materials and supplies, hiring and evaluating personnel, renovating space, and coordinating staff continually play themselves out in organizations. Such routines seem mundane and removed from the glamor of new technology, but they provide a vehicle for executing change. They must be invoked by managers trying to do something new as well as by the ones who are maintaining the status quo. Routines can also generate occasions for change. For instance, organizations have procedures for orienting newcomers. Those procedures can offer occasions for introducing newcomers to a new technology. Organizations have procedures for publishing newsletters. Those newsletters can offer occasions for debating the value of new technology.

Change is also affected by competence multipliers, the tendency for people to get better at what they practice, and to practice what they are competent at doing. An initial change attempt may be targeted equally at all organizational participants or at all people who hold particular positions. They might start out all equally competent. But for a variety of reasons including interest and circumstance, some people will spend more time with the innovation than will others. The time-spenders will find their competence increasing. They will practice more, and gain more competence. Over time the organization becomes increasingly differentiated with respect to experience and expertise with the innovation.

Through a combination of zeal and competence multipliers, a chosen innovation increasingly becomes a solution looking for problems to solve. Competent partisans can be counted on to offer their innovation as a solution to whatever the problem of the day happens to be. Because they are competent, their proposals are often taken seriously. Every new one adopted increases their competence yet again. It also increases instances of that solution in the organization.

Because change is driven by routines, competence multipliers, and solutions looking for problems, an initial "innovation" is an unstable phenomenon. It will change shape and purpose as it moves through an organization and through time, even as it changes the organization. For example, an office buys computers with secretarial work in mind, and at first the main effect is to improve the looks of letters and documents. But all documents flow through managers, some of whom try producing letters or reports on their own. Some of these experiments succeed, with the result that computing (albeit in different form) enters the management function.

In sum, the particular course of a given innovation is heavily dependent upon ordinary organizational routines, arbitrary occurrences that produce competence multipliers over time, solutions looking for problems, and a mutual transforming of innovation and organization. This is a very organic view of the process of change. It does not accord a dominant place to an organization's managers or leaders. Leadership is important in providing or acquiring the conditions necessary for change – slack, expertise, and zeal. But leadership can rarely predict, let alone produce, the exact course of a complex innovation over time.

Social Consequences of Computing

Despite difficulties in predicting the exact course of any complex innovation, certain consequences of technology innovations commonly arise. Following the framework introduced in Chapter 2, we distinguish among levels of effects. We first distinguish between intended and emergent effects. Intended effects of computing are the hoped-for technical effects of using computing as a tool, such as to establish computer links with branch offices or to automate an assembly line. In addition to these intended technical effects, significant unanticipated changes emerge as well. Emergent effects are highly variable and hard to foresee. First, the technology itself is changing; computing is a highly tractable technology and a multiplicitous resource that people can use in many ways. Also, emergent effects depend on the symbolic significance of computing in the organization and on how people are using computing as an occasion for doing other things. One example of how differently computing can emerge (despite the same basic technology) comes from observations of how people learn computing in different organizations. There are some organizations in which computing is learned in formal training programs. Frequently these are places where computing is used by clerks or blue-collar workers in repetitious tasks. Computing may have negative symbolic connotations. What do these classes look like? The participants are low-status workers or their supervisors. The curriculum is rigid and targeted to specific jobs; workers learn how to perform specific tasks using a computer. They do not learn to use computing for other, more general purposes. And among administrators, talking about computer "training" is an occasion for ongoing labor-management bargaining and conflict. Learning computing is a starkly different affair in places where computing is discretionary and has positive symbolic connotations. People may never go to classes; they will learn on their own because it is considered a good thing to instruct others and to learn about computers. Classes are considered education, good for personal competence and self-advancement as well as for the job. People learn general as well as specific skills. And talking about computer classes among administrators is an occasion for discussing the goals of education.

Among emergent effects, we make a distinction between transient and more permanent social effects. The emergent effects of new technology are frequently transient problems that disappear or are alleviated in time, as when an organization improves computer training programs. Other emergent effects are longer lasting. These are social effects that occur as a secondary outcome of people's having to pay attention to different things or having social contact with different people. We emphasize the secondary social effects because they are largely independent of any particular technology or innovation plan.

Change in attention means change in how people spend their time and what they think is important. Change in social contact patterns means change in who people know and interact with. When attention and social contact patterns are changed, so are roles, norms, and social structure. Social roles codify patterns of social interaction and attention. New social roles emerge as a result of computing: for example, hacker, user consultant, PC store manager. Also existing roles are altered: secretaries become PC experts and teach their bosses how to use the machines; high-level administrators who have never used a computer come to be viewed as backward; librarians become information-processing specialists. New and changed roles affect not only those who occupy them but also those who interact with them. Patterns of information exchange are changed. So are working and social relationships. Thus, social structure is changed. So are perceptions of who is important, what is legitimate, what is prestigious.

Organization structure can also be altered. The organization of computational facilities is important for two reasons. First, organization influences how tasks such as computer acquisition are accomplished, who achieves high attention and influence, and especially who depends on whom to accomplish necessary tasks. Second, organization confers legitimacy in that the existence of organizational units symbolizes acceptance of the functional utility and autonomy of computing. For example, a PC Store symbolizes the notion of user independence in hardware and software acquisitions – in contrast to the days when central Computation Center staff governed all acquisitions.

The computer is not the first technology to change patterns of attention and social contact. Consider the railroad. While the railroad increased the speed of interurban transportation, it also profoundly affected attention and social contact. Train travellers' attention was caught by a uniquely new view of the land, a continuous blur passing by a train window. This view led Impressionist painters to experiment with capturing on canvas the fragmented nature of passing events. The results of these experiments changed our aesthetic values of light, color, and motion. The railroad also changed social contact patterns through bringing strangers together safely for the space of a journey. Thomas Wolfe described a train journey in *You Can't Go Home Again*:

One looks at all the pretty girls with a sharpened eye and an awakened pulse. One observes all the other passengers with lively interest and feels he has known them forever

... all are caught upon the wing and held for a moment in the peculiar intimacy of this Pullman car which has become their common home for a night. (Quoted in Stilgoe, 1983: 68)

One modern equivalent of the Pullman car is the terminal room or computer room. Students and other computer users gather there at all hours of the day and night to do computer work. In the process, they meet friends, strike up acquaintances, or just observe other folks hunched over their machines.

When you go into the computer center for the first time, you get intimidated by some people who are always there. They want to show you what to do while you're trying to learn yourself. They come and say, "Oh, I know how to do this." ... It seems that some people are there just to be there.... People are just hanging around, talking, and laughing and joking. (Student interview, spring 1982)

In addition to introducing new patterns of temporary social contact, railroads substantially altered more permanent patterns of social contact as well. The growth of the suburbs, fostered by metropolitan railroads and then automobiles, increased the spatial distance between work and home and therefore changed social contact patterns. The suburbs became a place of women and children during the day; husbands and fathers appeared only on nights and weekends. In 1902 the wife of a railroad commuter described "life in the [metropolitan railroad] corridor, life revolving around the departure and arrival of her husband, her daily and seasonal activities outdoors, and her growing hatred of occasional visits to the city, the place of congestion, dirt, and noise" (Stilgoe, 1983: 283).

Computing can also create new social contacts and lead to new social relationships. A small number of computer romances has made the headlines. But a more significant form of sustained social contact occurs on special interest electronic bulletin boards or conferences. These are electronic forums accessible from one's own terminal or workstation where people with similar interests can exchange news or opinions. They may be accessible to only one geographic location or, through long distance networks, they may be accessible to people across the country and abroad. A hint of what electronic groups might be like in the future may be found in the list of computer interest groups available to students on the computer science network at CMU. Computer science students work in a computer-intensive environment, so in observing their community we surmise what our own future might be like. A partial list (A–H) of interest groups reads as follows:

- Arms-D (discussions of war, weapons, nuclear policy)
- Arpanet-BBoards (address of electronic bulletin boards)
- Astronomy Events (tells people about astronomical events)
- Aviation (for everyone interested in commercial or military aviation)
- Chess (a newsgroup)
- Cluster (technical discussions of cluster computers)
- Cube-lovers (Rubik's Cube mailing list)

- Dolphin-users (for people who use a Xerox 1100 workstation)
- Editor-people (for people interested in computer text editing)
- Energy (discussion group on energy and energy policy)
- Extended-Addressing (technical discussions)
- Forth (discussions of computer language)
- Franz-Friends (discussions of computer language)
- H19-People (discussions of H19 terminals)
- Header-People (discussions of electronic mail formats)
- Home-Sat (for those interested in home earth satellite receivers)
- Human-Nets (Discussions of many topics, all of them related in some way to the theme of a worldwide computer and telecommunications network usually called WorldNet)

New patterns of attention and social contact can create uncertainties about proper behavior and lead to embarrassment in social relationships. New norms or shared standards of conduct arise to ameliorate these uncertainties. Advice on "train manners" appeared as early as the 1880s and offered counsel on "what sorts of clothes to wear, what types of cosmetics to bring, how to direct the Pullman porter, and how a man and woman must arrange themselves at a dining car table" (Stilgoe, 1983: 70). We are just beginning to see advice on "computer manners": for example, "how to be a constructive, courteous sender and receiver of electronic messages" (Shapiro & Anderson, 1985: 18).

A new technology leads to a new way of life for some people, who become engrossed in exploring the limits of the technology and who develop deep social bonds with others who are doing the same. Highballers, hotroders, and hackers have in common that they are members of a subculture with values, norms, and behaviors that set them apart from others. Members of the computer culture have passionate opinions about hardware and software; their world is divided into people who can operate in the culture (wizards, wheels, nerds) and people who can't (clones, randoms). Cultural members are often viewed with some alarm by mainstream society. Even the telephone, a technology taken for granted in today's society, had its high priests in the early days. Surprisingly, given their contemporary reputation for unfailing politeness, telephone operators were once castigated for rudeness to novices. The *Times of London* complained that "too many of them [operators] seem to regard the telephone user as their natural enemy and treat him with utter nonchalance, if not with an insolence and impertinence which are all the more irritating because there appears at present to be no remedy for them" (*Times of London*, December 27, 1905: 7). A technology-centered culture is an important component of the social aspects of any technology – in its own right, as a source of innovation, and as an alien environment for technology novices.

We are not interested simply in what computers people use or what programs they run. Although they are not irrelevant to our interests, they are only the starting point for our concern. For instance, there must be hardware and software for electronic communication in order for people actually to communicate electronically. Once people begin communicating electronically, then we can trace how attention and social contact change as a result of that communication. Attention, social contact, norms, social structure – these are fundamental strands in the social fabric of any university, any organization, or the larger society. Computing may have profound effects on all of them.

The University Context

Carnegie Mellon University (CMU) has about 4,000 undergraduates, 1,500 graduate students, 500 teaching faculty, and 1,600 staff. It consists of four colleges (engineering, science, fine arts, and humanities and social sciences), two professional schools (business and public policy), and many interdisciplinary programs and research centers. Over the past ten years the university has transformed itself from a good regional university with two or three nationally prominent departments to a nationally recognized university. One of the key ingredients in this transformation is computers. The 1984 undergraduate catalog describes some of the importance of computing at CMU:

Almost every department at Carnegie Mellon uses computers as part of its curriculum, and nearly three-fourths of the students use computers in some way. Engineering and science students find that the computer is often used as a problem-solving tool or teaching aid; business students simulate corporate management and planning problems on computers. Humanities and social sciences students learn techniques for computerized statistical analysis and word processing. Fine arts students, depending on their majors, may work with computerized painting, graphic design, solfege instruction, or stage lighting design systems.

Carnegie Mellon is regarded as one of the nation's leaders in computer science research. In 1981, the university announced the opening of its Robotics Institute, an interdisciplinary project where research on integrated systems promises to have wide-ranging impact on industry. The project, which evolved from ongoing research in artificial intelligence in the Computer Science Department, involves engineers, scientists and management specialists from the campus community. Computer-automated manufacturing systems, underwater and space exploration, and inspection and maintenance of nuclear systems are just a few of the areas in which researchers will study the potential use of robots.

On October 20, 1982, Carnegie Mellon University and International Business Machines (IBM) signed a three-year agreement to develop a prototype personal computing network. Successful completion of this project will enable all students, faculty, researchers and professional staff at CMU to have access to personal computer workstations, each between 20 and 100 times more powerful than current home computers. The development plan would allow several thousand personal computer workstations to be in place by 1986, and 7,000 by 1990. (Undergraduate Catalog, 1984: 11)

Where does CMU stand with respect to the three conditions for change identified in the previous section – slack, competence, and zeal? As a private research university in relatively good financial health, CMU is near one end of

the slack continuum. It is also near one end of the competence continuum.
With a first-rate computer science department and a long-standing commitment
to computing in other parts of the university, CMU houses a relatively high
proportion of people with computing expertise. Its tradition of supporting mul-
tidisciplinary research centers and teaching programs reflects the relatively
permeable organizational subunit boundaries across which expertise can
propagate. CMU certainly houses computing zealots. One important example is
CMU's president, Richard Cyert, who prophesied:

> Maybe in the year 2000, when people look back ... I think the little project that we
> started here with IBM will be viewed as perhaps the most significant development in
> higher education in the 20th century. ("Distributed Personal Computing Environment,"
> 1986, p. 15)

As later chapters will demonstrate, the overall campus attitude toward computing is also quite positive.

It was in fact at Carnegie Mellon University that the concept of a "computer-
intensive" campus was born in 1980 (Updegrove, 1986). The concept entailed
providing thousands of powerful workstations linked together by a campuswide
communication network. Rather than take a casual approach to this idea,
CMU's strategy was decidedly aggressive in pursuing and shaping the new
computer technology. As happened at some other universities and colleges such
as Brown University, Reed College, and University of Houston, CMU administrators believed that being first would uniquely position their organization.
Being first would inspire enthusiasm and attract resources to offset the risks.
The CMU strategy for building a computer-intensive campus included providing
substantial computing resources, using "market" incentives, and encouraging
entrepreneurs. Providing computing resources entailed acquiring funds and
equipment from outside donors and hiring expertise to develop and support
those resources. It also entailed establishing organizational subunits to manage
and support their development and use. Market incentives included manipulat-
ing the price of mainframe services to discourage their use and providing deep
discounts on PCs to encourage their use. While most market incentives were
concretely related to computing services and equipment, some were more subtle.
For instance, departments knew that new computing-related majors like Information Systems or Chemistry and Computer Science attracted students in
droves. CMU has long encouraged entrepreneurship in research and teaching.
In the eighties computing entrepreneurship led every college and professional
school to seek major external grants for educational computing. It led individual
faculty members to establish computing-related research and acquire funds for it
(for instance, computer-based historical studies of Irish contentious gatherings
and management studies of how information systems reduce the range of information used in decision making). It also led groups of faculty members to

establish research centers related to computing (for instance, the Center for Technology and Productivity and the Center for Advanced Computing, for research using supercomputers). (Part II describes in some detail the growth in computing resources, activities, and positive attitudes resulting from this strategy.)

Examples from CMU can illustrate the four processes of change described in the previous section – routine-driven change, competence multipliers, solutions looking for problems, and mutual transformation. One relatively early instance of routine-driven change comes from the history department. In 1981 a university-wide committee on the future of computing at CMU found "an extraordinary penetration of computing" in the history department (Task Force on the Future of Computing archives, meeting notes 10/29/81). The department was using computing extensively in both teaching and research and wanting to use it even more. This use and enthusiasm had its impetus in the annual budgeting routine five years earlier. In 1976 the chairman of the history department requested authorization from the dean of his college to hire additional secretaries to type manuscripts and course materials. The dean refused the request but said he would provide a terminal to anyone who wanted to learn text editing. Furthermore he would underwrite development costs for any undergraduate courses that used computing extensively. The department need not have taken the dean up on his offer. Professors could have continued to use existing routines to prepare manuscripts and course materials. But several professors did acquire terminals in 1977, more did in 1978, and the process was launched.

An instance of competence multipliers comes from the membership of the Task Force for the Future of Computing, a university-wide committee established in 1981 to "attain a broadly based view and a sense of perspective about where [CMU] wants to go" with respect to computing (Cyert, 1981, p. 1). The task force, whose 17 members were drawn to be widely representative of the campus, met intensively throughout the fall of 1981 and canvassed the entire campus. In the spring of 1982, it issued a report on the future of computing at CMU that importantly influenced the then-developing idea of a computer-intensive campus. By 1985, of the 14 faculty and staff who had been task force members and were still at CMU, 6 (43%) had taken on new major responsibilities with respect to computing. They were: director of the Computer Center, head of the Computer-aided Design Center, head of the Center for the Design of Educational Computing, assistant director of the Software Engineering Institute, head of the Committee for Social Science Research on Computing, and vice-provost for research computing. Only the first of these positions had even existed at the time of the task force. Of course task force membership did not directly cause people to take on these new responsibilities. But it did cause them to spend relatively more time than their peers thinking, talking, and writing about the future of computing. And it caused them to be identified with those ideas by senior administrators who later made or approved the new appointments to computing-related positions.

The library provides instances of solutions looking for problems and mutual transformation of technology and organization. During the 1970s the university began transforming itself into a national research university, but the size and scope of the library collections lagged far behind. The quality of the library was acknowledged to be a university problem. Computing was seen by central administrators as a way to upgrade the quality of the library. Over the first half of the 1980s the library began investing heavily in computing. In the process the library began to be transformed from a repository for books and journals to an information broker. Simultaneously, library personnel began modifying the technology they had acquired and acquiring other technology that had not been part of the original plans. Certainly the library changed during this five-year period, but it would be a mistake to assume that the technology innovation remained stable over that period. It changed and evolved as library personnel increased their competence and aspirations with respect to computing. (Chapter 9 describes the computerization of the library in more detail.)

And what of social consequences? The remainder of the book describes in some detail changes in attention and social contact patterns resulting from computing at CMU. It describes changes in how people view themselves and changes in roles and social structure. Chapters 1 and 2 suggested that the most profound long-run effects of computing may be on how we view ourselves as people and on the organization of knowledge. It is too early in the spread of powerful computing to produce real data on these effects. But in the studies reported in the rest of this book we do see tantalizing glimpses that computing changes how people think of themselves. And we see that the organization of knowledge about computing is certainly changing.

Part II

Components of Change: Resources, Behavior, and Attitudes

Part II describes three fundamental components in the social process of technological change. They are resources, behaviors, and attitudes. Each is both an outcome of previous change and an input to current change. The level of computing resources at CMU in 1981 was the outcome of many previous years of resource allocation and decision making. That level also served as the base around which new resources could be deployed and the baseline for measuring the change in resources from 1981 to 1985. People's computing behavior (e.g., what programs they used on what machines) was an outcome of the resources available and procedures for managing those resources. Similarly it was the impetus for acquiring new resources and changing procedures for managing them. People's attitudes about computing (e.g., how positively or negatively they viewed it) were both an outcome of their previous experiences with computing and an influence on how they anticipated further experiences with computing and on how they wanted to change the resources.

Chapter 4 enumerates computing resources at CMU and how they grew and changed form during the years 1981 to 1985. Chapters 5 and 6 describe how people use these resources, that is, what programs people run. Chapters 6 and 7 describe people's attitudes about computing. Chapter 6 describes their personal attitudes; Chapter 7 describes "public" attitudes as indicated by the contents of campus newspapers.

Technological change includes changes in the amount of technology and changes in how the technology is organized, both of which are documented in Chapter 4. Organizational theorists for years have wondered if computerization leads to centralization of authority. In this chapter we examine one kind of centralization, the centralization of computer administration. We find fairly good evidence that just the opposite of centralization has been occurring, at least in the time frame of this research. When "technology optimists" talk about the effects of computers, they frequently ask about productivity improvement. Unfortunately, measuring productivity is no simple matter. Should we measure efficiency in student learning by counting the number of instructors who can be dismissed? Should we try measuring the proportion of time instructors have for research? Productivity is an abstract and value-laden idea. We did not feel prepared to say that something learned in 15 minutes is more efficient than something learned in 1.5 hours. On the other hand we can find out how people actually use computers and then let the reader decide if these uses are productive. Chapters 5 and 6 use two different methods to investigate how people use computers. One of the findings of these chapters is that nearly everyone who uses a computer uses it primarily for text processing and communication with other people. Numerical computation is a subsidiary use. The last chapter in this section is a study of the news about computing within CMU. We include this chapter here because the news documents technological change and also illustrates the enormous symbolic importance of computers at CMU. As Chapter 2 predicts, the "hoopla" about computers is considerable and may overshadow and obscure its actual technical and social effects for many years to come.

The chapters in Part II represent a broad range of methods for studying the components of change. Chapter 4 relies upon organizational archives such as inventory reports, organizational charts, and personnel records to analyze changes in resource levels over time. Chapter 5 uses data that were automatically collected by mainframe computers to analyze what programs people run on those machines. Chapter 6 uses questionnaire-based self-reports of people's computing behaviors and attitudes. Chapter 7 uses content analysis of campus newspapers to assess public attitudes about computing. All of these methods together yield a much richer picture of computing components for change than would any one method alone.

Three themes weave across all of the chapters in Part II. One is that computing is a multiplicitous technology. In the CMU case this means that many computing resources are available and their form changes over time. It also means that there are many strategies for acquiring computing and many ways of using it. And it means that computing has many different organizational meanings. It is a resource like instructors. It is a tool like the telephone. It is a symbol like admissions statistics. It is an occasion for debate over values. A second theme, evident in Chapters 5 and 6, is that computing is used not only for calculation and data analysis. Text editing, communication, and even jokes are important uses of computing. These uses imply a broad role of computers in organizational life, and increase the likelihood of secondary social effects. The third theme is that computing is positively valued. This is not to say there are never complaints or doubts. But across many people and settings a generally positive attitude toward computing prevails.

4   The Computers Are Coming!

Suzanne Penn Weisband and Jane Siegel

In Part I we suggest some of the potentially profound effects computing may have on organizations. In order for those effects to occur, the amount of computing available to people must increase. Although simple increases in the amount of available computing power is surely not a sufficient condition for important social effects, it is just as surely a necessary condition. This chapter describes the technology of computing at Carnegie Mellon University from 1981 to 1985 to set the context for the subsequent chapters in this book. We enumerate increases in the total computational resources (hardware, software, and human work) during the period and describe changes in the distribution of these resources through the university. Total resources and resource distribution reflect the community's access to computation and the distribution of that access. Understanding the level of resources gives a sense of what is required to begin to establish an electronic community. Understanding the distribution of access is necessary to understand and evaluate the computational infrastructure. A university in which only 10% of the people use 95% of the computing resources hardly seems an "electronic community." Further, distributional data provide a basis for examining hypotheses about social and organizational effects. For instance, a computer network that connects art professors with engineering professors can have different social consequences than a network that connects the art professors only with one another.

During the period of our study none of our computational resource measures had zero baselines. That is, computing was already quite prevalent on campus in 1981. By 1981, 27 years had passed since CMU had acquired its first mainframe computer, an IBM 650. It was 16 years after the computer science department had been created, 10 years after the time-shared system had been installed, and 1 year after the liberal arts college began requiring that all freshmen take a course in computer programming. These bits of history suggest that by 1981, CMU was already heavily committed to computing. Possibly CMU was, even then, the most computerized university in the world.

Our study began just prior to an important turning point in the history of computing at CMU: In 1982 the president announced a joint venture between the university and IBM to build a powerful distributed computer network. This was an explicit decision to move the university toward a saturated computing

43

environment, an electronic community involving the entire campus. The new electronic community would represent a quantum leap in computation, both quantitatively and qualitatively. Although the operational goal of the joint venture was (and is) to build a distributed computer network of powerful workstations, accessible by all and educationally productive, we did not limit our study to the planned technical changes brought about directly by the joint venture. As we discussed in Chapters 2 and 3, adaptations surrounding a major technology introduction frequently surpass and exert a greater total impact than the new technology that was envisaged initially. For that reason, we attempted to sample all aspects of computer technology change at CMU – hardware, networks, computer professionals, and the like. As it turns out, this approach was fortunate. The distributed network that was planned at the beginning of the decade is just being implemented as we approach 1988, but Carnegie Mellon University is undeniably a vastly different computing environment now than it was in 1981. In the sections that follow we describe the nature of this change.

Computing Components

The physical basis of a modern computing facility is embodied in three main components: computers that process and store information; interfaces, such as terminals and printers; and some means of communication. To represent the first two tangible aspects of CMU's computing facilities, we enumerated computers, terminals, and printers owned by the university. To investigate communication, we looked at local area networks and campus connections to long-distance networks.

Hardware

In the spring of 1981, most of the 131 computers at CMU were large mainframes (e.g., DEC-20s) and minicomputers (e.g., VAX), although scattered around campus were some microcomputers such as Apple, Commodore, and Hewlett-Packard personal computers. Terminals were used to connect the general campus community to a group of mainframe computers, the DEC-20s. The computer science community used terminals to interact with its own group of mainframe computers. The printers on campus were generally line printers and daisy wheel printers. Computer Science and Robotics used prototype laser printers from Xerox Corporation. Figure 4.1 shows the number of computers, terminals, and printers in 1981 and in 1985.

By spring of 1985, CMU owned 2,789 computers. This does not include several thousand personal computers sold to students, faculty, and staff by the campus PC Store and other computer stores in the city. Although the change includes an increase in mainframe and minicomputers, the largest part of the

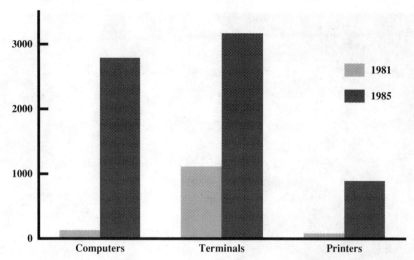

Figure 4.1. Total number of computers, terminals, and printers in 1981 and in 1985.

increase derives from an influx of microcomputers on campus. (Table 4A.1 in the Appendix to this chapter shows how the computers were distributed across the university in 1981 and 1985.) The 1,000% increase in number of computers is huge by any measure, but it is especially impressive in light of other organizational changes during the same period: The physical size of the campus increased only 10%. The student body increased only 5%. The size of the staff and faculty increased 15%. The budget increased 60%.

One of the debates over the large joint venture with IBM concerned whether it would cause a decrease in technology choice on campus and an increased dependence on a single vendor. Yet not only did the number of computers increase, but the diversity of manufacturers increased as well. In 1981, 21 different computer manufacturers were represented by equipment at CMU; in 1985, 100 manufacturers were represented, an almost 400% increase. (Table 4A.2 lists the 100 different computer manufacturers represented at CMU.) Not only has the number of manufacturers proliferated, but campuswide access to machines from different vendors has also increased. In 1981 almost all educational computing took place on large DEC time-sharing systems. By 1985, while those systems were still heavily used, campus clusters of IBM PCs, Hewlett-Packard workstations, and Apple Macintoshes were also in place and widely used.

In comparison to the 20-fold increase in computers from 1981–1985, the number of terminals increased only three-fold: 1,113 terminals in 1981 versus 3,169 in 1985. Also, terminal technology had changed little. The new terminals differed from older models only in having detachable keyboards and larger screens. Nonetheless, the change is significant. Connecting terminals to mainframes and

By spring of 1985, CMU owned 2,789 computers.

minicomputers gave many new groups, especially from the humanities, social sciences and the arts, ready access to computing for the first time in their offices, dorms, and homes. Crowding in terminal rooms was much reduced. And for the first time in its history CMU found it necessary to carry out detailed inventories of computer hardware located off campus.

The campus community also acquired access to more printers, with 81 in 1981 and 893 in 1985. Most of the printers acquired after 1981 were for the IBM PCs and for the Macintoshes. Also, during this period, the university acquired Xerox laser printers for the general campus community. The new print interfaces gave anyone on campus the ability to produce documents of fine print quality and to experiment with fonts and illustrations. (During this period, at least one professor forbade use of the laser printer for term papers because, he said, laser-printed term papers gave a misleadingly good appearance.)

The enumerations above bear generally on the distribution of computing resources. This distribution can be characterized by both dispersion and penetration. How widely dispersed was the spread of computational facilities across different departments? How deeply did computational facilities penetrate into departments and reach all individuals? Clearly, the general trends were in the direction of both broad and deep distribution. More total groups acquired access to computer hardware. And groups acquired access to more computer hardware.

Software

Along with its physical components, a computing facility requires software: an operating system and programming environment, programming languages, and tools such as editors, computer mail, statistics packages, and data base management systems. At CMU, the software situation was complex even in 1981. In 1981 the mainframe campus computers held 26 public directories containing 2,789 files available to the average user. These public files included such computing tools as programming languages, tutorials, and statistical packages. By 1985, computing tools had increased in number by more than one-third: 30 public directories contained 3,729 files available to the general computing public. There were new tools such as graphics packages, data base packages, and spread sheets; many of these tools were used on PCs as well as on mainframes. The campus PC Store, established in 1983, sold about 4,000 software packages from May 1984 to May 1985. Figure 4.2 displays types of software programs sold by the PC store. Text-processing programs like Epsilon, WordStar and MacWrite were most popular at the PC store.

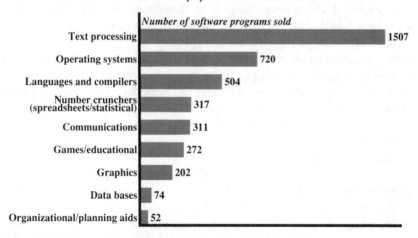

Figure 4.2. 1985 Personal Computer Software Sales (May 1984–May 1985).

Tools also increased in complexity and demand or support higher skill requirements. People who switch from line editors to Emacs and Scribe (still the standard editing and document production tools) must learn the equivalent of two new programming languages. People using the newer statistical packages to their capability should be familiar not only with traditional statistics such as

stepwise regression and univariate analysis of variance but with the proper use
of more complex applications such as multivariate analysis of variance and log
linear analysis. Even the computer mail options were more various and complex
in 1985 than they were in 1981. The documentation for tools available on the
mainframes lengthened by 20% during the period of our study.

Just as Chapter 2 suggested, CMU's "housekeeping" was affected by computing. Computer-based administrative tools grew on CMU's campus. Generally,
these tools are information systems that provide ways for administrators and
their staffs to organize and to store administrative data, for example, personnel
applications for jobs on campus. The systems also provide for querying records
in the data base, for updating them, for producing reports and forecasts. Figure
4.3 shows that in 1981, 19 departments at CMU used computer information
systems. All were data base systems implemented on mainframe computers. In
1985, 24 departments used computer information systems. Fourteen of these
were implemented on mainframe computers and the rest were implemented on
minicomputers and microcomputers. In addition, applications were spreading
from the financial domain (57% of the applications in 1981, 47% in 1985) to the
domains of personnel administration and building and property maintenance.

Communication

Some views of computer-intensive environments picture many independent
users, each with his or her personal computer, unaffected by general system
crashes and strains on capacity. However, communication to and among computers can contribute immeasurably to their usefulness. Communication made
possible by computer networks increases people's access to shared information
and services, such as data bases, printers, and help files. Even more important
perhaps, communication facilities permit person-to-person communication
through computer mail, computer bulletin boards, and computer conferencing.
Historically, as we pointed out in Part I, technologies such as the telephone and
the automobile that changed the nature of direct communication and contact
among people had significant long-term social effects. We expect that direct
electronic communication will be one of the major ways that the electronic
community is forged and that it will affect the social and intellectual fabric of
the university. For that reason we monitored the growth of demand for communication facilities.

At CMU, communication facilities take two forms, local area networks and
long-distance networks. A network allows people to send mail or other files to
anyone with an account on the same computer or on any other computer linked
through the network. In 1981 there were two local area networks, an Ethernet
linking Computer Science machines and a DECNET linking Computation Cen-

Figure 4.3. Information systems for business and service functions.

Functional area	Spring 1981 Computers	Spring 1981 Applications	Spring 1985 Computers	Spring 1985 Applications
Planning	Mainframe	Buildings	Minicomputer	Buildings
Administrative systems	Mainframe	People	Mainframe, Minicomputer	People, People
Telephone	Mainframe	Money	Minicomputer	Money
Stores				
Child care				
Housing	Mainframe	Buildings	Mainframe	Buildings
Food	Mainframe	Money	Mainframe, Microcomputer	Money, Money
Parking	Mainframe	Buildings	Microcomputer	Buildings
Budget	Mainframe	Money	Mainframe	Money
Purchasing	Mainframe	Money	Mainframe, Mainframe, Local area network	Money, Money, Money
Accounting	Mainframe	Money	Mainframe	Money
Cashier	Mainframe, Mainframe	Money, Money	Mainframe, Mainframe, Mainframe	Money, Money, Money
Payroll	Mainframe, Mainframe	Money, Money	Mainframe, Mainframe	Money, Money
Audit				
Federal regulations			Microcomputer	Buildings
Personnel			Minicomputer, Local area network	People
Physical plant	Mainframe	Buildings	Minicomputer, Minicomputer	Buildings, Buildings
Security			Microcomputer	People
Treasurer	Mainframe	Money	Microcomputer	Money
Endowment	Mainframe	Money	Mainframe	Money
Alumni relations	Mainframe	People	Mainframe	People
Fund raising				
Admissions	Mainframe	People	Mainframe	People
Registrsation	Mainframe	People	Mainframe	People
Placement			Microcomputer	People
Financial aid	Mainframe	Money	Mainframe, Local area network	Money, People
Public relations			Minicomputer, Minicomputer	People, People
Publications	Mainframe	People	Mainframe	People

KEY:
- Mainframe computer
- Minicomputer
- Microcomputer
- Local area network
- Buildings
- $ Money
- People

ter machines. Four mainframe computers were connected to the DECNET
network. By 1985 the university DECNET connected 8 mainframe computers
and 4 minicomputers, and it was linked to 49 different DECNET sites (see
Figure 4.4). These included at least twelve more local area networks which had
been added on campus (e.g., the Information Technology Center's development
network, the Library network).

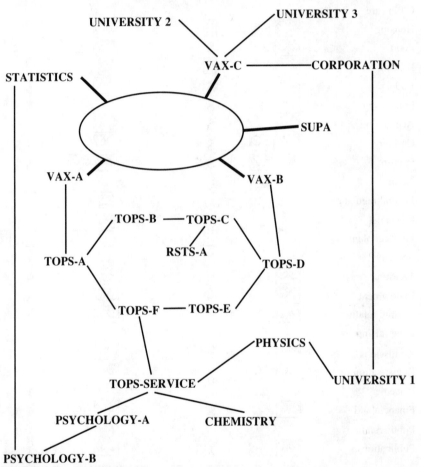

Figure 4.4. CMU DECNET, 1985.

The first long-distance network used on campus was ARPANET, the network
established by the Department of Defense to permit research computing at
remote sites. (It was soon observed that the ARPANET was more frequently
used for person-to-person communication and information exchange.) By 1981,
people at CMU also had access to TELENET, a commercial long-distance net-

work owned by General Telephone and Electronics. In 1985 network connections had been established to BITNET, CCNET, and MAILNET, all established for nonprofit, academic purposes.

In addition to people's sending electronic mail and transferring files, groups could also establish computer bulletin boards to communicate through the network. In spring 1981 only the Computer Science Department and Robotics Institute had established computer bulletin boards on their machines; there were no bulletin boards on the campus DECNET network. The first computer bulletin board on the DECNET was established in late 1981 by the Task Force on the Future of Computing. Since that time, the number of computer bulletin boards on the DECNET has grown rapidly. By 1985 there were 82 bulletin boards with topics ranging from academic coursework and computer clubs to recipes and sports (see Table 4A.3 for the complete list).

Access and Use

When the Task Force on the Future of Computing published its report in 1982, it listed access as the first issue in any expansion of computational facilities: "We have purposely placed access first on our list of issues. This is primarily because enhancing computing means enhancing computation usage, which means good access. However, we are also responding to the universal cry of frustration we have heard from the campus community about the current state of access (p. 9)." So we must address whether, along with the large increase of computer hardware, software, and communication, there is a corresponding increase in access and usage. This is a nontrivial question, because accessibility is driven not only by available resources in the computing environment but also by the desires of people to use them. As resources increase, desires tend to increase also.

A sample survey we conducted in 1984 showed that students, faculty, and staff reported using a computer about 3.5 hours on the average weekday. This is a substantial increase over the 1.5 hours that was estimated in 1981. In Chapters 5 and 6 we discuss computer use in more detail.

Organization and Expertise

Organizational Structure

Changes in organizational structure consisted of new computing units, new names for units, and new conceptions of computer services. These changes reflect the growing influence of computing as tool, as symbol, and as occasion for basic social processes at CMU. In 1981 there were five computer-related central administrative units; in 1985 there were 10. (See Figure 4.5.) This

number does not include units located at the college level, such as the Center for
Technology and Productivity or the Center for Arts and Technology. It also
does not include preexisting units whose names were "computerized." For
example, in 1983 the Electrical Engineering Department renamed itself the
Electrical and Computer Engineering Department. Telephone Services was part
of the Computing and Planning Department in 1981; in 1985 it was renamed
Telecommunications to reflect the notion that communications and computing
systems must be integrated, and that cable is as important to computing as to
traditional telephony. At least two noncosmetic organizational changes increased resources for research in computing and elevated the status and authority of computer science and engineering from their already high position.
The first was the creation, in 1984, of the Software Engineering Institute supported by the Department of Defense. The Institute, whose purpose is to find
ways of applying software research in defense systems and in industry, may
ultimately employ up to 500 people and account for a substantial minority of the
university budget. The second important change gave the Computer Science
Department university status as an independent department reporting directly to
the provost rather than one within the Science College reporting to its dean.

Computer Administration

As organizational units concerned with computing proliferated at CMU, decision making about computing became more diffuse. The domain of computer
acquisitions illustrates this increasing diffusion. In 1979 five groups were involved in important computer acquisition decisions at CMU: the Computation
Center director and staff; the Vice-Provost for Computing; the Computer Policy
Committee, made up of senior faculty representatives from some colleges and
schools; the Computer Board, composed of top officials and faculty; and the
Capital Allocation Committee, also composed of top officials and faculty. By
1985, deans, department heads, research directors, and faculty had independently acquired computers for their units. Paradoxically, this decentralization
was helped along by a tightening of central control over mainframe computing.
In 1983 and 1984, just prior to the influx of minicomputers and microcomputers,
mainframe computing had become very popular. If the demand for mainframe
computing were to be satisfied, mainframe computer acquisition and maintenance costs would have overwhelmed the university budget. So top officials
centralized the locus of decision making about mainframe computing. The
Computer Policy Committee, which prior to 1983 had made acquisition decisions, became the Computer Policy Advisory Committee (CPAC) and lost its
decision-making authority. The Computer Board, composed of the Senior
Vice-President for Academic Affairs, the Provost, and the Vice-Provost for

1981

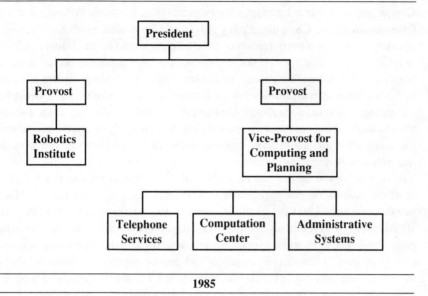

1985

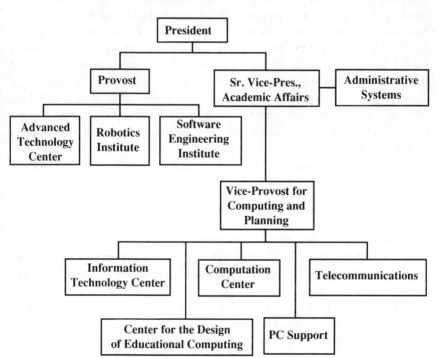

Figure 4.5. Computer-related administrative units at CMU.

Computing and Planning, the Vice-President for Business Affairs, and the Chairperson of the Computer Policy Advisory Committee, made the decisions about what new computer resources would be presented to the Capital Allocation Committee, which would decide how to apportion computer capital acquisitions and other capital decisions. At the same time, one vice-president at CMU took on formal responsibilities for computing and hired a new vice provost for computing. In sum, a smaller, more central administrative group came to control decisions about central services and large machines. This effectively slowed the acquisition of mainframe computers and inhibited new investments in mainframe software and services.

At this point, the central administration also decided to impose much higher costs on mainframe computing and to stop improving services for it. Many people complained, but useful minicomputers and microcomputers had become affordable even to relatively impoverished departments. Since mainframe computing was becoming more expensive and overcrowded, the obvious choice was to acquire departmental minicomputers and microcomputers. Research faculty in engineering, psychology, and statistics started a trend that spread across the university by acquiring minicomputers and hiring professionals to operate their computer systems. They supported these acquisitions from research grants. New subunits within the Computation Center – the Personal Computer (PC) Support Group and the PC Store – began operations in the fall of 1983. One of the first activities of these units was to invite all departments to buy discounted IBM PCs. By 1985 acquisition decisions were being made by administrators in 4 colleges with 24 departments, among them 2 professional schools and 4 institutes. In addition, such decisions were made by the Computer Board, the Computer Policy Advisory Committee, the Computation Center, the Information Technology Center, the Center for Educational Computing, the Computer Club, and several offices within the central administration such as the Administrative Systems Department.

Expertise

A computing facility is only as sophisticated as the people who support it and use it. Therefore, we care about the degree to which CMU employs computing experts, and the degree to which expertise and support are spread through the community. Also, the presence of experts is an indicator of the presence of a computer culture, that is, of specific values, norms, and skills that influence computing attitudes and behavior.

We operationalized "expertise" by formal job titles and job categories that specified computing as a main activity (e.g., programmer or software engineer), or specified managing computer-related departments as a main activity (e.g.,

Director of Computing). We did not include anyone holding a teaching position in our count. The number of computer professionals doubled from 1981 to 1985. Table 4.1 shows that in 1981, full-time computer professionals numbered 169; in 1985, full-time computer professionals numbered 359.

One debate surrounding increased computing in 1981 was over the possibility that technicians residing in a powerful computation or technology center would dominate computer-related policies and developments. Our data do not answer this question, but they do suggest that expertise is becoming decentralized. In 1981, six academic departments employed full-time computer professionals whereas in 1985 ten departments employed full-time computer professionals. In Chapter 6 we show also the growing computer expertise of students and faculty. In nearly every department, nonprofessionals among the students, staff, and faculty act as in-house computer experts and consultants.

Another measure of computational expertise is support services. Support includes hardware and software acquisition, installation and maintenance, education and training, consulting, systems analysis, and preparation of documentation and directories. CMU has employed both students and part-time and full-time staff to provide these support services. The data in Table 4.2 suggest that human support has grown significantly. For example, from 1981 to 1985 the number of full-time support staff grew from 60 to 144 persons, a 140% increase. Again, this contrasts with an overall staff increase at the university of only 16%. As we have shown earlier (Figure 4.7), computer support services have been reorganized to reflect the increasing variety in the kinds of computation on campus.

Core Activities

It is possible to conceive of a dynamic, growing university computing facility that nevertheless fails to affect the core activities of the university: education and research. We should therefore ask whether the rapidly expanding computation activity at CMU reflects commensurate growth of educational computing and research computing.

Unfortunately, we do not have adequate data to compare educational and research computing with computing done for other purposes – to make social contacts, say, or to do administration. The versatility of computers makes sorting out its functions as difficult or more difficult as sorting the functions of other multifunctional tools one finds in a university such as books, telephones, typewriters, and calculators. Furthermore, we do not have a common yardstick for evaluating the relative significance of "more" research computing and of "more" educational computing. Is it significant that in 1985 a sociologist used a computer to conduct an electronic survey whereas in 1981 he used a paper and

Table 4.1. *Computer Professionals at CMU in 1981 and in 1985*

Organizational units	No. of computer professionals	No. of other computer professionals who manage computing units
1981		
1. Central administration		
Administrative systems	3	13
Computation Center	7	27
Hunt Library	0	1
Total	10	41
2. Centers and institutes		
Design Research Center	0	2
Mellon Institute – Research	2	2
Robotics Institute	0	28
Total	2	32
3. Academic departments		
Carnegie Institute of Technology – Dean's Office	0	1
Computer Science	1	73
Graduate School of Industrial Administration	0	3
Mechanical Engineering	0	2
Psychology	0	2
School of Urban and Public Affairs	0	2
Total	1	83

continued

pencil questionnaire to accomplish the same purpose? Is it significant that a social psychology professor has developed a computer tutor to help her teach research methods? We know that such changes took place, but we do not know how significantly they changed the fundamental practices of teaching and research.

Given the difficulties, we simply report what we know about changes in educational and research behavior and leave the comparative question open. One method we have employed is to "self-report," that is, asking people how they expect computers to change their own research and teaching or how computers have already changed these activities. Chapter 6 presents data on how faculty and students answer these questions.

Apart from self-report, another measure of core change is change in educational curricula. At CMU in 1981 there were six majors or concentrations that

Table 4.1. *(cont.)*

Organizational units	No. of computer professionals	No. of other computer professionals who manage computing units
1985		
1. Central administration		
Administrative systems	3	18
Computation Center:		
Administration	2	3
Data communications	1	6
Hardware	0	5
Operations	2	8
Software	0	·7
User services	1	7
Hunt Library	0	5
PC Support	2	10
Registrar	0	1
Telecommunications	2	0
University planning	2	1
Vice-Provost for Computing and Systems	1	1
Total	16	72
2. Centers and institutes		
Advanced Technology Center	1	0
Center for Design of Educational Computing	1	2
Design Research Center	0	3
Information Technology Center	0	19
Mellon Institute – Computer Engineering	2	10
Robotics Institute	0	52
Software Engineering Institute	5	18
Total	· 9	104

continued

were described in the Course Catalog as computing-related; in 1985 there were nine such majors or concentrations. Also, in 1981 there were 60 courses whose course titles or course descriptions were designated explicitly as computing-related; in 1985 there were 82 computing-related courses. The largest increase in educational computing (using courses as the measure) was in non-science or engineering courses (art, business, history, etc.). For example, by 1985 there were computer-related courses in art ("Art and the Computer"), industrial management ("Management Information Systems"), and philosophy ("Ethics

Table 4.1. *(cont.)*

Organizational units	No. of computer professionals	No. of other computer professionals who manage computing units
3. Academic departments		
Architecture	2	3
College of Humanities and Social Sciences – Dean's Office	1	1
Computer Science	3	110
Electrical & Computer Engineering	1	20
Engineering & Public Policy	0	2
Graduate School of Industrial Administration	0	6
Mellon Institute of Technology – Dean's Office	0	1
Physics	0	1
Psychology	0	6
School of Urban and Public Affairs	0	1
Total	7	151

and Computer Technology''), where in 1981 there were none. (See Table 4A.4 in Appendix to this chapter for the complete course list from 1984-1986.) This large relative increase can be attributed to a statistical artifact, that is, to the very low number of computing courses in the humanities, social sciences and art when the decade began. Still, the trend is toward closing the gap between educational computing in science and engineering vs. other disciplines.

Conclusion

CMU has seen a remarkable increase in computing resources over four years. Many of the changes were unforeseen when the decade began. They emerged as an interaction of technology advances and organizational process, including those emphasized in Chapter 3: routine-driven change, competence multipliers, solutions looking for problems, and mutual transformation of technology and organization. An example of unanticipated routine-driven change was the enormous growth of access to computers by nontechnical faculty. One reason for this change was that secretaries used computers to produce documents, which led to the faculty discovering text editing, document preparation programs, and printers. At CMU we used to hear people make a distinction between ''real'' computing like programming and ''fake'' computing like text editing. With the entry of nontechnical people into computing, and of some of them into sophis-

Table 4.2. *Central Computer Services at CMU*

Organizational unit	Staff (No.)
1981	
Administrative systems	18
Computation Center	33
Telephone Services	6
Vice-Provost for Computing and Planning	3
Total computer services staff	60
Managers and directors of computer services	8
1985	
Administrative systems	24
Center for Design of Educational Computing	5
Computation Center	
Administrative	8
Data communications	8
Hardware systems	7
Operations	12
Software systems	8
User services	9
Information Technology Center	40
PC Support	17
Telecommunications	8
Vice-Provost for Computing and Systems	3
Total computer services staff	144
Managers and directors of computer services	17

ticated computing, the definition of real computing expanded to include making documents. This change illustrates how cultural as well as technical transformation of technology can be instigated within routines.

An example of unanticipated change with competence multipliers was the growth at CMU of national (and international) networks and facilities for sending mail and documents across them. At first only the computer scientists accustomed to ARPANET used national networks. Then administrators decided to assign people free computer accounts for classwork, teaching, and administration. People with computer accounts learned to send computer mail. Some of them did it frequently. The frequent users wanted more and broader access to mail networks. Access to networks stimulated demand for even more mail facilities.

An example of unanticipated change as solution was the creation of new computer-related curricula such as the information systems major in the Department of Social Sciences. Administrators encouraged initiative and entrepreneurship in computing at the departmental level. Department heads adopted computer-related curricula as a way to solve or alleviate departmental problems. Computer-related curricula increased enrollments in social sciences, modernized the Philosophy Department, and reduced isolation of the Art Department.

Nearly all of the unanticipated technological changes at CMU increased ordinary people's access to new technology, and therefore changed the organization itself. Some writers have claimed that computers are an important organizational resource, and therefore will be captured by the technical and managerial elite and used disproportionately for their benefit (Boguslaw, 1981; Danziger, Dutton, Kling, & Kraemer, 1982). At CMU higher-status people received new computers first, but the larger effect was the increasing dispersion of computation and computational resources across statuses and types of people along with decentralization of services and expertise, and expansion of individuals' technology choices. This suggests that elitist domination of technology is not inevitable, and that technology growth can occur along with democratization of technology access in organizations.

Of course, democratization is not always a good thing in all aspects of an organization. For example, free use of computer mail entails some risk that people will embarrass managers with complaints they make public (Trebig, 1985). The debates over "democracy" at CMU concerned decentralization of control in two areas of computer administration, computer purchasing and support services. CMU has created either a mess or an opportunity depending on how you view decentralization (for general analyses of decentralization see Simon, 1977; Mintzberg, 1979; McLaren, 1982).

With respect to computer purchases the question was whether to allow individuals and departments to buy their own computers. Decentralized purchasing is attractive because it is fast and reflects local needs. It is motivating, because it demonstrates the faith of top administrators in the capabilities of department heads. It increases local competence. The disadvantages of decentralized purchasing are inconsistency of purchases and costs across the organization and inattention to overarching organizational goals such as network compatibility. At CMU decentralized purchasing created a babble of computers, which created compatibility requirements for the new distributed network that were never envisioned initially.

Decentralization of computer services was another issue. Decentralized services are attractive because they allow local helpers to resolve crises quickly without disrupting other units. But decentralized services are duplicative and encourage neglect of common problems. At CMU many computer services such as major repair and maintenance and operation of the mainframe computers were (and still are) centralized; decentralization increased mainly in smaller jobs such as PC installation and in jobs that many people could do such as running statistical programs. The Computation Center represents a major source of centralized services. It is typically slower to respond to problems than department staff are. Difficulties in its systems affect the whole university. When repairs are made to its air conditioners, everyone using a mainframe computer stops work. Compare the Computation Center with Professor Elliott Clark, a typical department computer guru. When something in the department breaks or someone has a computing problem, he is a sympathetic helper. He not only fixes problems, he also teaches people about computers. On the other hand, he cannot repair the computer network and he does not have the clout to acquire a computational laboratory for students. Democratization, or decentralization in this example, is therefore a problematic variable. As long as computation implies large common problems, then decentralization of purchasing and services wastes resources. But where local experts can handle the work, centralization wastes talent. At CMU and possibly in most other organizations, computation services need to be both centralized and decentralized, and this is probably what will happen in the coming years.

Epilogue

When we wrote this chapter in 1986, the most recent compilation of CMU computers indicated that CMU owned 2,789 computers. In May, 1987, just before publication of this book, the inventory indicates that CMU owns 5,513 computers. Other aspects of the computing infrastructure have increased as well (e.g., network connections, information systems, courses). Many of the new computing resources are connected with the development and deployment of "Andrew," the major computer system developed by CMU with IBM. The changes and learning connected with introducing this new system seem significant, frequent, and likely to continue over months and years. Central administrators and service people are developing programs to provide people with the expertise (and bravery) to participate in this new stage of technology. The culture of diffused technological change seems as robust as it was in 1982.

Appendix

Table 4A.1. *Computers at CMU in 1981 and 1985*

Organizational units	Number 1981	Number 1985
1. Central administration		
Accounting		10
Action Program		2
Administrative Systems		32
Admissions		13
Auxiliary Services – Administration		1
Benefits Office		1
Budget Services		2
Career Services and Placement		2
Cashier		2
Children's School		2
Computation Center	20	390
Controller		1
Counseling and Student Development Center		1
Credit Union		1
Faculty Senate		1
Federal Compliance/Safety		2
Financial Aid		18
Foundations and Corporations		1
Housing System		3
Parking System		1
Payroll		1
Personnel		5
Physical Plant – Administration	2	1
Physical Plant – Construction Design		1
Planning	2	
President		3
Property Management		1
Provost		4
Publications and Campus Printing		11
Public Relations		1
Purchasing		2
Registrar		12
Research Contracts		2
Security		1
Senior Vice-President, Academic Affairs		15
Student Affairs – Dean		23
Summer Studies Program		4
Systems Control		3

continued

Table 4A.1. *(cont.)*

Organizational units	Number 1981	Number 1985
Telecommunications		6
Treasurer		2
University Dining Service		3
University Libraries:		
Administration		9
Automation and Planning		4
Engineering and Science Library		1
Fine and Rare Books		1
Hunt Library		20
Mellon Institute Library		2
University Planning		8
Vice-President, Business Affairs		9
Vice-President, Development		4
Vice-President, University Relations		8
Vice-Provost, Computing & Systems		11
	—	—
	24	666

2. Centers and institutes

Academic Advisory Center		4
Advanced Technology Center		5
Center for Design of Educational Computing		21
Center for Energy and Environmental Studies		4
Design Research Center		13
Hunt Institute for Botanical Documentation		5
Information Technology Center		416
Mellon Institute:		
Administration		6
Computer Engineering		6
Professional Services		2
Rail Systems		5
Sponsored Research	1	13
Technical Services	2	3
Robotics Institute		191
Software Engineering Institute		16
	—	—
	3	710

continued

Table 4A.1. *(cont.)*

Organizational units	Number 1981	Number 1985
3. Colleges		
Carnegie Institute of Technology:		
Dean		18
Biomedical Engineering		3
Chemical Engineering		29
Civil Engineering		45
Electrical and Computer Engineering	6	124
Engineering and Public Policy		16
Mechanical Engineering	9	67
Metallurgical Engineering and Materials Science	4	40
College of Fine Arts:		
Dean		5
Architecture	4	20
Art		20
Design		18
Drama		9
Music		11
College of Humanities and Social Sciences:		
Dean		22
English		38
History and Philosophy		34
Psychology	9	98
Social Science		39
Statistics		13
Graduate School of Industrial Administration		172
Mellon College of Sciences:		
Dean		6
Biological Science	2	39
Chemistry	10	40
Computer Science	49	329
Mathematics		17
Physics	9	57
School of Urban and Public Affairs	1	81
	—	—
	104	1,410

Note: This list does not include terminals and printers.

Table 4A.2. *The 100 different computer manufacturers represented at CMU in 1985*

APL	Data I/O	Lobo	Tandy
Accurex	Data General	Lockheed	Teleserve
Aerometrics	DEC	MDB	Televa
Ampex	Digital Pathway	MDI	Tektronics
Apple	DISA	Masscomp	Teralk
Aptec	Dynex	Matrex	Three Computers
Array	EAI	Maxtor	3-M
Atari	Eagle	Morgenthaler	Three Rivers
BBN	Epson	Mosaic Tech	Texas Instruments
Bruter	Evans & Sutherland	Motorola	Timeplot
CMU	Four Phase	NB	Troy
Carberra	Fujitsu	National Semiconductor	Unimation
Charles River	General Data	Nicolet	Varian Instruments
Christian Industries	Grid System	Ohio Scientific	Varian Systems
Citoh	HBS	Omnibyte	Vicom Systems
Columbia	Hewlett Packard	PAR	Victor
Commodore	IBM	Panasonic	Wang
Compaq	IS	Perkin Elmer	Waters
Compugraphic	Ikegar	Polymorphic	Wavetek
Computex	Infotron	Pring	Weather Measure
Cromenco	Integrad	Processor Tech	Xerox
Cybsystem	Intel	Ridge	Zenith
Cybtronics	Interdata	Science Research	
DSC	Iris	Silicongraphic	
Daisy Systems	LSI	Sun	
Data Machines	Lancer	Symbolics	

Table 4A.3. *Computer Bulletin Boards at CMU in 1985 (excluding Computer Science bulletin board)*

BBoards for scheduled courses:

12-631	15-1xx
15-200	15-211
15-212	15-381
18-101	21-199
33-113	66-100
76-271	82-103

General BBoards:

Aac	Ad451
Advanced-scientific-computing	Afrotc
Apartments	Aphio
Army-rotc	Asian-club
Bhac	Bib-myth
Cmu-mac	Computer-club
Cooking	Corporations
Cs-312	Csw-99-101
Cycling	Dec-pro-350
Dept-of-drama	Fluids
Focus	Foundations
Gamers-club	General
Graphics	Hss-computing
Humannets	IBM-3083
IBM-announcements	IBM PC
Icec	Ieee
Im	Info-kermit
Info-sci	Info-sys
Ingres	Is1
Itc	Job-postings
Library	Macintosh
Mcs-frosh	Mcsfss
Mech-e	News-cc
Off-campus-jobs	Opinion
Pc-user-group	Peaa
Peace-alliance	Personal-computing
Philosophy	Physics-iie
Pronumerate	Public-relations
Region	Registrar-information
Research-information	Robotics-club
Scribe	Sflovers
Space	Student-senate
Tennis	Uds
Uds-comments	Vax-vms
Workstudy	Wrct

Table 4A.4. *Computer Courses at CMU, 1984–1986*

Academic department	No. of computer courses
1984–1986	
Architecture	2
Computer Modeling in Design	
Introduction to Computer-Aided Design	
Art	1
Art and the Computer	
Biomedical Engineering	1
Bioinstrumentation and Bioinformation Processing	
Carnegie Institute of Technology	1
Real-Time Computing in the Laboratory	
Chemical Engineering	5
Economics and Optimization	
Process Dynamics and Control	
Process Design and Economics	
Simulation	
Process Engineering and Synthesis	
Civil Engineering	2
Structures	
Computer Methods in Civil Engineering	
Computer Science	17
Introduction to Computing B	
Introduction to Computing C	
Discrete Mathematics of Computer Science	
Survey of Programming Methods and Applications	
Fundamental Structures of Programming I	
Fundamental Structures of Programming II	
Combinatorial Analysis	
Comparative Languages	
Artificial Intelligence: Representation and Problem Solving	
Artificial Intelligence: Vision and Manipulation	
Compiler Design	
Operating Systems	
Software Engineering Methods	
Applied Algorithm Design	
Formal Languages and Automata	
Computer Graphics	
Special Topics	

continued

Table 4A.4. *(cont.)*

Academic department	No. of computer courses
1984–1986	
Electrical and Computer Engineering	6
Analysis and Design of Analog and Digital Circuits	
Introduction to Computer Architecture	
Fundamentals of Control	
Concurrency and Real-time Systems	
Logic and Processor Design	
Computational Methods for Electrical Engineering	
Engineering and Public Policy	1
Robotics: Applications, Cost and Benefit	
English	2
The Computer in Literary and Linguistic Studies	
The Computer and Rhetorical Studies	
Industrial Management	3
Management Information Systems	
Computer Graphics in Communications	
Advanced Computer Graphics in Communications	
Mathematics	4
Linear Algebra	
Numerical Methods	
Algebraic Structures	
Mathematical Logic	
Music	1
Electronic and Computer Music	
Mechanical Engineering	5
Manufacturing Science	
Dynamics of Physical Systems	
Feedback Control	
Dynamics	
Numerical Methods	
Philosophy	3
Logic and Computers	
Ethics and Computer Technology	
Computer Programming Projects in Philosophy	

continued

Table 4A.4. *(cont.)*

Academic department	No. of computer courses
1984–1986	
Physics	6
Introduction to Computational Physics	
Electronics II	
Advanced Computational Physics	
Special Problems in Computational Physics	
Principles of Instrumentation I	
Principles of Instrumentation II	
Psychology	6
Cognitive Psychology	
Information Processing Psychology and Artificial Intelligence	
Research Methods in Cognitive Psychology	
Cognitive Processes and Problem Solving	
Intelligent Computer-Assisted Instruction	
Advanced Seminar in Cognitive Processes	
Social Science	7
Information Systems I	
Information Systems II	
Information Systems III (project course)	
Computer-Based Models of Social Phenomena	
Emerging Social Issues in Computing	
Computers in Organizations	
Communication, Science, and Society	
Statistics	9
Statistics Concepts with Computer Applications	
Statistical Methods for Data Analysis	
Introduction to Probability and Statistics I	
Introduction to Probability and Statistics II	
Experimental Design for Behavioral and Social Sciences	
Advanced Data Analysis I	
Advanced Data Analysis II	
Simulation and Monte Carlo Methods	
Statistical Software Packages	
Total	82

5   Electronic Observations of Computer User Behavior

Mike Blackwell

Chapter 4 documented that there are thousands of computers at CMU. What do people do with them? At CMU, artists draw pictures using graphics workstations. Engineers design bridges using computer simulations. Students write term papers and play games using personal computers. But we can only guess at the prevalence of these behaviors because there have been no comprehensive studies of computer behavior across an entire organization. If systematic studies were available, the information would help us anticipate likely social effects and plan future systems.

In 1983, when the research reported in this chapter began, many computer centers collected statistics about *computer cycle use*, that is, the number of hours of computer time that people use. Administrators in computer centers monitor computer cycle use to anticipate demand for computer capacity. A different statistic, and one that is gathered less frequently, is *computer program use*, that is, the functions for which people use computers. Monitoring computer program use along with cycle use – the "what for" as well as the "how much" – would help administrators anticipate demand for computer functions and services, a question of increasing importance now that computer capacity has expanded so markedly. Fortunately, computers can be programmed to collect data both about cycles and programs. One purpose of this research was to explore the kinds of information these data can provide.

Another reason to study computer use is to put the computer to better application as a tool for social science research. When people interact with computers, they are writing, reading, solving problems, communicating, and otherwise emitting behavior that social scientists are interested in studying. By monitoring the programs people are running, we can ascertain the relative importance of different computer functions as well as differences in computing behavior among groups of people. Using the computer as a research tool has the potential of collecting data that would otherwise be impossible to obtain.

At the very lowest level observable by a person, the computer performs just one function, executing programs. Of course, this one function has many varied and complex side effects, but simply examining which programs a person has the computer run provides an objective measure of how the computer is being used. Then we can ask how different people behave: what types of programs do different kinds of people run, how often, when, and for how long? What is required then is a method of collecting these data.

Typically, studies of how people use computers rely on self-report data from interviews or questionnaires. These methods are useful, but they require active participation of the people being studied, which may lead to biases in the data. Also, they limit the quantity of data that can be collected by the researcher. People cannot be observed constantly, nor can we expect them to maintain accurate records of everything they do. An alternative is to use the computer as a passive observer of what programs it is running and for whom. The computer can observe constantly, collecting as much data as desired, without any effort from either the researcher or the people being studied. An additional benefit of this method of data collection is that the data are already stored in the computer, ready for analysis, relieving the researcher of tedious data entry.

Until recently the most popular and accessible computers on campus were the six DECSystem-20 mainframe computers maintained by the university's computation center for the general campus community. The Computer Science Department and the Robotics Institute also used one DECSystem-20 mainframe, along with many smaller mainframe computers. Hence, the DEC-20 machines were a logical choice as a site for studying campus computer users.

Study 1

Do group differences exist?

The DEC-20 operating system collects a variety of statistics on all files stored on the system, including the programs that people run. These statistics include the date when each program was created and the number of times the program has been run since its creation. Thus, the average number of times per day that each program is run is easily determined. This number is the average for all of the users of the particular mainframe on which the measurement is taken. If different groups use different mainframe computers, then comparing the measurements for two different mainframes will give an idea of the way different groups use computers. At CMU, the groups on the campus mainframes tend to be similar because the Computation Center distributes student users alphabetically across its mainframes. Thus, a comparison of users between two campus machines should not yield much difference. Fortunately, one mainframe has a very different user group, the Computer Science DEC-20, which is used solely by Computer Science and Robotics faculty, staff, and graduate students. By comparing the average number of times per day that programs are run on the Computer Science mainframe with the same measure on any one of the Computation Center mainframes, it is possible to find out if computer use differs

Functional category	Program name	Use
Executive	Exec, Cmexec, Clock, Sysdpy	Logged in but idle
Text processing	Emacs, Zemacs, Edit	General text editing
	Scribe	Document preparation
	DoverQ, Print	Printing
	Spell	Text correction
Communicating directly	MM, MS	Computer mail
	BBoard, Clxbbd	Group communications
Programming	APL, Basic, Bliss, COBOL, Macro, Pascal, SNOBOL	Computer languages
	Link, DDT	Program preparation and debugging
Data processing	SPSS, Minitab	Statistics
	Macsyma	Symbolic data manipulation
	Dbmsf	Data base management
	Plot	Data display
Using networks	NFT, FTP, Cmuftp	Transfering file with another mainframe
	Host, Telnet, Tn, Chat	Logging in on another machine
	Kermit	Transfering file with a PC
Having fun	Joke, Cookie, Bye	Tells jokes, fortunes
	Coke	Status of coke machine
	Various games	Computer games
Finding people	Finger, Where	Locating users

Key to figures and tables: Programs run on CMU mainframe computers.

between groups. Additionally, because the Computer Science users represent an extreme case of a "computer competent community," their behavior provides an interesting standard against which to compare that of other users. This exercise was accomplished using a program called Rdstat which computes the average number of times per day each program on the mainframe is run.

Results

The Rdstat program ran on the main system program directories of two mainframes, the Computer Science machine and one of the Computation Center machines. For the Computer Science group, 77 system programs were run at least once per day. For the general campus group, 102 programs were run. The

25 most frequently run programs for each of the two groups are plotted in Figure 5.1 with a logarithmic axis to scale them in to a smaller range.

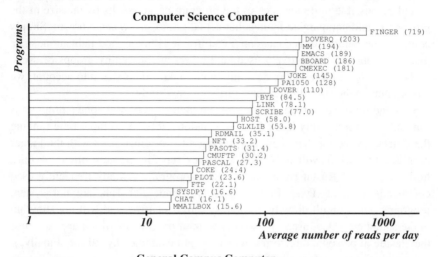

Computer Science Computer

FINGER (719)
DOVERQ (203)
MM (194)
EMACS (189)
BBOARD (186)
CMEXEC (181)
JOKE (145)
PA1050 (128)
DOVER (110)
BYE (84.5)
LINK (78.1)
SCRIBE (77.0)
HOST (58.0)
GLXLIB (53.8)
RDMAIL (35.1)
NFT (33.2)
PASOTS (31.4)
CMUFTP (30.2)
PASCAL (27.3)
COKE (24.4)
PLOT (23.6)
FTP (22.1)
SYSDPY (16.6)
CHAT (16.1)
MMAILBOX (15.6)

Average number of reads per day

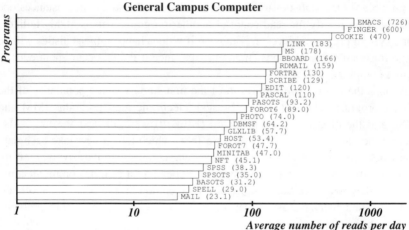

General Campus Computer

EMACS (726)
FINGER (600)
COOKIE (470)
LINK (183)
MS (178)
BBOARD (166)
RDMAIL (159)
FORTRA (130)
SCRIBE (129)
EDIT (120)
PASCAL (110)
PASOTS (93.2)
FOROT6 (89.0)
PHOTO (74.0)
DBMSF (64.2)
GLXLIB (57.7)
HOST (53.4)
FOROT7 (47.7)
MINITAB (47.0)
NFT (45.1)
SPSS (38.3)
SPSOTS (35.0)
BASOTS (31.2)
SPELL (29.0)
MAIL (23.1)

Average number of reads per day

Figure 5.1. Program use on the time-sharing computer systems.

Before describing the results further, we must be aware of four limitations of the data. First, the sizes of the two groups are different. Because of this, direct comparisons of program usage are not valid, but relative comparisons are. For example, Finger is the program that "points a finger" at who is logged in, tells where they are located, and other data about them. It is not correct to say that the computer science group runs Finger more often than the general campus group does, even though the Finger program has more average reads per day for computer science. But it is correct to say that the computer science group runs

Finger much more often than it runs Emacs, the text editing program, whereas the general campus group runs Emacs slightly more often than it runs Finger. It would be possible to divide each of the program usage results by the size of the groups to yield comparable figures, but actual group size was unknown. Simply counting the number of accounts on a mainframe is not a good indication, since many accounts are not actively used, and others are shared by groups of users. Since plans for a more elaborate study would take group size into account, we did not pursue the size of the groups further in this study.

A second limitation is that Rdstat gives no indication of how long a program is run, only how frequently it is run. Users undoubtably spend more time running the Emacs text editor than they do scanning a list of other users with the Finger program, but Rdstat will only show that they run Finger more often. A third limitation is that Rdstat counts only system programs. Many frequently used commands such as Type, Print, Directory, Send, and Talk are not system programs but are built directly into the system executive, and will not show up in the statistics. Also, users' personally written programs will not appear, since they reside in personal directories, which are not examined by Rdstat. Finally, it is possible for the statistics to be incorrect, since under some circumstances one program can modify the read count of another program. This is highly unlikely for a system program, however. But even if it does happen, the statistics will be valid for relative comparisons among groups since it should occur about equally across computers.

Perhaps the most interesting result of the first study was the popularity of the Finger program. The text editor (Emacs), electronic mail programs (MM and MS), and the electronic bulletin board (BBoard) were all near the top. Also among the most popular programs were Joke, which tells a new joke each day, and Cookie, which tells a fortune. These data, collected unobtrusively, reaffirm two facts of organization life. First, people spend a lot of time communicating. Second, they will have fun if they can. If we could observe behavior in offices, factories, and hallways as we can on computer systems, we would probably discern the same phenomena.

How different were the two groups? This is easier to answer if we divide the programs into functional categories. The categories we used in this analysis are:

1. Text-processing programs: Programs used to create, manipulate, and process text, such as Emacs, Scribe, and Spell. For text editing, there is no way to distinguish between editing text for a human (such as a manuscript) or a computer (such as a program).
2. Communication programs: Programs that allow people to communicate directly with one another: MM, MS, and BBoard.
3. Fun programs: Programs that are playful in nature: Joke, Cookie, Bye, Coke, Gloria and games.
4. Programming programs: Programming languages (Pascal, FORTRAN, Bliss, Basic, COBOL, Macro, SNOBOL, APL), and programs used in conjunction with the pro-

gramming languages (Link, DDT). This class does not include the run time libraries, such as PA1050, Pasots, or Forots.

5. Network programs: Programs that allow people to move information across the networks: NFT, Host, FTP, Telnet, Tn, Cmuftp, Chat, and Kermit. These programs are generally used to transfer files between computers, or to log into another computer, as apart from programs that send mail and BBoard messages between users (categorized as communication).

6. Data-processing programs: Programs used to process data (in particular, numbers), such as SPSS, Minitab, Macsyma, Plot and Dbmsf.

7. Finger: Finger does not fall neatly into any of the other classes.

A few programs that could not be identified were left out; none of these programs ranked very highly in total usage. For each category, the average number of runs per day for its programs was totaled. To make the results for the two groups comparable, each category total was divided by the total number of programs run per day for the entire group, which gives an estimate of the average number of times per day each kind of program is run. These data are displayed in Figure 5.2.

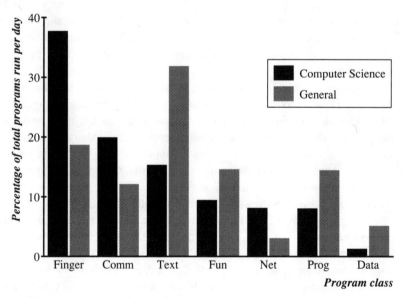

Figure 5.2. Program class usage from the first study.

Figure 5.2 shows that the Finger program is used frequently by both groups. Finger performs a variety of social functions. Typed with a person's name (e.g., "Finger Blackwell"), it is a way to find out where he is, if he is logged in, and likely places to find him if he is not. It shows what he is doing and possibly even his philosophy of life. (Finger reveals a person's "plan" file, which many people use to communicate more than just their work plan.) Typed alone,

Finger lists everyone who is logged in. Hence, it is a way for someone using a computer to remind himself that he is not really alone. Finger finds others who are in the same situation, and it reassures one that the "real" world hasn't disappeared. (I find myself running Finger late at night, alone in my office, while waiting for a program to finish, or after a long editing session. Often, Finger will reveal friends who are logged in elsewhere on campus. We'll send messages between our terminals for a while, perhaps to arrange to order a pizza, or just to waste a few minutes before plunging on with whatever we were doing.) Perhaps the reason why the computer science users run Finger proportionally more often than the general users is that so many of them work alone in their offices for long periods. By contrast, many of the general users, who are undergraduates, work in one of the public terminal rooms, where contact with the social world can be made in person.

Figure 5.2 shows other similarities between the groups. Most striking is the high frequency of communication and text processing. Within that, the computer science group uses the computer more often for communication than the general users do. This phenomenon may result from the fact that the computer science and robotics users are a natural and close-knit group, whereas the general users are a diffuse society who have been assigned to their particular computer alphabetically.

For the general users, text processing is by far the major function of the mainframe. These users include many faculty from the humanities, as well as students who have to write term papers. Fun programs are used next most frequently by both groups in relation to all other programs. Many users have the computer tell them a joke every time they log on or log off. We have no way of calibrating this result against the results of other studies in organizations. Organizational research has not focused on fun. It may be that people run the joke programs about as often as they trade jokes with colleagues in person.

Networking programs are used more often by the computer science users than by the general users. The computer science mainframe is connected to several different networks: ARPANET, local Ethernet, and local DECNET, but at the time we studied it the general mainframe was connected only to the local DEC-NET. Programming, on the other hand, is done more often by the general users because of the large number of students taking programming classes. The final category of programs, data-processing, is little used by both groups, a surprise when one considers that university computer centers used to be considered data processing centers.

Study 2

Study 1 has several limitations, due both to the type of data collected and to the method of collection. In Study 2, random samples of equal size from four social groupings were selected. Each sample consisted of 20 computer users with active computer accounts on one of the mainframes. The four groups were: (1) undergraduate students, (2) faculty in the College of Humanities and Social Science (H&SS), (3) faculty, staff, and graduate students in the Department of Computer Science and Robotics Institute (CS/RI), and (4) faculty in the Department of Electrical and Computer Engineering (ECE). Because ECE faculty were discovered to use their own VAX computers rather than the computation center mainframes, observations were terminated on the group and a group of administrators was added.

A new program, called Cstat, collected the data as follows. Every minute, Cstat automatically takes a snapshot of the computer system, recording the names of every person logged in at the moment, and the names of the programs they are currently running. (This information is readily available to any user from the operating system. It is reported by the Systat and Finger utilities, for example.) Cstat then searches its snapshot for the users belonging to the four sample groups. For every subject who is logged in, Cstat makes an entry in a computer log file for that group. This entry consists only of the current time and the name of the program the group member is running. Cstat checks for all group members, then goes back to sleep for another minute. Cstat ran as a detached background job for one week on three mainframes used by people in the four groups. Cstat ran 24 hours a day, except when a mainframe crashed. Then Cstat stopped and had to be restarted by hand when the mainframe came back up. Nevertheless, the statistics were collected over a large fraction of the week for all of the groups.

One important feature of Cstat is that it does not keep a record of the names of the users it discovers using the computer. There is no way to tell from the log file what particular person was running any program, just his or her membership in one of the four groups. By disassociating the data from any individual, the privacy of the group members, who were not informed that they were being electronically observed, was protected completely. A second important feature is that, as described earlier, Cstat collected only data that were publicly available to any system user. Insofar as individuals were not identified and only public behavior was recorded, the procedure used was like that used by social scientists who observe groups of people in natural settings, as when they study shoppers in department stores or children on playgrounds.

As an automated research assistant, Cstat has advantages over Rdstat. First, the sizes of all of the groups can be the same, so direct comparisons of program usage are valid. Second, Cstat estimates how long a program has been run, rather than how frequently, giving a better idea of how much time people spend running different programs. Third, Cstat records any action run by the user, including built in system functions like Print, Directory, Send, and Talk. Fourth, unless a user goes to extreme lengths to hide what he or she is doing, Cstat always reports correct statistics. Cstat does have one drawback. Because of its one-minute granularity, programs that take less than one minute to run, such as Finger and Directory, will be caught infrequently in Cstat's snapshot.

Results

Running Cstat for one week in fall 1983 produced approximately one million bytes of data. One method of analysis was to count entries in the data log files. Counting the number of times snapshots were taken, the number of times group members were logged in, and the number of different programs used by each group elicited the data in the top panel of Table 5.1.

Based on the average number of users logged in when the observations were made, one can see that the computer scientists use the computer most often. However, the undergraduate students use the computer nearly as much as the computer scientists do and more than twice as much as the H&SS faculty do. Comparing the number of different programs each group used is also interesting. The computer scientists and students, who are logged in often, use a much wider variety of programs than the H&SS faculty do.

Another way to organize the data is to sum the amount of time each program was used by the different groups. These data are presented in Table 5.2. The same program categories used in Study 1 were applied, except that the fun category was omitted since most of the fun programs (like Joke) run for less than one minute, and thus they are not well represented by the data. Likewise, Finger also runs for less than one minute. Nonetheless, Finger is run so frequently that it still shows up in these data. The Finger statistics are included so comparisons of its use among groups can be made. A new category, Executive, is the TOPS-20 top-level monitor. When a user is running "Exec," he is logged in but is not running any programs and the computer is idle.

One potential problem in classifying the data collected by Cstat is that all of the programs run by a user are recorded, including any personal programs he or she may have written. Fortunately, users rarely give their personal programs the same names as system programs, so any unrecognizable program name in the data was assumed to be a personal program and was not classified. As it turned out, the number of unclassifiable programs was very small, accounting for well under 1% of the total program usage, so we felt it was safe to ignore them in subsequent analyses. Another potential pitfall with the program names is that it

Table 5.1. *Data collected by Cstat computer program*

Group observed (n = 20 / group)	Number of observations	Number of users observed	Average number of users	Number of programs observed
Fall 1983				
Computer Science faculty and graduate students	9,374	22,729	2.42	97
Undergraduate students	6,839	14,620	2.14	104
Humanities and Social Sciences faculty	6,839	6,741	0.99	34
Spring 1984 [a]				
Computer Science faculty and graduate students	9,927	17,763	1.79	77
Undergraduate students	9,853	2,447	0.25	49
Humanities and Social Sciences faculty	9,853	6,084	0.62	39
Administration	10,253	5,505	0.54	22
Spring 1985				
Computer Science faculty and graduate students	10,365	21,146	2.04	63
Undergraduate students	9,410	4,419	0.47	43
Humanities and Social Sciences faculty	9,412	2,152	0.23	33
Administration	10,342	2,704	0.26	29

[a] Spring Carnival week.

is possible for a user to give a program the same name as a system program, to conceal its true identity. A few years ago there was a rise in the number of people playing a "Star Trek" game cleverly named "Emacs," the name of the most common text editor. The operations staff is wise to this trick now and assures me that it doesn't happen anymore. Still, the possibility is there.

The data in Table 5.2 show that text processing is the major use of the computer by a factor of two or three to one over all other uses of the computer. Although surveys suggest computers are popular as text processors, neither our own survey research nor the computer literature had led us to anticipate the

Table 5.2. *Program usage (and rank order of usage) from Cstat data*

Computer program category	Computer Science faculty and graduate students	Undergraduate students	Humanities & Social Science faculty	Administration
Fall 1983				
Text processing	7,117 (1)	7,009 (1)	3,024 (1)	
Executive	6,638 (2)	2,595 (2)	1,136 (3)	
Programming	1,989 (3)	1,192 (4)	101 (6)	
Communicating	1,914 (4)	1,877 (3)	516 (4)	
Network	959 (5)	314 (5)	201 (5)	
Data processing	467 (6)	273 (6)	1,213 (2)	
Finger	130 (7)	125 (7)	7 (7)	
Spring 1984				
Text processing	2,959 (3)	711 (2)	2,853 (1)	382 (3)
Executive	7,099 (1)	725 (1)	1,859 (2)	3,298 (1)[a]
Programming	3,031 (2)	173 (4)	0 (7)	0 (7)
Communicating	2,715 (4)	627 (3)	306 (4)	552 (2)
Network	711 (5)	40 (5)	312 (3)	320 (4)
Data processing	78 (7)	0 (7)	254 (5)	318 (5)
Finger	92 (6)	23 (6)	9 (7)	3 (6)
Spring 1985				
Text processing	3,534 (2)	1,977 (1)	1,103 (1)	112 (5)
Executive	13,440 (1)	769 (2)	336 (3)	1,246 (1)
Programming	0 (7)	97 (4)	77 (5)	6 (6)
Communicating	3,109 (3)	754 (3)	454 (2)	239 (4)
Network	137 (4)	39 (5)	79 (4)	800 (2)
Data processing	53 (6)	0 (6)	6 (6)	268 (3)
Finger	62 (5)	0 (6)	0 (7)	0 (7)

[a] Of these, 1,291 are idle programs.

extremely high degree to which all groups would use computers for this purpose in relation to other purposes. Hindsight, of course, explains that verbal communication, on paper and directly, is a major organizational activity, and especially so in universities. When a technology helps people prepare and communicate verbal information, they will use it for that purpose. Furthermore, as we noted in describing the results of Study 1, the general text editors are used for preparing communications to the computer, that is, writing programs as well as preparing communications to people.

The usage characteristics of the computer science group and the student group are remarkably similar. The biggest difference is that the computer science group spends more time doing nothing at the Exec. This is an artifact of the fact that at CMU computer scientists are not charged for computing and usually have terminals on their desks that they can log into and keep running all day. Undergraduates who do this would use up their computer time allotments, or find other people using their directories. The H&SS faculty group differs from the other groups in that this group uses the computer for data processing more than for programming. These data indicate that faculty are using the computer in their research, which at CMU is highly quantitative in both humanities and social sciences.

Change over time

The computing situation at CMU is far from static, as we documented in Chapter 4. Prices of computers are falling. People are buying personal microcomputers. Departments are buying minicomputers. To observe how computing at CMU is changing over time, it would be ideal to monitor what programs people use with Cstat on all of the computers, personal and mainframe. Unfortunately, Cstat at the time of this study was useful only for collecting data on the mainframe computers. Nonetheless, its data will yield an estimate of how computing may be changing. It is highly unlikely that the *amount* of computing done by people is decreasing. Indeed, it is probably increasing. Hence, any change in the computing behavior of a user group on the mainframes will be indicative of the functions that are and are not attracting users to newer, cheaper computing facilities.

With this hypothesis in mind, Cstat was run twice more, in the spring of 1984 and in the spring of 1985. The members of each group remained the same with the exception of a few users whose accounts had expired or had become entirely inactive and were replaced. A new, fourth group consisted of 20 members of the university's top administrators at the level of college deans to president.

At the outset, two anomalies in the data need to be explained. First, the usage ratio measure for the undergraduate student group (Table 5.1, second panel) suggests that the students plummeted from being one of the heaviest mainframe users to being one of the lightest. There were not enough personal computers on campus to account for this drop. We believe the explanation is Spring Carnival weekend, which occurred in the same week the second Cstat run was made. In any case, the third Cstat run was done a week earlier in the following year, and the student usage rate moved up.

The other surprise occurs in the data for the administration group. Administrators appear to use the mainframe computer about as much as humanities and social sciences faculty do (Table 5.1), but administrators spend a lot of this time with their terminals logged in but sitting idle (Table 5.2). Two computation center policies to deal with overcrowding make this behavior understandable. First, a person was not allowed to log in if there were more than a certain number of people already logged in, or if the computational load on the computer was above some specified limit. If either of these two limits was exceeded when a person attempted to log in, he was placed in a queue, sometimes for as long as four hours in the spring of 1984. Second, once a person was logged in, if his job was idle for about 15 minutes, his job would be automatically logged out. Administrators circumvented these policies by logging in once in the morning, when the computer was lightly loaded. But since they were not going to use the computer actively all day and they did not want their jobs automatically logged out, they played a trick on the computer. They ran one of several programs that uses enough computing to keep them logged in while they are really idle. One of these programs was a clock program in which the computer kept a constantly updated picture of a clock on the terminal screen – a quarter-million dollar digital clock! Another program merely kept a display of the mainframe's activity on the terminal screen, updated every few seconds. This active idleness behavior was not seen in the student and H&SS faculty groups because it would have been prohibitively expensive to run a program that did nothing for hours. Computer scientists did not have restrictive policies on their computer. By spring 1985, after administrators had been informed about their own behavior and the load had lessened on the mainframes, this behavior disappeared from the record. In any case, because of this idleness behavior, the usage ratio for the administration group reported in Table 5.1 is actually higher than it ought to be. The data in Table 5.2 show that administrators use the mainframe most for direct communication, whereas the other groups use it mostly often for text processing.

Change over time in average usage is plotted in Figure 5.3. These data show that computing on the mainframe computers decreased as personal computers became available. The group that changed least was the computer science group, which reflects their exclusive access to uncrowded mainframe computers. The decrease is most marked among the students (even taking into account Spring Carnival). The mainframe usage for the faculty group decreased, but the number of programs that they used on the mainframes stayed constant, indicating that although they used the mainframes less, they did not substitute some functions more than others with personal computers. (Chapter 6 corroborates this finding.)

It would be surprising if all mainframe uses decreased at the same rate over time. At the time of the studies, most personal computers did not gracefully manage network and communication functions such as electronic mail and bulletin boards. On the other hand, personal computers are very good for text

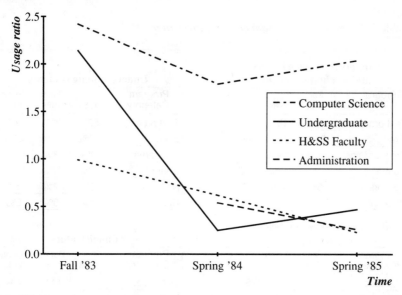

Figure 5.3. Change in program use over time.

editing and graphical representation. The percentage of total usage in each program category represented over time is shown in Table 5.3. These data suggest that fluctuations in program usage are relatively minor and are not patterned regularly. Hence, while people may be switching to personal computers, they have neither abandoned mainframe computing entirely nor have they assigned some uses strictly to personal computers and others strictly to the mainframe.

Table 5.4 shows the programs that accounted for the top 95% of the total usage by each group over time. Only 20–30% of all the programs used account for 95% of the program usage. This percentage remained constant over time, even though the total number of programs decreased. The table also shows that the use of the major programs, the executive (Exec), the editor (Emacs), the mail manager (MM or MS), the bulletin board (BBoard), and a few others, did not change markedly. Rather, as the total computing on the mainframes decreased, lesser programs, many of which performed the same functions as the major programs but with different features or interfaces, were abandoned. Since the programs that disappear are not programs performed well by personal computers, a reasonable hypothesis is that evolution is working – the strongest programs survive. A key argument is that the student "hackers," who formerly improved weaker programs and created new programs to compete in the available program pool, have moved from the mainframes to the personal computers where they have greater access and control. (Usage in the programming cate-

Table 5.3. *Change in program category over time*

Computer Science faculty and graduate students

Program Category	Fall 1983	Spring 1984	Spring 1985
Text proc.	37%	18%	17%
Exec	35%	44%	66%
Programming	10%	19%	0%
Comm.	10%	17%	15%
Network	5%	4%	1%
Data proc.	2%	0%	0%

Undergraduate students

Program Category	Fall 1983	Spring 1984	Spring 1985
Text proc.	53%	31%	54%
Exec	19%	32%	21%
Programming	9%	8%	3%
Comm.	14%	28%	21%
Network	2%	2%	1%
Data proc.	2%	0%	0%

Humanities & Social Sciences faculty

Program Category	Fall 1983	Spring 1984	Spring 1985
Text proc.	49%	51%	54%
Exec	18%	33%	16%
Programming	2%	0%	4%
Comm.	8%	5%	22%
Network	3%	6%	4%
Data proc.	20%	5%	0%

Administrators

Program Category	Fall 1983	Spring 1984	Spring 1985
Text proc.		11%	4%
Exec		56%	47%
Programming		0%	0%
Comm.		15%	9%
Network		9%	30%
Data proc.		9%	10%

gory declined among students and computer scientists, the major sources of hackers.) Exciting new locally developed programs are now appearing on the personal computers, rather than on the mainframes. Old (but still very useful) programs are maintained on the mainframes by a small number of paid support staff.

When Do People Compute?

Cstat data can also be analyzed to learn when people compute. Because all of the data recorded are time stamped, it is possible to tell what time of day group members were logged in, and what programs they were running at that time, hence, when during the day they perform different types of computing. For this analysis, the data from the first run of Cstat was used for the Computer Science, H&SS faculty, and undergraduate student groups, and the data from the second run of Cstat was used for the administration group. (The reason for mixing the two data sets is that the administration data was not recorded for the first run, and the student data from the second run were tainted by Spring Carnival.) To

Table 5.4. *Individual program usage over time (by percent of total use)*

Computer Science faculty and graduate students

Fall 1983		Spring 1984		Spring 1985	
Program	% of usage	Program	% of usage	Program	% of usage
EMACS	23.49	EXEC	39.85	EXEC	63.56
EXEC	14.98	LISP	15.45	MM	10.77
CMEXEC	14.23	EMACS	12.22	EMACS	6.85
MM	6.97	MM	10.75	ZEMACS	5.01
#'(LAM	6.32	ZEMACS	3.55	BBOARD	3.75
CLIS	5.70	BBOARD	3.43	FINE	3.30
DETACH	3.57	DETACH	1.64	SCRIBE	1.48
SCRIBE	2.89	LEDIT	1.45		
ZEMACS	2.85	TN	1.35		94.72
HOST	2.59	HOST	0.97		
LISP	2.00	CLXBBD	0.93		
LEDIT	1.94	KKJOB	0.92		
PLOT	1.75	SCRIBE	0.64		
BBOARD	1.17	PTYCON	0.55		
FTPSRT	0.92	TELNET	0.54		
NFT	0.85	FINGER	0.52		
DOVERQ	0.85				
COMPLR	0.67		94.76		
FINGER	0.57				
PRESSE	0.53				

Total programs   94.84

95% of usage:	20 (20.6%)		16 (20.8%)		7 (11.1%)
100% of usage:	97		77		63

Humanities & Social Science faculty

Fall 1983		Spring 1984		Spring 1985	
Program	% of usage	Program	% of usage	Program	% of usage
EMACS	24.55	EXEC	30.56	EMACS	29.97
EXEC	19.82	EMACS	30.01	MS	19.56
SPSS	17.82	EDIT	14.61	EDIT	18.26
EDIT	14.09	SPSS	4.17	EXEC	15.61
MS	6.81	MOUNT	3.58	SNOBOL	3.49
SCRIBE	6.10	MS	2.93	KERMIT	3.39
DUMPER	2.15	NFT	2.37	SCRIBE	2.42
SNOBOL	1.42	SCRIBE	2.10	TYPE	1.72
KERMIT	1.42	KERMIT	1.05	MM	1.02
HOST	1.02	MAIL	1.76		
		TYPE	1.00		95.44
	95.20				

Total programs   95.14

95% of usage:	10 (29.4%)		11 (28.2%)		9 (27.3%)
100% of usage:	34		39		33

continued

Table 5.4. (*cont.*)

Undergraduate students					
Fall 1983		Spring 1984		Spring 1985	
Program	**% of usage**	**Program**	**% of usage**	**Program**	**% of usage**
EMACS	43.65	EMACS	26.32	EMACS	41.32
EXEC	15.29	CMEXEC	16.39	EXEC	17.40
MS	10.15	MS	15.69	BBOARD	9.50
LEDIT	3.30	EXEC	13.24	ASSM	7.97
MACLIS	2.59	BBOARD	7.89	MS	7.38
CMEXEC	2.46	APL	6.38	REMARK	6.38
APL	2.35	SCRIBE	2.21	SCRIBE	3.17
LISP	2.05	MM	1.51	PASCAL	1.67
BBOARD	1.92	HOST	1.10	KERMIT	0.59
DBDRIV	1.66	TYPE	1.02		
SCRIBE	1.29	LOTS	0.98		95.38
	1.29	WHERE	0.94		
TYPE	0.96	PDS	0.74		
KERMIT	0.94	REMARK	0.57		
WHERE	0.85				
NFT	0.80		94.98		
REMARK	0.76				
VDIREC	0.62				
PASCAL	0.59				
MM	0.51				
LINK	0.49				
	94.52				

Total programs
95% of usage:	21 (20.2%)		14 (28.6%)		9 (21.0%)
100% of usage:	104		49		43

Administrators				
		Spring 1984		Spring 1985
		Program	**% of usage**	**Program**	**% of usage**

Program	% of usage	Program	% of usage
EXEC	36.46	EXEC	46.08
SYSDPY	23.45	KERMIT	20.78
MS	10.03	MS	8.21
BBOARD	9.94	TELNET	5.95
EMACS	6.61	ADSHOW	5.29
KERMIT	5.81	EMACS	3.51
ADSHOW	3.18	AD1ZX	3.22
	95.48	ADSUMN	1.41
		NFT	0.92
			95.37

Total programs
	Spring 1984	Spring 1985
95% of usage:	7 (31.8%)	9 (31.0%)
100% of usage:	22	29

determine when group members were logged in, the number of people logged in was averaged over every hour that data were recorded. These data are shown for each group in Table 5.5.

For the Computer Science group, computing was spread fairly evenly throughout the day, with a decrease in the early morning hours, and maximums in the late afternoon. (Also, but not shown, the weekend days did not differ greatly from the weekdays.) The undergraduate students also used the computer evenly across the day and night. By contrast, the H&SS faculty and the administrators showed a clear "9 to 5" pattern in their computer use. (Also, they did little computing during the weekends.) With few exceptions, particular categories of computing are not relegated to certain times of day. One notable exception: For all of the groups, communicating was more likely during the daytime than at night. These data may indicate that face-to-face interaction during the working day stimulates electronic communication or that people are using electronic communication as integral to their work and not just as discretionary communication. We hope to explore this idea further in future research.

Discussion

The Cstat program used in this research has several limitations. One problem is that the program is indiscriminate about how a user is logged in. If a user's job were detached (the job is still logged in, but the terminal is no longer connected to it), or if a user were running a program under a batch job, Cstat recorded that user as being logged in. This is not desirable, since what is really of interest is when an actual human is sitting at a terminal, logged in. It is a minor change to have the Cstat program skip over detached and batch jobs, or at least specially flag them in the log file. To keep all of the runs consistent, this change was not implemented, but it should be done for future studies. Another problem is the small size of the sample groups and the short duration of the runs. Using groups larger than 20 members will make the data more representative of the group as a whole, and collecting data for more than one week will smooth out inconsistencies in the data (Spring Carnival, for instance). Because Cstat has a very low computational overhead, these changes would not significantly increase the load on the subject mainframes (it would not do to antagonize the users while studying them). The only limiting factor is storage space for the data, which could quickly become overwhelming. A possible solution would be to run Cstat at intervals longer than one minute, or perhaps one day per week over the course of an entire semester. While this latter solution would lose some data, such as how computing changes over the week, it would be better suited to answering questions such as whether students change their computing behavior over the course of the semester.

Table 5.5. *When programs are run*

**Computer Science faculty
and graduate students**

Program Category	Time of day		
	Morning (12 - 9)	Day (9 - 5)	Night (5 - 12)
Text proc.	26%	34%	40%
Programming	26%	33%	40%
Comm.	10%	51%	38%
Network	43%	27%	30%
Data proc.	26%	12%	62%
Exec	25%	43%	31%
Finger	6%	61%	33%
Total comp.	27%	37%	37%

Undergraduate students

Program Category	Time of day		
	Morning (12 - 9)	Day (9 - 5)	Night (5 - 12)
Text proc.	40%	33%	26%
Programming	47%	31%	22%
Comm.	20%	44%	37%
Network	18%	19%	62%
Data proc.	15%	24%	62%
Exec	23%	42%	35%
Finger	10%	38%	52%
Total comp.	33%	36%	31%

**Humanities & Social Sciences
faculty**

Program Category	Time of day		
	Morning (12 - 9)	Day (9 - 5)	Night (5 - 12)
Text proc.	8%	83%	9%
Programming	0%	100%	0%
Comm.	7%	63%	30%
Network	0%	59%	41%
Data proc.	26%	46%	28%
Exec	4%	79%	17%
Finger[a]	29%	29%	43%
Total comp.	10%	73%	17%

Administrators

Program Category	Time of day		
	Morning (12 - 9)	Day (9 - 5)	Night (5 - 12)
Text proc.	5%	33%	62%
Programming[a]	0%	0%	0%
Comm.	16%	62%	22%
Network	0%	100%	0%
Data proc.[a]	0%	0%	0%
Exec	29%	51%	20%
Finger[a]	0%	0%	100%
Total comp.	22%	60%	18%

[a] Number of hits for category << 100

As was noted previously, the computing situation at Carnegie Mellon is constantly changing. Soon, many people will use the campus wide network of distributed personal workstations. Unfortunately, programs like Cstat, while ideal for studying users assigned to one or to a few mainframe computers, become increasingly less useful for collecting information on users who move from computer to computer at their convenience. In order to continue to collect data on computer user behavior automatically, a new method is required. Two different schemes might be useful for collecting data on a distributed computing system. The first is similar to Cstat. Programs for collecting the desired data on a selected group of users would always run in the background on all of the computers on the network, waiting for one of the selected users to log in. Once a day or so, each program would send any data it collected to a central data base. The trick to this method is that the data collection program must be installed into the operating system of every computer. Technically this is feasible, since all of the computers retrieve their operating system from the central file servers residing on the network. However, it might be difficult to obtain the required cooperation of the users and the staff and it could be considered a breach of security and privacy. The advantages of this method are that it is invisible, will not increase the load on the computers noticeably, and cannot be circumvented by users.

The second scheme is to construct a program that monitors the behavior of any user who starts the program running on his or her workstation while logged in. This program could then be started automatically by placing the proper instructions in a user's log in command file. All users to be observed would have to be instructed as to how to change their log in command file to accommodate the monitoring program. This method transfers the approval from the system administrators and large groups to individual users. It also makes salient to users that they are being observed, and provides them with a means to avoid the monitoring program on selected computing sessions.

Our effort at using the computer to collect behavioral data produced some surprises. One stereotype of mainframe computing shattered by these data is the notion that computing is mainly programming and data processing. In this university, over the three years studied, the mainframes were used for programming and numerical analysis, but they were not primarily used for those purposes. All kinds of people – computer scientists, students, humanities and social science faculty, and administrators – used the computer mainly to compose, edit, and print verbal text. They used the computer to send computer mail and to read computer bulletin boards. They used the computer to play games and to read fortunes. Our data suggest that computer use is verbal, social, informal, and fun. Consider, for example, the pervasiveness of Finger. This is a much different picture than is usually given of computer use, and implies a much greater potential for social effects.

6   Faculty and Student Observations of Their Computing Behavior

Paul Anderson

Chapter 4 reported that there are thousands of computers at CMU; Chapter 5 reported what programs are run on the mainframes by various groups of users. But the data collection methods used in Chapter 5 did not directly measure anything about PC use. Nor did they measure anything about people's attitudes toward the computers they were using or the computing they were doing. This chapter describes the results of a questionnaire-based study of faculty and student attitudes toward computing and their uses of PCs as well as mainframes.

Beginning in the fall of 1983, students, individual faculty members, and departments were able to purchase PCs at a substantial discount. If large numbers of faculty and students did acquire access to PCs, then several things might occur. One: their attitudes toward computers and computing might change as a result of exposure to a different kind of computing. Their attitudes might become more positive because they used friendlier machines that were under their own control. Their attitudes might become more negative because they worked with machines that were smaller and less powerful than the mainframes. Two: the total amount of time they spent computing might change. Their time might increase because they had more control over their computing environment. Three: the kinds of tasks they used computers for might change. Faculty and students might customize their computing environments to do things they had never done before. This chapter explores these hypotheses.

Method

This chapter is based on the results of a 1985 survey that addressed three topics: the nature of computing on the campus, the use of personal computers, and the ways in which different types of personal computers are used. The survey identified three different types of computer users: those who do not use personal computers (PCs), those who use PCs but do not own or have exclusive use of one, and those who either own or have exclusive use of a PC. Everyone in the survey answered questions about their use of computers and their attitudes toward computing at CMU. Those who used PCs more than three hours each week were also asked questions relating specifically to their PC use. The entire questionnaire was 13 pages long and consisted of 61 questions.

90

The CMU community was divided into four groups: faculty, staff, undergraduates, and graduate students. A random sample was generated for each group roughly in proportion to its total size, yielding a total sample of 1,000 people. The survey was distributed in the late spring of 1985. Of the 150 surveys sent to faculty, 54% (81 surveys) were returned. The sample size of 81 provides a .05 confidence interval of greater than 11% on either side of a reported value. Of the 490 surveys sent to undergraduates, 30% (147 surveys) were returned. The sample size of 147 provides a .05 confidence interval of greater than 8% on either side of a reported value.

Results

Attitudes toward Computing

According to this survey, both faculty and students view computing and technological change positively. (Tests not reported here indicate no statistically significant differences between faculty and students in their attitudes toward computing.) As shown in Table 6.1, 87% of faculty and 94% of students believe in universal access to computing resources. Seventy-four percent of faculty and 83% of students believe everyone should learn how to use computers. Faculty and students also indicated a reasonable degree of satisfaction with the state of computing at CMU. Sixty-four percent of faculty and 67% of students report that computing access is one of the things they like about CMU. Sixty-four percent of faculty and 70% of students believe CMU's computer environment is better than that at many schools. Responses to questions about emphasis on computing, anticipation of new powerful workstations, the Computer Center attitude toward users, and mainframe availability were approximately equally divided between those expressing agreement, and those who disagreed or expressed indifference. Despite their relatively positive orientation toward computing, computing is not simply an end in itself for the faculty as a whole. Only 42% like to experiment with computing systems and 38% would like to use computers more than they do now. Students display slightly more fascination: 53% like to experiment with computer systems and 51% would like to use computers more than they do now.

Eight of the attitude items in the 1985 survey repeated questions asked in a similar survey of the campus community conducted in the spring of 1983. Differences in the percent of faculty and students expressing agreement with the attitude statements are displayed in Table 6.2. The results suggest a small increase in the perception that there is too much computing at CMU, a small decrease in anticipation of the new workstation, and essentially no difference in the perception of the Computer Center, the access to computing at CMU, and the relative standing of CMU computing facilities relative to other schools.

Table 6.1. *Percentage of faculty and students who agree with various attitudes*

Attitude statement	Faculty who strongly agree or agree	Students who strongly agree or agree
Everyone at CMU should have full and easy access to a computer.	87.3	93.9
Almost everyone should learn how to use a computer.	73.8	83.0
One of the things I like about CMU is the access I have to computing.	64.0	67.4
In general, I would like to see more practical uses of computers made at CMU in my courses or in my job.	51.9	62.6
I like to experiment with computer systems.	42.3	53.1
I'm looking forward to the new powerful personal computer workstations being developed at the ITC.	39.5	41.3
I would like to use a computer more than I do now.	37.5	51.0
The mainframe time-sharing systems seem more available now than ever before.	36.4	27.0
There is too much emphasis on computing at CMU.	32.0	21.8
The people at the Computation Center don't seem to care about users.	30.0	26.4
I'm afraid that moving to personal computers will mean sacrificing some of the features I like about computing on larger machines.	27.8	33.1
I would use the mainframe time-sharing system more if the loads weren't so high.	18.8	25.7
Lots of schools have a better computing environment than CMU.	13.9	5.0

Note: Faculty *n*s range from 66 to 80; student *n*s range from 137 to 147.

There was a striking change in the perceptions of mainframe time sharing computing. In the 1983 survey, no faculty agreed with the statement that the mainframe was more available than ever before. In the 1985 survey, 36% expressed agreement with the statement. Similarly, the demand for mainframe computing services appears to be less of a hindrance than in 1983. Thirty-four percent fewer faculty and 39% fewer students indicated that high loads were preventing them from doing all the mainframe-based computing they desired. In conjunction with this shift fewer people perceived that PC-based computing entails sacrificing desirable features found on larger computing systems. These data suggest that general attitudes about computing are relatively stable across time and are not markedly changed by the introduction of new machines. The only attitudes to change are ones about specific machines.

Amount of Computer Use

A majority of faculty (69%) and students (52%) reported using a computer daily, and about 25% of both faculty and students reported using more than one computer every day. The behavior of daily users revealed in this study reinforces the observation made in Chapter 4 that computing is becoming more decentralized. Fewer than half of the daily users use machines provided by the central campus computing facility. PCs have become an important source of computing resources for the faculty and students. Forty-one percent of CMU faculty and 26% of students owned a PC in 1985. The average hours of PC use among the faculty in 1985 was 11 hours per week among those who reported some PC usage and 6 hours a week for the comparable group of students. Of those faculty who used microcomputers, 77% used IBM PCs, 9% used Apples, and 14% used other brands. Of the students who use microcomputers, 55% used IBM PCs, 32% used Apples, and 12% used other brands.

Kind of Computer Use

Faculty and students report using computers mostly for work. Eighty percent of faculty reported using computers frequently for job-related work. Sixty-eight percent of students reported using computers frequently for school work. Faculty and student program use across a variety of computing tasks is displayed in Table 6.3, which is organized by the same categories employed in Chapter 5.

As reported in Chapter 5, text processing and communications programs are quite popular. Text editing receives the highest reported use with 68% of the faculty and 56% of the students reporting frequent use. Over 56% of the faculty and 49% of the students report using computer mail frequently. In contrast with the data in Chapter 5, a relatively high proportion of faculty and students report using computers for programming and calculation. Forty-four percent of faculty and 48% of students report using computers for programming frequently. Twenty-eight percent of faculty report using computers for statistical analysis frequently.

The discrepancies between the electronic data reported in Chapter 5 and the

Table 6.2. *Change in faculty and student attitudes from 1983 to 1985*

Attitude statement	Faculty who strongly agree or agree(%)	Students who strongly agree or agree(%)
The mainframe time-sharing systems seem seem more available now than ever before.	36.4	-3.9
There is too much emphasis on computing at CMU.	11.6	6.6
Lots of schools have a better computing environment than CMU.	1.7	1.3
The people at the Computation Center don't seem to care about users.	-1.0	-3.0
One of the things I like about CMU is the access I have to computing.	-7.0	-7.3
I'm afraid that moving to personal computers will mean sacrificing some of the features I like about computing on larger machines.	-10.4	-.2
I'm looking forward to the new powerful personal computer workstations being developed at the ITC.	-10.5	-20.0
I would use the mainframe time-sharing system more if the loads weren't so high.	-34.4	-39.4

self-report data presented in this chapter could be produced by underestimates of programming and statistical analysis in the electronic data or overestimates in the self-report data. Blackwell acknowledged that system data on text-editor use do not distinguish between editing prose and editing programs. Writing and editing programs are included in his "text editing" category, leading to a total for the programming category that is artificially low. In other contexts, self-reports commonly overestimate socially desirable behavior such as contributing to charity or wearing a seat belt; such behavior is commonly overestimated by 10–30% of all respondents (Sudman & Bradburn, 1982, pp. 56–62). At CMU, programming and data processing are socially desirable uses of computing. Professorial salaries and honors and student SAT scores are correlated with working in fields where programming or statistics are studied or used heavily. Therefore faculty members and students may have consciously or unconsciously

Table 6.3. *Percentage of faculty and students who report using a computer frequently for different purposes*

	Faculty(%)	Students(%)
Kinds of use		
Job-related work	79.7	30.4
Personal work	43.4	48.3
Recreation	16.2	35.9
School		67.4
Kinds of programs		
Text processing		
Editing	67.9	55.8
Communication		
Electronic mail	56.8	49.0
Bulletin boards	33.3	25.9
Programming	44.4	47.9
Data processing		
Statistics	27.8	8.2
Data base applications	21.3	8.9
Financial management	8.3	2.1
Design	12.7	4.1
Graphics	19.7	10.9
Fun		
Games	6.8	24.0

Note: "Frequently" means 1 or 2 on a 5-point scale. Faculty ns range from 71 to 79; student ns range from 138 to 147.

overestimated their frequency. Possibly both underestimates in the electronic data and overestimates in the self-report data produced the discrepancies noted here.

Although the concept of "computer literacy" does not necessarily imply a working knowledge of a programming language, 73% of the CMU faculty and 88% of the students report they are comfortable writing programs in at least one language. Forty-three percent of the faculty and 56% of the students report a working knowledge of two or more languages. The only statistically significant difference between faculty and students in their computing behavior is that students ($M = 2.25$) report they know more programming languages than faculty

$(M = 1.56, t (226) = 3.21, p < .01)$. Among faculty who report a working knowledge of a programming language, the most widely known language is Fortran; 73% report knowing it. Forty-one percent of faculty know Basic; 31%, Pascal; and fewer report knowing other languages. Among students the most widely known language is Pascal; 78% report knowing it. Fifty-nine percent of students know Basic; 21%, Fortran; and fewer report knowing other languages.

PC Users. The personal computer represents a seemingly striking change in the nature of computing. The cost of computing has fallen to the point that computing no longer is viewed as an expensive centrally provided resource. It is now practical for individuals to have exclusive use of a machine, and for that machine to sit idle while the user does other tasks. The ways PCs are used by those who use PCs at least three hours per week or have exclusive access to one are shown in Table 6.4. The two most frequently rated activities are text editing (79% for faculty and 71% for students) and programming (44% for faculty and 47% for students).

Because the survey contained questions about general computer use and microcomputer use it is possible to determine how using a PC differs from using other, larger computers. The survey respondents were asked to rate the frequency with which they used PCs and other kinds of computers to perform a variety of tasks. By excluding those who reported they never performed a task using any form of computing and by comparing the ratings of the rest, we can identify those tasks for which the PC is used more frequently and those for which the PC is used less frequently than other computers. The comparison is shown in Table 6.5. The results of the comparison indicate that PCs are a general purpose substitute for computing on other machines. A majority of faculty and students report that for job tasks, schoolwork, personal tasks, and recreation, they use PCs and other computers about equally. A majority of students report using PCs and other computers equally for all classes of use. A majority of faculty members report they use PCs and other computers equally for programming, games, data base applications, graphics, text editing, and financial management. Only for statistics and design did less than a majority of faculty use PCs and other computers equivalently. For statistics, PC use dominated; while for design, 40% used the PC more while 40% used the PC and other computers equally.

User Groups

The increased application of computers in education has injected technology into areas that have traditionally been nontechnical. It is a common belief that attitudes toward computing and the amount and purpose of computer use vary substantially between technical professionals and nontechnical professionals,

Table 6.4. *PC task frequency for faculty and students*

	Faculty(%)	Students(%)
Kinds of use		
Job	86.7	36.7
Personal	55.8	65.2
Recreation	9.8	56.3
Schoolwork		73.8
Kinds of programs		
Text processing		
Editing	78.6	71.2
Programming	44.2	47.0
Data processing		
Statistics	23.8	4.6
Data base applications	24.4	9.1
Financial management	19.0	3.0
Design	10.0	28.8
Graphics	31.7	24.2
Fun		
Games	4.8	44.6

Note: Faculty *n*s range from 40 to 45; student *n*s range from 60 to 66.

and between males and females. Hence we tend to assume that a male engineering student or professor will be a more enthusiastic computer user than would a female English major or professor. This survey shows some differences between faculty and students in traditionally technological disciplines and those in nontechnical disciplines and between men and women, but the differences are not nearly as large as might have been supposed.

To examine the difference between technical and nontechnical faculty and students, the respondents were grouped according to their college affiliation. Faculty ($n = 37$) and students ($n = 92$) in the engineering and science colleges were categorized as technical and faculty ($n = 42$) and students ($n = 55$) in the fine arts, humanities, and social sciences were categorized as nontechnical. The responses of groups to 30 attitude and behavior questions were compared using t tests (applying the Bonferroni correction for lack of independence across tests). There were no differences between technical and nontechnical faculty. Technical students ($M = 2.78$) know more programming languages than do nontechnical students ($M = 1.36, p = t (140) = 6.10, p < .01$).

Table 6.5. *Percentage of faculty and students who use a PC for different tasks more or less frequently than they use other kinds of computers*

| | Frequency of using a PC and other kinds of computers | | |
	Use a PC more(%)	Equal use(%)	Use a PC less(%)
	Faculty		
Kinds of use			
Job	18.6	81.4	0.0
Personal	23.1	66.7	10.3
Recreation	21.1	68.4	10.5
Kinds of programs			
Text processing			
Editing	22.5	70.0	7.5
Programming	27.5	66.7	6.1
Data processing			
Statistics	45.5	36.4	18.2
Data base applications	30.8	53.8	15.4
Financial management	5.0	65.0	30.0
Design	40.0	40.0	20.0
Graphics	19.2	57.7	23.1
Fun			
Games	11.8	64.7	23.5

continued

Similar tests were performed to determine whether there were distinguishable differences between male faculty ($n = 67$) and female faculty ($n = 11$) or between male students ($n = 103$) and female students ($n = 44$). There were no differences between male and female faculty. Male students ($M = 2.55$) know more programming languages than female students do ($M = 1.55$, $t (145) = 3.50$, $p < .00$) And male students ($M = 5.93$) used a microcomputer for more hours a week than female students did ($M = 2.79$, $t (118) = 3.42$, $p < .01$).

Conclusion

The short story about computing among faculty and students at CMU is that they do a lot of it and they generally like what they do. In 1985, 69% of faculty

Table 6.5. *(cont.)*

	Frequency of using a PC and other kinds of computers		
	Use a PC more(%)	Equal use(%)	Use a PC less(%)
	Students		
Kinds of use			
Job	45.5	51.6	3.0
Schoolwork	18.1	74.5	5.4
Personal	31.7	61.4	7.1
Recreation	19.7	64.7	15.8
Kinds of programs			
Text processing			
Editing	33.4	52.6	14.1
Programming	41.8	50.9	7.2
Data processing			
Statistics	38.6	58.0	3.2
Data base applications	46.6	53.2	0.0
Financial management	31.7	63.2	5.3
Design	23.0	53.9	23.1
Graphics	19.1	50.1	31.0
Fun			
Games	21.7	60.9	17.4

Note: Faculty *n*s range from 15 to 40; student *n*s range from 19 to 57.

and 52% of students reported they used a computer every day. Seventy-three percent of faculty and 88% of students reported they knew at least one programming language. Seventy-four percent of faculty and 83% of students believed everyone should learn how to use computers.

The new PC technology has not made a big difference in the way faculty or students think about or use computers. General attitudes about computing did not change as a result of PCs. Only attitudes about specific machines changed. (It is amusing that one of the biggest attitude changes resulting from PCs is to make people less negative toward the mainframes!) The amount of time people spent computing, which was already over ten hours a week prior to PCs, did not seem to increase much. And the kinds of tasks people used computers for did not seem to change greatly.

It was difficult to distinguish between technical and nontechnical faculty in their computer attitudes, amount of use, or kind of use. Also, male faculty were indistinguishable from female faculty with respect to computing. Technical students knew more programming languages than did nontechnical students. Male students knew more programming languages and used a PC for more hours a week than did female students. But those were the only differences across a large number of attitude and behavior measures. These findings contrast with the widespread expectations that high levels of computing must widen the traditional separation between technical and nontechnical disciplines, and exaggerate differences between men and women.

Although the faculty and students at CMU are hardly a representative group, these results suggest that for faculty and students, busy with research and schoolwork, the computer is a tool. What drives the demand for computing are the tasks that faculty and students need to perform, not some intrinsic fascination with hardware or an undying allegiance to quill pens. In an environment rich in computing resources, everybody computes in ways appropriate to the tasks they need to get done. This chapter's findings emerge from a context in which faculty and students already had relatively good access to computing prior to and in addition to the introduction of PCs. In that light the findings demonstrate the folly of predicting the impact of any technology without considering the organizational context in which it is introduced. For an organization that has had little or no computing, the widespread introduction of PCs might lead to more dramatic changes in attitudes and behavior than were noted in this chapter. But such changes will be relative to people's existing patterns of work, not produced by features of the technology alone.

7   What's News About Computing?

Suzanne Penn Weisband and Teresa Gardner

Chapters 4, 5, and 6 documented day-to-day computing on campus, enumerating who uses what computers and what programs, and analyzing how these patterns have changed over time. In addition to using computers, people can also talk about computing. This chapter analyzes something of the talk about computing at CMU to broaden the behavioral perspective of the previous three chapters. Although technological change frequently occurs with no fanfare in organizations, it sometimes attracts attention and debate. Organizational newspapers are one indicator of events that excite gossip locally. Gossip is an interesting problem for managers who have to introduce new technology. One advantage of gossip is that it heightens people's involvement and it prepares them for change. A disadvantage of gossip is that it elicits rumors and invites dissent. In some cases this dissent helps forestall foolish technological change.

In this chapter, we examine the published news at CMU about computing to answer three general questions. First, to what extent did the news reflect what was really going on? Second, how did the news change over time? One hypothesis was that news about computing might become less frequent with time as people got used to the idea of computerization. Or news about computing might increase as more people used computers. Third, we asked if new computing technology invited public controversy. If so, what was the nature of the controversy? In Chapter 3 we proposed that computing is a solution looking for problems. An organizational change of such magnitude as the "fully saturated computer community" might offer many choice opportunities where the match of computer solutions to problems could be debated. These debates would create an arena for playing out ongoing organizational conflicts and negotiations. In this study, we examined organizational news about computing controversies at CMU with the idea that they might reflect computing as an occasion for airing organizational differences.

Of course, official newspapers and minutes represent only one source of talk about computing or any other organizational topic. And that source does not represent any simple mapping of all possible stories or opinions having to do with computing. Campus reporters, just like all others, must select their stories and editorial topics out of a very large pool of potential topics (Gans, 1980, pp. 78–81). Furthermore, even that pool of topics is constrained by the reality of the

101

organizational environment. For instance, in the CMU case we would be unlikely to find a story saying, "President asks students to choose between computers and football," because this particular organization never makes such
choices explicit. Nevertheless the official news about computing at CMU does
provide one indicator, albeit an imperfect one, of what people were saying about
computing during the period of this study.

We carried out a content analysis of computer-related topics in all the articles,
editorials, and announcements in the weekly student newspaper, in all the articles in the monthly faculty-staff newsletter, and in all the agenda items of the
faculty senate meetings that appeared in minutes from the fall semester, 1981,
through the spring semester, 1985. We categorized each article, editorial and
announcement as good news, bad news, or news reflecting controversy. We
present findings for each publication in turn, and then we discuss how our data
answer the three general questions we set out to examine initially.

The Student Newspaper

We collected the news items (articles, editorials, or announcements) about computing by searching all 75 issues of the student newspaper published from fall
1981 until spring 1985. The computer news consisted of 191 items including
105 articles (55%), 48 editorials (25%), and 38 announcements (20%). We also
recorded the semester and date of publication and number of pages in each issue.
For the time period studied, the student newspaper averaged 25 pages per issue,
with a range of 12–36 pages. The computer news represents about 5% of all
news items, including announcements but not paid advertisements, which we did
not study.

We grouped computer-related items into three content-based categories: good
news about computing, bad news about computing, and reports of controversies
about computing. Good news items included announcements of achievements
or milestones in computerization on campus such as the delivery of new kinds of
computers. Bad news reported problems in using computers and negative social
or educational effects (reported as fact). Any debates having to do with computing were categorized as news of controversy. Items in the controversy-news
category include editorials, letters to the editors, and featured articles presenting
one side of a controversy, as well as items presenting balanced news about a
controversy. Among the articles, there were 83 coded as good news, 11 coded as
bad news, and 11 coded as news of controversy. The editorials contained 8
coded as good news, 7 coded as bad news, and 33 coded as controversies. All
38 of the announcements were coded as good news. Table 7.1 illustrates news
in each category.

Figure 7.1 shows the number of good news items, bad news items, and items

Table 7.1. *Definitions, examples, and frequency of three categories of news items used for content analyses in the student newspaper*

Category definitions and examples	No. of news items pertaining to each category definition
Good news	128
News items that	
• report new computers on or around campus, new uses of the computer, new organizations and committees concerned with computing (e.g., "UCC welcomes public with open house," 4/17/84)	57
• provide helpful hints for using the system and list available features or services (e.g., "Some neat tricks for printing TOPS-20 files," 11/23/82)	19
• announce seminars or demonstrations (e.g., "'Robot-town' hosts exposition," 3/15/83)	38
• tell mainly of the people involved in using the computers (e.g., "Grad student shows research at conference," 4/30/85)	14
Bad news	18
News items that report	
• problems involved with using computers. For example, space, hardware, software, and building maintenence problem (e.g., "Builders find crack in UCC," 1/31/84)	8
• persons involved in misuses and people directly affected by problems with the system (e.g., "Freshman faces CMU suspension," 11/15/83)	8
• misuses of the system (e.g., "Password-stealing program uncovered," 1/15/85)	2
Controversies	45
News items that involve	
• debates concerning the building of a campus environment saturated with powerful computing computing and electronic communication equipment. These include:	28
information given to the student body, (e.g., "Computer plans should be studied, communicated," 10/26/82)	11
academic aspects, (e.g., "DEC-20 withdrawal; learning to use a pen," 11/2/82)	8
cost, (e.g., "Personal computing funds should be spent elsewhere," 5/4/82)	5
and social implications (e.g., "Comp Center changes further isolate community," 9/14/82)	4
• debates centered around the existence of the Software Engineering Institute (e.g., "Moskowitz challenges professor's belief on SEI," 10/2/84)	12
• debates about hackers (e.g., "Redefining the 'hacker'," 1/22/85)	5

reporting controversy over time. Three general themes can be discerned. First, good news dominated throughout the period studied. Second, the news encouraged and revealed increasing student use of computing as a tool. Third, there was more controversy about organizational commitments to future computing resources than about computing performance itself. For example, at the beginning of our observation period, in the spring of 1981, the Task Force for the Future of Computing issued its interim report advocating a fully saturated computing community. This report elicited a whole year's articles, virtually all positive, on the coming computer revolution. In this same year, demand to use the computer system grew so rapidly that the system crashed and ground to a halt nearly every evening. Yet no headline announced, ''Campus computer crashes 47 times in 2 weeks.'' Our findings reflect the positive symbolic significance of computing at CMU, and the CMU community's view of computing as solution rather than problem.

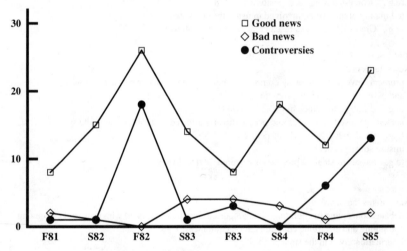

Figure 7.1. Good news, bad news, and controversies about computing in the student newspaper.

Bad news about computing was reported infrequently in the student newspaper. One brief spate of news was about a computer crime. In 1983 a freshman used methods he learned in his introductory computer programming course to cause the computer system to crash repeatedly. He was suspended. In response students wrote about the social control of computing. Some students supported computer policies that would protect ordinary computer users (''Inconsideration hinders use of computing,'' 11/15/83). Other students supported computer policies that would promote people's explorations of computer technology (''[The suspended freshman] not told he was wrong,'' 11/15/83).

Much more controversy emerged over two organizational decisions, the deci-

M. SUSSMAN

" A SUBDIRECTORY? WELL, IT'S
A DIRECTORY CREATED WITHIN
ANOTHER DIRECTORY USED TO... "

In 1983 a freshman used methods he learned in his introductory computer programming course to cause the computer system to crash repeatedly. Cartoon from the student newspaper.

sion of CMU in 1982 to form a joint venture with IBM and the establishment, in spring of 1984, of the Software Engineering Institute (SEI). Ostensibly, opposition to the joint venture was based on opposition to the university making stronger connections with business and to more computers in education. Some students worried that CMU values and student life would change.

By computerizing, Carnegie Mellon was said to be "racing to become the first college in the country to replace the student–faculty ratio with a student–computer ratio in their admissions brochures" (12/7/82). Students were most outraged over having had no warning of what the university was planning ("Damn the students, full speed ahead," 10/26/82). They wanted a chance to suggest other uses of funds ("CMU needs something more," 2/14/84). They demanded to know whether CMU would require students to purchase their own personal computers ("Computer package unfair," 9/25/84). CMU ad-

Some students worried that CMU values and student life would change. Cartoon from the student newspaper.

ministrators reassured the students of the rationality of the joint venture and claimed that any new financial charges for computing would be levied against future freshmen, not current students.   However, debate continued over the principle of surcharges and, more generally, over administrative authority versus student participation.   The script was unique, but the theme and roles were traditional.

The SEI controversy was an occasion for arguing general values of the university and society.   The SEI was created with Department of Defense funds to improve software in the military and in industry.   Opposition to the SEI was based on objections to military funding in the university, to President Reagan's so-called Star Wars defense program, and to nuclear war. The ostensible players in this drama were political groupings (liberals versus conservatives), but these groupings are correlated with organizational position at CMU, and students generally represented the liberal, anti-SEI side.

Ongoing controversy flowed through academic years. During the academic year 1981–1982, talk began over the report of the Task Force for the Future of Computing. This is when gossip first surfaced about the negotiations with IBM. Controversy abated somewhat once the joint venture with IBM was begun. The next controversy over the Software Engineering Institute was still escalating when we ended our study.

The Faculty–Staff Newsletter

As we had done with the student newspaper, we collected all articles about computing from the monthly faculty–staff newsletter. We analyzed 89 articles from 30 different issues during the time period, fall 1981 to spring 1985. On average, each issue of the newsletter contained eight pages, one or two pages of which featured an interview with a faculty or staff member. We found no editorials or announcements about computing in the newsletter. However, one-third of the featured interviews concerned a faculty member's involvement with computing ("[John Doe] speaks on computer graphics," 11/81). As before, we categorized the 89 articles as good news, bad news, and news reflecting controversy. Table 7.2 gives examples of the 48 good news items (54%), 9 bad news items (10%), and 32 reports of controversy (36%).

The faculty–staff newspaper, like the student newspaper, presented a steady flow of good news about computing, reports on computing as a tool, and controversy as response to new organizational commitments to computing. The faculty–staff news differed from the student news in that less of it was purely how-to information and more was about controversy.

Controversies about computing were on three topics: the IBM/CMU joint venture, a change in organizational policy governing intellectual properties, and the establishment of the SEI. The newsletter's depiction of the joint venture debate centered on how CMU and university life would change ("Coal research gives way to IBM," 11/82). Among faculty and staff, this controversy seemed mild. The intellectual property policy controversy was more heated. It concerned a proposed policy to require significant profit sharing between originators of software and the university. Many staff members objected to changing the traditional policy that people own full rights to their writing, art, and software. In this case, publicity contributed to revision of the proposal and seems an instance of public attention preventing foolish change. The public controversy that lasted longest was over the SEI. Some staff members strongly supported

Table 7.2. *Definitions, examples, and frequency of three categories of news items used for content analyses in the faculty–staff newsletter*

Category definitions and examples	No. of news items pertaining to each category definition
Good news	48
News items that	
• report new computers on or around campus, new uses of the computer, and new organizations and committees concerned with computing (e.g., "Million dollar 'clean room'," 5/82)	40
• tell mainly of the people involved in using computers (e.g., "Retail sale of used computers wins award," 5/84)	7
• relate humorous accounts of the positive aspects of computers (e.g., "A day with a live-in campus computer," 2/82)	1
Bad news	9
News items that	
• report problems involved with using computers (e.g., "Mainframe educational accounts are cut," 3/84)	5
• relate humorous accounts of the negative aspects of computers (e.g., "1989 or half-an-hour in a small dorm room," 3/82)	4
Controversies	32
News items that involve	
• debates centered around the existence of the Software Engineering Institute (e.g., "SEI stirs grassroots debate," 1/85)	14
• debates concerning the building of a campus environment saturated with powerful computing and electronic communication equipment (e.g., "Waiting for the PC's," 1/84)	13
• debates centered around policies for assessing ownership of intellectual property, like software design and development (e.g., "A new policy for intellectual properties?" 10/82)	5

the SEI as an opportunity for the university to do important and worthwhile research in computing. Others opposed it on grounds of opposition to academic research for military purposes and university reliance on military funding. Participants in all of these controversies tended to be senior faculty and administrators, reflecting the use of these discussions as an occasion for organizationally vested people to argue university values and directions.

The Faculty Senate Agenda

We collected agenda items from the minutes of the faculty senate meetings in order to study what administrators and faculty members said about computing in these meetings, and to compare these discussions with talk in the student newspaper and faculty–staff newsletter. The data are from 28 faculty senate meetings from fall 1981 to spring 1985. Meetings were usually conducted once a month. They contained an average of 7 agenda items, ranging from 4 to 11. All of the meetings began with the minutes of the previous meeting and announcements; then people presented reports from various councils and committees, news of faculty appointments and tenure decisions, and, occasionally, of elections. For each faculty senate meeting, we counted the number of agenda items and the number of agenda items related to computing. Then we performed content analyses on the minutes of the meetings. Because the minutes are summaries of decisions, we could not use evaluative categories. In 28 meetings there were 193 agenda items, 14 of which were related to computing (7%). This is only slightly higher than the percentage of news about computing. Each of the agenda items about computing concerned one of the three major controversies reported in the faculty–staff newsletter. However, the distribution of talk was different. Only 3 items were about the joint venture and 1 was about the Software Engineering Institute; 10 of the 14 were about the intellectual property policy. Since this latter is the only one of the issues whose outcome the faculty senate might have influenced, the data suggest that faculty meetings, as compared with news media, were an occasion for both political action and general debate over values.

Discussion

The first question we asked when we began this study was how public talk about computing compares with actual technological change. We found that the news did inform people about major organizational changes such as the joint IBM – CMU venture. The news announced new computing resources, such as the delivery of new computers, and new behavior, such as faculty software research. This news was overwhelmingly positive and rarely touched on problems or negative attitudes and reactions.

The second question we asked was how computer news changed over time. Our data do not show that news about computing increased or declined over time. Despite the vast increase of computer facilities and access over the four-year period, the volume and flow of computer news was stable. Perhaps an implicit newspaper policy is to constrain the amount of news about computing. If the normal routine is "Print one or two pieces on computers each issue," our data would show stability over time.

Finally, we asked if computing was controversial. We found that controversy did parade through the news. Controversy was always provoked by doing something new, but not all new actions were controversial. For example, people did not argue about the Robotics Institute, the new Philosophy Department (which was highly oriented toward computation), or new curricula in information systems and computer art and music. Controversial topics were ones having broader appeal and implications. They attracted participants from the entire campus. They were occasions for debating general policies and general values.

We have no evidence that talk about computing was problematic for CMU managers. The news generally represented computing activity in a positive light and helped socialize people to using it as a tool and applying it as a solution. Except in one case, that of the proposed software ownership policy, controversy generated more excitement than it mobilized dissent. We think the news helped to make computing an entertaining and interesting topic of conversation. Public attention is not always auspicious for an organizational change, but the CMU atmosphere was one of zeal and increasing competence. The news at CMU reflected these conditions and contributed to high expectations for future computing.

Part III

Workers and Managers

Part II characterized three fundamental components in the social process of technological change – resources, behaviors, and attitudes. These components are common and necessary across the entire organization and are independent of any particular jobs, tasks, or organizational structures. In Part III we turn to the social processes and effects of computerization within particular work settings. We look at secretaries in Chapter 8, the library in Chapter 9, and top administrators in Chapter 10. In Part III we are more specific about particular kinds of attitudes, resources, and behaviors that may be found in one work setting but not another. We also investigate outcomes of particular computerization processes.

The general positive attitudes about computing that we documented in Part II are important both as causes and consequences of the behavior of particular workers and managers. In two of the work settings reported in Part III, a top administrator who believed in the importance of computing pushed for new computing applications for an organizational group – in one case for top university administrators and in the other case for the library. Thus those two administrators' positive attitudes were important in conditioning the kind of computing and the response to it that we found in those groups. It has already become a truism in studies of computer system introduction that "top management support" is critical. But the CMU case allows us to better understand what that means. One part is top management's supporting and fostering a general ideology about the positive value of computing. A second is top management's belief that particular functions, people, or groups would benefit from more computing. Action in both areas is more potent than in either alone.

In only one of the three cases reported in Part III, that of the library, were any special computing resources acquired for the particular group. In the other two cases – top administrators and secretaries – their increased use of computing simply occurred within the general multiplicitous and expanding computing environment described in Chapter 4. Significantly, though, the top administrators *thought* they were acquiring special resources. That sense of specialness was an important part of the implementation strategy for that group. Secretaries and librarians, as we describe in Chapters 8 and 9, felt special in comparison with their peers in other universities who did not have access to as much computing as they did.

We document three kinds of outcomes related to increased computing for workers and managers: outcomes related to attitudes, work processes, and social structure. In all three studies people exhibit quite positive attitudes toward computing. This finding may be most interesting for the secretaries who often are reported in other studies to be negative about computing (e.g., Glenn & Feldberg, 1977). Chapter 8 discusses why secretaries might feel so positive. In addition to producing positive attitudes about computing, using computers in the CMU environment seems also to produce positive attitudes about oneself. Secretaries report that using computing makes them feel more competent and confident in their roles as working women. Librarians report that computing enhances their prestige within the library profession. Administrators report that using computers makes them feel "with it" and modern.

All three groups report that the pace of their work has changed as a result of computing; they say computing saves them time. Secretaries and administrators report little change in the kind of work they do as a result of computing; librarians report more change. All three groups, though, report changes in their communication behavior as a result of electronic mail and bulletin boards. Each group reports communicating with more people.

Social structure (i.e., the distribution of information, rewards, and status across organizational positions) is both reinforced and altered by computing. Computing reinforces social structure when high status people receive the best and newest computing resources and amenities. This occurred in the cases of the library and top administrators. Social structure is altered when communications no longer flow only through the hierarchical chain of command, as occurred in the case of the library. Social structure is also altered when new patterns of expertise emerge, as in the case of the secretaries.

The data collection methods in Part III are primarily questionnaire and interview. Chapter 9 demonstrates the value of longitudinal survey research in which the same people are questioned at two points in time. Chapter 9 also demonstrates the folly of assuming that a "technology innovation" can be studied in isolation from other changes occuring concurrently. We document in the library how technology change occurs around, beside, and beyond any particular "technology innovation." This means that investigators must exercise caution in attributing change in behavior or attitudes to a particular innovation.

The chapters in this part also illustrate a way in which inference from case studies is difficult. In each of the chapters we report that people's attitudes toward computing are positive. And we imply that their computing experiences are what caused the positive attitudes. But we cannot rule out the possibility that people who are positively disposed to computing self-select themselves into this organization. That is one reason that longitudinal data are useful. If we can learn that people become more positive to computing over time, then we are more confident that self-selection is at least not the only factor operating. We have some evidence of both individual change and selection effects in the library, where we took measures two years apart.

People work in or around a strong computer culture at CMU and increasingly share vast computer resources. In this part we discuss how working in a place that values computers affects people's ambitions and their sense of self. We discuss the spread of computer language and computer metaphors and mores. (An epitaph in an administrator's public computer plan reads, "A kimono, formerly open, now lies crumpled in the corner of the room, discarded like so many mainframes.") And we consider the spread of computer expertise. Secretaries now routinely train their bosses in how to use new hardware or software. Computing seems to offer many opportunities for people to expand or change their organizational and professional roles.

8   Secretaries and Computers

Karen Hartman

This chapter is about CMU secretaries. The U.S. secretarial population has grown in the years 1960–1981 from 1.5 million to close to 4 million (Feldberg & Glenn, 1983). Yet with a few exceptions (Glenn & Feldberg, 1977; Kanter, 1977) analyses of secretarial work (including computing) and the organizational functions that secretaries serve are rare. If, as the advertisements proclaim, the office of modern times has arrived, it is important to explore the effects of computers on a population segment that is among its principal users, secretaries.

The few studies of advanced technology in offices that include secretaries have centered primarily on implementation problems, ergonomic issues, or on traditional job characteristics such as task variety, satisfaction, autonomy, and productivity (Arndt, Feltes, & Hanak, 1983; Gunnarsson, 1984). These studies essentially view the secretarial task in isolation from other work and other goals of the organization. Some research has moved beyond this more narrow perspective to place secretarial computing in an organizational context. Bikson and Gutek (1983) describe how white-collar workers, including secretaries, use computers, and they also address organizational characteristics that affect implementation and people's use of computers. For example, they found that people's satisfaction and use of a computer system was significantly predicted by the organization's orientation toward technological change. Amick and Damron (1984) have studied the office as a system of working relationships, noting that people's perceptions of the impact of computers on their work was dependent on their organizational position and role. In carrying out this study, I began with the premise that the secretarial job exists in an organizational context of many jobs, some of which are closely interdependent, and all of which are interrelated by status. I therefore gave attention to two issues not usually discussed in the literature: the impact of computers on work relationships within and across different levels of the organizational hierarchy and the effect of computers on secretaries' views of themselves as workers.

Procedure

All 233 secretaries who worked on campus were divided into three groups. One group consisted of secretaries in academic departments such as Chemistry and

114

English. A second group consisted of secretaries in administrative and support offices such as the Controller's Office and the University Dining Service. The third group consisted of secretaries in computer research organizational units such as the Computer Science Department, the Robotics Institute, and the Software Engineering Institute. To compare secretaries working in three different types of office environments, the secretaries were sampled proportionately from these groups. I sent 47 secretaries letters inviting them to participate in the study in the fall of 1985. Three were no longer on campus, 4 were sick or on vacation, and 2 had been reclassified to different job categories. Of the remaining 38, 10 said they were too busy and 3 refused to participate without giving a reason. This left 25 (66% of those contacted) in the interview sample; 12 were from academic departments, 9 were from administrative and support offices, and 4 were from the computer research units. Preliminary analyses showed no differences among these three groups, so no further mention of the groupings is made. The 45-minute interview contained 24 open-ended questions about the secretaries' daily use of computers, their feelings about computers, and how computers affect workplace relationships. Prior to the interview the secretaries completed a 15-item questionnaire that measured additional attitudes and feelings about the computer. The interviews were tape recorded and the transcriptions were entered into computer files for text analysis.

All 25 secretaries were female and all were classified as non-exempt employees. Their mean age was 37 (range, 23–60) and the average tenure at CMU for this group was 5.5 years (range, 9 months–23 years). Six secretaries had used computers prior to taking their present job at CMU. At the time of the interview all 25 used computers in their work. Seventy-two percent were familiar with the time sharing system at CMU as well as microcomputers such as the IBM PC or the Apple Macintosh. All but two secretaries had either terminals or personal computers on or near their desks. On average the secretaries used computers 4 hours a day (range, 1–6).

The first set of findings described below presents the secretaries' initial experiences with the computer and how they learned to master it. Next, we look at what the secretaries do on the computer. The third and fourth sections place the secretary in an organizational context, focusing on the impact of the computer on work relationships and on the secretaries' suggestions for improving productivity. Last, a discussion of the consequences of computer use on the secretaries' perceptions of themselves is presented.

Findings

Learning to Use Computers

When secretaries talked about the first time they used a computer at CMU, 13 of 25 described their first encounter as a negative one. Words such as frustrating, terrible, awful, and fearful dominate their comments, reflecting a general sense of loss of control over their work. A recurring theme was fear of deleting all their work by mistake. (The letters in parentheses are unique secretary identifiers.)

I was afraid I would lose all the material I had typed in. (G)

I was scared, really scared. I just thought any little button that you would push would wipe everything out. (K)

We were all very much afraid of it. I think the big fear with computers is deleting your data ... (Q)

People often try to make sense of an aversive situation by constructing explanations for their distress (Thompson, 1981). This was the case for several of these secretaries. One secretary attributed her loss of control to the computer, anthropomorphizing the machine in the process:

I was petrified. I mean you worry about everything. Every time you'd use it, it'd give you all kinds of error messages. I swear it knows when a novice logs in because it picks on you. (D)

Another secretary blamed herself for the frustration the experience evoked:

...I would do things and it would not respond. Not knowing the computer I would be frustrated because, "well what did I do?" (W)

And a third secretary, who had prior computer experience, attributed her problems to the well-intentioned actions of others that took control of the learning process away from her:

I was nervous because what I did at Pitt, although it was similar, there was still... And everyone here who was already working on it when I started said, "No, do it this way"... I had people coming over with their arms over my shoulders, "No, do this," type, type, type ... And that made me crazy ... I don't like someone to type in front of me ... That made me nervous. Because everyone here is so used to the system, and they're so at ease with – "Let's experiment. Let's try this." I think they don't realize sometimes that new people don't want them just coming in and "Type this in and you'll never have to do it again." I didn't know what I was doing in the first place. Let me learn that first. (Y)

For many of the secretaries the feelings of confusion and loss of control extended well beyond their initial contact with computers. Two women recalled feeling that grappling and struggling with the computer would be endless and mastery would never arrive:

I hated it and I thought I would never like it ... Many a times I would have liked to put my fist through it. People wanted things in a hurry and I couldn't do them in a hurry and I would think about it all night "Oh my God, I have to go back there." I really hated it. (V)

...I felt like there would never be a point where I would be able to sit down and work on a computer without having a lot of manuals next to me. (B)

Of the 11 secretaries who did not report a negative initial experience, 4 claimed that because of their prior experience they were not intimidated. Six secretaries described in a neutral way the experience of working with a new, strange tool and they referred to the touch of the keys, the commands, and other new skills in their answers. The remaining secretary took an assertive stance, and defined the situation as good and necessary:

...It was a challenge, and I guess I, as they say, coming to CMU, I figured I was going to have to work with computers, and I better learn it. And I didn't let it throw me. (X)

All the secretaries eventually achieved mastery through a variety of means, most of which were informal and self-initiated. Eighty-four percent reported they learned primarily through trial and error and practice on their own. In response to the question, "How did you eventually learn?" one secretary said:

Just by using it. The more you use it, the more you understand, I think. (R)

And another secretary remarked:

Doing it. Nobody can tell you how to do it. You have to do computers. (F)

Learning on their own included staying overtime or coming in on weekends. Some secretaries printed out graduate students' manuscript computer files and studied them. Some read manuals (although manuals were described frequently as indecipherable). Six secretaries specifically mentioned they helped each other:

...We all grew with it, so, if we didn't understand, someone else over here would know and would tell you. So it was a learning together process. (Q)

CMU does provide computer education classes for the staff, and 92% of the secretaries reported they had taken at least one class. Many, however, voiced complaints. They described the classes as moving too fast, and as glossing over subjects rather than providing depth or detail. They said the classes were taught at a superficial level. Several secretaries wanted more variety in the type of classes offered and the level at which they were taught, especially classes for more experienced users. Secretaries criticized instructors for not providing enough practice time and attention in class, and for their insensitivity to the fact that what they were teaching was a "foreign language" to many of the secretaries. The alien culture metaphor, introduced in Chapter 11, seems particularly appropriate here. One secretary gave a vivid description of her experience in the classes:

Most of the time the instructor was talking maybe an hour and you had half an hour to play with it. And you got stuck, there were so many people in the room – everybody would be asking questions. But they never really went into detail about it, so you still didn't get the understanding of the answer and then you had to leave, because you had to go back to your job. (J)

Another secretary focused on the language difficulties:

But I think they should be taught by someone who had to learn the hard way also – somebody that can explain it in everyday language. Explain on the same level as the people who are coming in and looking at this thing and saying "Oh my God, what am I going to do with this thing?" They really need someone like that. Not somebody who had been around computers and talks like a computer.... They just seem to think everybody knows this language and this is what they are going to tell them. I think they need somebody who has definitely learned the hard way, to help them understand. (V)

Four secretaries also expressed the difficulties they encountered when they tried to strike a balance between going to class, practicing what they'd learned, and doing their job. For example:

...When you go to class you've got to come back to work and you're behind in work because you've taken up some of your hours. So you really don't have time to come back and sit down and go over what they taught you ... Faculty think when you go to these classes and you come back you know everything. "Put my vita on the computer." Sure! (B)

This same secretary, however, goes on to find something constructive in the pressure she feels:

But I guess if you didn't have people asking for things you wouldn't be able to get the time to actually learn procedures and how to do it. (B)

In summary, over half of the secretaries reported initially experiencing confusing and negative interactions with the computer. Moreover, as a group they found the formal training provided by the university to be limited. They relied mainly on their own internal resources (e.g., persistence and patience) and the help of other secretaries to learn the necessary computer skills. But they were largely successful. At the time of the interview, 72% of the secretaries reported they had a good deal of mastery over the computer as compared to when they first began using it. The secretaries reported similar learning experiences and feelings of mastery regardless of their age or tenure at CMU.

Secretarial Computing at CMU

The secretaries at CMU, like most secretaries elsewhere, work for people rather than for production units. Most work for more than one person. The average is 3.5 bosses. The secretaries' work is not highly routinized; they perform a wide variety of duties for their bosses. These include typing and producing documents as well as performing social and organizational functions such as briefing visitors, helping students register, answering phones, and arranging luncheons, meetings, and seminars. Judging by the number of secretaries who wanted to be interviewed but had no hours free, and by the number who had visibly large piles of work on their desks when interviewed, the secretaries have little slack time and indeed they report a heavy paper load.

CMU secretaries use computers to do many of their tasks, which can be sorted into three broad categories: text processing, data management, and communication. Examples that fall into each category are shown in Table 8.1.

Although the computers available at CMU are multifunction machines and, as Table 8.1 indicates, secretaries use the computer for a variety of jobs, the majority of these tasks involve managing text information and use only the word-processing capabilities of the computers. Document production is, of course, one of the traditional secretarial tasks, and it is not surprising that secretaries at CMU use computers primarily for this purpose. Using the document production programs is not a trivial task, however. The most popular text editor (Emacs) is a command-oriented system that allows a range of tasks from deleting material in a file to moving material between two different manuscripts using different windows. Most secretaries know at least 100 commands that may be used on this system. Similarly, they are familiar with the text formatter (Scribe). This document preparation system is also command oriented and can be quite complex. For example, commands for printing a mathematical equation can run 20 lines. The text formatter is frequently revised and secretaries must keep up with new versions. Additionally, those secretaries who work on both the mainframe computer system and personal computers use a protocol (Kermit) to transfer files between mainframe and personal computers over phone lines. Thus, document production at CMU requires far more technical proficiency than is necessary in the office equipped with only a typewriter. Although the task itself is no different from what secretaries have traditionally performed, computing seems to have increased secretaries' skill levels and not decreased them as a deskilling theory would suggest.

Two tasks other than text processing are performed on the computer by a significant number of secretaries. Nine have learned to use LOTUS or similar spreadsheet programs, suggesting an expansion of their responsibilities that is in part possible because of the presence of computers. The secretaries also use the electronic mail system that connects them with people and departments across campus. Eighty percent of the secretaries reported they used the mail system: 13 have used it both socially and for work, 6 have used it only for work, and 1 secretary said she used it only socially. Several secretaries mentioned that they use the mail system much less frequently than in the past because of cost and difficulties connecting to the mainframe system from their microcomputers. More or less simultaneously with the widespread introduction of microcom-

Table 8.1. *Examples of secretaries' computer work*

Text processing	Data management	Communication
preparing coursework	making graphs/charts	electronic mail &
preparing slides	student registration	bulletin boards
making schedules	employee records	
typing resumes	bookkeeping (LOTUS)	
typing bibliographies		
preparing agendas for visitors		
preparing the graduate catalog		
dealing with promotion cases		
preparing annual reports		
typing speeches		
making lists		
making labels and name tags		
typing letters/memos		
typing papers/manuscripts/reports		

puters on campus, the Computation Center raised the cost of using the time sharing system. Also, connecting to the mainframe from the microcomputers is somewhat difficult. Thus, secretaries who previously had easy access to the time sharing system via terminals now face both financial and system stumbling blocks to using the mail system. This barrier will be removed as the new distributed network is installed.

These alternate computer based tasks constitute a small part of the average workday and overall, the secretaries' jobs are relatively constrained. The secretaries (76%) report that by and large computing has not changed the type of work they do. But within the limited range of tasks flexibility of execution and responsibility exists; there are instances when the secretaries take the initiative and are not simply responding to the standard demands of their job. For example one secretary said:

I like to invent things. I'm the one that put the graduate student list, graduate form letters on there [the computer]. I did it without any one asking me. I put the annual report on there without anyone asking me. You know, just for my benefit. (B)

Another secretary commented:

I've created a lot of forms that we use in our office to handle inter-office problems. (O)

Many of the secretaries do try to experiment with the computer, primarily exploring document production options in formatting and tabulating, and making documents more presentable. They complain, however, that they do not have the time to really play with and explore the computer's capabilities; they fit it in when they can:

Not during office hours... I have fooled around on it, say, on my lunch hour... (S)

All 25 secretaries said they liked computing in their work. Most of the reasons given for their positive attitudes focused on the word-processing functions of the computer. Many remarked that the editing capabilities made changes easier (36%), the turnaround was fast (44%), and their documents always turned out nicely (24%). The reduction of paperwork was also cited as a positive feature of using computers (8%) and several secretaries noted that generally it was a timesaver and they accomplished much more using the computer (20%). The comments below are representative of their opinions:

...I think they're much faster. It's a lot easier to go back and change your mistakes or to switch a paragraph here a paragraph there if they want it instead of retyping the whole thing. (L)

I think that you get more of your employee for the 8 hour period. You get so much more done. (Q)

It makes my job a lot easier. You can do some thing so quick on the computer... It's just a timesaver and at times that's real important. (M)

Several secretaries volunteered more personal reasons why they liked computing in their job, noting it was challenging, fun, creative, and they liked learning something new. Finally, two secretaries specifically mentioned the ease with which they could now reach people and have them respond by using computer mail instead of repeatedly trying to connect with people by the telephone.

The secretaries were also asked what they disliked about computing in their job and 44% could not think of anything they disliked. The answers of the remaining 14 secretaries generally fell into two categories. One set of responses referred to functional problems with the system. Ten secretaries cited as irritations the mainframe crashing and difficulties getting on the system, printers that are slow and not of the best quality, formatting difficulties, and/or problems interpreting software and getting a program to run. One secretary clearly described the problems associated with trying to produce a document using the existing system:

I think sometimes it's frustrating. You try to do some things, try to format, and you can't do everything, you have some problems trying to get it to run and that's frustrating. You go down and get your printout and something doesn't come out right then you have to sit and fool around with it – that's frustrating. That part of it I can see whereas if you had done it on the typewriter you could have formatted it the way you wanted. But I still prefer the computer. (V)

And the one secretary of those interviewed who was the least enamored with computers vividly expressed her irritation with the document program:

The fact that you've got to keep giving all of these little itsy, bitsy commands, you know, before it does anything. And on the typewriter you just automatically do it. If you want to underline a word you've got to give it a command to do that. And then remember to un-command it, so to speak. (I)

The second category of responses centered on negative health outcomes associated with computer use. Five secretaries expressed complaints that included eyestrain, noise from the printers, and sitting for long stretches.

In summary, CMU secretaries generally reported feeling that the computer had not brought fundamental changes in the type of work they performed; their principal job is still text management. Some secretaries, however, have learned to use a spreadsheet program to perform bookkeeping tasks and to aid data management (e.g., student records). This could be considered a computer-wrought expansion of secretarial skills. Interestingly, despite the general view that the nature of their work has not changed, 72% of the secretaries feel the volume of work they produce has increased. Why they have this perception is unclear. As a secretary suggested above, because the computer enables one to do work faster, more work can possibly be accomplished during the average work day. The behavior of the secretaries' bosses may also contribute to the impression that they are doing more work on the computer. Since the editing capabilities of the computer make changes easier, bosses might be more willing to ask repeatedly for revisions on papers with which in the past they would have been satisfied. Furthermore, 52% of the secretaries felt their bosses were producing more work on their own computers, leading perhaps to increased work for the secretaries. Of course the secretaries' self-reports should be supplemented with objective measures of the amount of work they perform. Yet their perceptions are important if we are to understand secretarial reactions (both positive and negative) to the introduction of advanced technology in the office.

Work Relationships

Many people believe that office automation has detrimental effects on clerical workers and secretaries (Braverman, 1974; Glenn & Feldberg, 1977; Machung, 1983). Computer-based clerical work is described as standardized and isolated; the word-processing pool is typically used as an example. Some writers argue that computers simply exacerbate an existing negative situation in organizations where work has been highly specialized, such as the insurance and telephone industries (e.g., Kraft, 1984). The conditions at CMU are very different from those that have been depicted in insurance and telephone companies. Secretarial work at CMU has never been highly routinized. As previously noted, the secretaries perform a variety of duties including many that require interpersonal skills. They have considerable autonomy allocating their time and attention within the day and week. They deal with people directly, not only with faceless documents or data. They work close to people in other jobs and help people cope with crises (such as late-registering students) and office problems. Indeed the interviews revealed that at CMU the computer, rather than making work life more isolated, has led to increased interaction among employees both within and across organization levels and subunits.

Secretaries at CMU do not sit isolated in front of their computer screens for hours on end. All 25 reported that they help one another with the computer and most say that the secretaries encourage each other.

The secretaries in the department are all very helpful. They interact a lot whenever someone seems to be having a problem. (E)

...if we get errors, we all get together – "What the heck is this?" (B)

Additionally, for one older secretary the computer provides a means of crossing age barriers:

...it's interesting that I feel that I can relate to the younger people in the office, because we have that common practice of using the computer – we have to talk about it. If I would sit in a corner and just work as I did years ago, in that same style, I think it might raise some barriers. But, I think this helps to develop an ease of relationships with the others who use computers. (O)

The computer affects secretaries' perceptions of other staff members' work capabilities. Sixteen of the women saw the secretaries in their office as equals on the computer. Nine reported they did envision a hierarchy in terms of computer skill and attributed the differences in skill to the type of work the secretary is asked to do by her boss, longer experience with computers, and more extensive training. Five of the nine reported feeling resentful of others who were less proficient if they were constantly being interrupted and asked for help. Nevertheless, even when negative feelings existed the secretaries continued to aid one another:

Once in a while with the other secretary in the office – because I don't think she really understands how the whole thing really works... I don't think she's really grasping the basic concepts. So she tends to ask me the same sort of thing over and over. And, I usually try and help her – but I know sometimes I'm short with her. I don't mean to be ... (U)

The proliferation of computers in offices on campus has not drastically changed the division of work among secretaries. Twenty-one of the secretaries responded that they do not informally divide up tasks among themselves on the basis of computer skill – they do their own work. However, the computer as a flexible tool has the potential for increasing sharing as one secretary in an academic department articulated:

...you can share the work. Which you could not do with the typewriter – if you had a fifty page paper that had a lot of different sections you were stuck with it. But now, someone can do a section and just merge them at the end. It puts less pressure on people. (F)

In addition to seeking help from one another, the secretaries also seek computer help vertically within the organizational structure. Besides turning to computer professionals who aid the staff as part of their job, the secretaries also call upon their bosses and graduate students. About half ($n = 12$) mentioned they have asked their boss for help and 6 responded they consult graduate students. The secretaries' help-giving behavior similarly crosses organizational lines. Twenty secretaries reported helping their bosses, primarily with word-processing. Graduate students also seek their help, and one secretary bemusedly reported that programmers have consulted her:

And I have programmers coming to me. Which is really strange because I would think they'd be able to figure it out. And yet they come. "I've been having a problem with such and such. How do you get it to work?" ... I think that perhaps the MAC is too simple. They expect to have to do something very complicated. (X)

Ninety-two percent of the secretaries' bosses use computers. Interestingly many of the secretaries find their bosses changing what they do on the computer with some bosses taking on tasks that were formerly the secretary's responsibility. Over half ($n = 14$) reported that their bosses have changed what they do as a result of having their own computers. The secretaries see their bosses typing more drafts of papers and memoranda on their own, and being more creative.

A lot of his outlines and engineering-type documents that he really knows how he wants it worded and set, he does himself so it's a lot easier for me. Then, when it's a bigger thing, I can take all his little pieces and figure out how I'm going to format into the larger piece. (Y)

Some things that I used to do on the typewriter or on the word-processor now the treasurer and assistant treasurer do themselves on the IBM PC. Graphs and charts and calculations, like forecasts. They used to do a lot of handwriting and then give it to me to type and, of course, now with the LOTUS 1-2-3 they are able just to do it themselves. (O)

I think he's more creative ... And he's doing a lot more statistical stuff. (T)

I'm sure the Dean has. He writes constantly on his MAC and he does most of his own editing, and I'm sure that would not have been the case before that happened. (U)

They seem to be doing like more drafts on their own and they will often come in and give me the disk to finish up. The ones that have computers seem to like them a whole lot. (H)

They've changed the way they work. One boss I work for now, he will type a lot of his own papers because he feels that he's more comfortable doing that because he will just put in thoughts to start with, and then expand on them. And then when he's satisfied with it, he gives it to me to put equations in, to format things, and have it run off for him. (D)

One secretary commented on both the positive and negative aspects of her boss doing memos, papers, and letters on his computer:

...it's nice too because if it's just like a memo that's going to another person in the department, instead of him writing it out, giving it to me to type, he'll type it and say just put it out.

She continues with the following:

He's typing a majority of his letters. In a way that's good and in a way that's bad... because if he has a word "form" instead of "from" and I used SPELL, it's not going to catch that as a context error. If it's a real long letter I would have to proof it anyway if I type it, but sometimes I feel a little more comfortable if I typed it in first ... (G)

The preceding comment suggests that for this secretary having the boss do more on his own is a mixed blessing. She feels loss of control over the quality of the outgoing product (the paper) which previously she had seen as her clearly defined responsibility. Another secretary indicated that having the boss do more of his own work can create more work for her:

...they will do a draft and I will put the finishing touches on it. It all depends on what they are doing. But I will always go through and make sure that the commands are right, because they will screw up there, especially two of them. One does no commands whatsoever. So you always have to go in and make sure. (A)

How such role conflicts and tensions that arise out of the blurring of responsibilities are resolved is an important topic for future study.

Improving Office Productivity

Throughout the interviews the secretaries offered suggestions that they felt would improve office productivity. Almost all the secretaries made at least one comment that addressed administrative actions regarding training that could lead to improved secretarial efficiency. These included the following:

- provide classes for varying levels of users
- have peers who speak the secretaries' language teach the courses
- allow more time to practice during class
- make the classes mandatory regardless of prior computing experience
- provide regular workshops that allow secretaries to remain up to date
- survey the secretaries about classes they would like offered
- organize classes around functions, e.g., books, letters, bibliographies
- immediately sign up new employees in classes.

These suggestions are not unique to CMU. They reflect the types of issues and problems secretaries (or other new computer users) are likely to face in any organization.

A number of secretaries also mentioned problems they faced trying to obtain computing information. Secretaries described user consultants as unclear and unable to supply answers to secretaries' questions. They described manuals as unhelpful, and the administrative staff at the university Computation Center as difficult to reach. More generally, the secretaries felt their needs were not considered by the administrators in charge of computing. This is exemplified in a comment that refers to installing a new version of the document production program by the University Computation Center.

There's no rapport between the secretaries and the Comp Center. They don't consult secretaries who use the system. They should keep the same versions for the secretaries – don't change just for the convenience of the students. (E)

Secretaries offered two concrete solutions for some of these problems. One secretary suggested installing a helpline for secretaries that is staffed by people who do not speak computerese. A second secretary suggested the development of a system whereby a secretary could access and exchange information about computing with secretaries in other departments.

Computers and the Secretary's Sense of Herself

Potentially, the computer can change not only the structure of work, what is done, how rapidly, and by whom, but it may also have an effect on an individual's sense of self. For example, Turkle (1980) suggests that working with computers can lead people to feel more competent, confident, creative, and powerful. One way these changes may be manifested among secretaries is in their work aspirations and their perceptions of themselves as independent workers. Additionally, working with computers may affect the secretary's perception of her role within the larger work organization.

The secretaries were asked if they felt they had acquired marketable computer skills and if there were computer skills they would like to acquire. These two questions were used as indicators of the secretaries' aspirations. Twenty-two secretaries felt they were attaining marketable, transferable skills. Eighty-eight percent of the secretaries said there were computer skills they would like to acquire. Learning how to use other machines and operating systems (e.g., UNIX) was mentioned by 44% of the secretaries. Forty percent responded they wanted to gain knowledge of various software programs, with LOTUS cited most often. Learning to program was mentioned twice. The comments were characterized, in general, by a feeling of receptiveness:

I'd like to learn as much as I can about computers because it would only be for my benefit to do that. And now I'm not as afraid as I once was. (T)

The secretaries were also asked directly, "Has working with computers had an effect on how you feel about yourself as a working woman?" and 80% responded affirmatively. Two secretaries commented that working with the computer had intellectually stimulated them and made them feel smart:

Well, I'm certainly using a part of my brain that I have never used before – in a technical sense. And it feels good. (S)

The other secretary said that not only did she feel smart but that she believed using computers should change the perception of secretaries' work:

I think it kind of makes you feel smarter... All you have to do is talk to someone who doesn't know anything about computers and you feel like you know everything ... I think it also kind of dissolves the stereotype of secretaries as real stupid, just sitting there and filing their nails ... I think having these computers certainly – you might not have to know programming, but you have to know how to operate them, how to do the word-processing. So I think it adds some intelligence to the job ... it makes you feel a little more important that you have computers to work with. (M)

The secretaries also mentioned that they were feeling more competent, that they had pride in what they can and do accomplish, and that they were better and more accurate secretaries. These feelings are exemplified by the secretary who commented on the contrast between her feelings as a computer novice and her present sense of her capabilities:

...when you learn something new and you get better and faster it does make you feel good. You know, cause I can see the difference three years back and now. I mean it used to take me, it seemed like forever, to put one equation in ... I feel more confident and proud (J)

A worker's introduction and subsequent adjustment to a new technology such as computers may also affect her perceptions of her worth to and role in the organization. In an attempt to tap this, the secretaries were asked to, "Think of a secretary who does the same job but she does not use computers. Do you think you should be paid more than she?" Half of the secretaries responded yes to this question. When asked why, this group of women stated they possessed more knowledge and skill, they produced more and it was of a better quality, and they had put forth the effort to learn how to use the computer. One secretary noted:

...knowing a computer or learning the computer techniques and the different pieces of software out there is like attending school ... I certainly think I've got a Ph.D. in computing ... I should be paid for what I know. (S)

Another of the secretaries who answered yes focuses in her response on the special skill she possesses, a skill not held by everyone:

...anybody can just type on a typewriter – on a computer you have to know, you have to learn it. It's not something everybody can do. (F)

Six answered no, I should not be paid more. Five reasoned that it would be unfair or harmful to the other secretary, and two said the computer skills they had were neither unique nor special. As an example of the former, one secretary said:

In a way, if the secretary is just using a typewriter and doing the same amount of work that I am doing perhaps she should be paid more, because it would seem like it would take her longer to get the same type of thing done. (H)

Another secretary combined both explanations for saying no in her response:

Actually, as far as the amount of work goes, she's really doing more work than I am, probably, for not having a computer and I don't think it takes such a great amount of skill to be able to do what I do at least ... At this level that I'm at, I don't feel that I'm doing that much different, except that I turn on my computer instead of turning on the typewriter. (U)

Five secretaries were very ambivalent, answering both yes and no to this question. One secretary said she did not know what to say, and one secretary stated unequivocally, "I think secretaries in general should be paid more." (C)

Discussion

As noted at the beginning of this chapter, secretaries and their work have received little research attention. This study attempted to examine secretaries' feelings about and experiences with computing in their work. Interviews revealed that the secretaries at CMU are positive about using computers. They do a great amount of their work on the computer. Moreover, despite negative initial experiences with the computer as well as limited training, they have achieved a relatively high level of mastery and feel particularly good about this accomplishment. They want to learn even more.

These findings of positive outcomes and experience are at variance with the negative picture painted by most authors who address the impact of advanced technology on clerical workers. This is primarily due to the fact that previous analyses confused aspects of the technology with aspects of the workplace. A word-processing pool workplace, where secretaries sit typing documents or punching numbers all day, never working face to face with people who write the documents or produce the data, will hardly produce positive outcomes. In these places, also, secretaries often have no control over their time and attention, never face non-routine challenges, and are closely supervised, sometimes down to key stroke monitoring. The secretarial work at CMU is neither isolated, routinized, nor closely supervised. The secretaries perform a variety of jobs on multifunction machines. They are responsible for people (e.g., their bosses) not for particular jobs (e.g., insurance claims), and they interact with other secretaries with similar responsibilities. They rely on each other for computer help and are often the local computer expert for their bosses. They also work for an organization that values computing; as Bikson and Gutek (1983) note, the organization's positive orientation toward technological change can positively influence satisfaction with, and use of, computers.

The data reported here are clearly limited to one organizational setting: a small research-oriented university. They are, however, representative of that setting; a survey of secretaries at CMU conducted previously reports similar computing experiences and attitudes (Giovengo, 1983). It is possible, although unlikely, that secretaries with a strong, positive bias toward computers are disproportionately represented in the university's personnel pool. There is no way, in a study of one organization, to address this point directly. We did find, however, that more recently hired secretaries were no different on measures of their learning experiences and feelings of mastery than secretaries whose tenure at CMU included the period preceding the widespread dissemination of computers on campus. It is also conceivable that the secretaries' experiences with the computer could be affected by the type of equipment they use. In this sample, the responses of the three secretaries who used only stand-alone PCs appeared not to differ from the responses of the four secretaries who used only the time-sharing systems in their work, although this could not be ascertained quantitatively because the n's of these two groups were so small. Certainly, future research needs to examine the impact of advanced technology on secretaries in other organizational settings. Continued attention needs to be given to the effect of new technologies on work relationships; advanced technologies such as computing can affect not only work productivity but also the system of work relationships that exist in an office. For example, at CMU computing help and expertise is sought both vertically and horizontally within the organization and many bosses are doing and/or sharing work that was previously their secretaries' responsibility. Unfortunately, in this study bosses were not interviewed. Investigating their perspective is important, as is examining over time the changes in work and relationships new technology brings to the office.

Several practical issues that could be addressed by the CMU administration were raised in the interviews. First, the secretaries leveled their greatest criticism at the computer training they received. The secretaries could benefit from classes taught by peers who are familiar with typical secretarial tasks and who speak their language. Additionally, a continuing computer education program would permit the secretaries to keep abreast of new developments, polish their existing skills, and provide an opportunity for those secretaries who are particularly interested in computing and their work to develop more special-ized expertise they could share with others in their office. Second, the development of local secretarial experts or liaisons would serve both administrative and secretarial interests. They could aid in the dissemination of information from the more centralized computer administration as well as communicate the needs of the secretaries to those computer managers. Third, the administration could capitalize on the secretaries' expressed desire to explore the work capabilities of the computer by guaranteeing them compensated time for courses and giving them access to free accounts.

An intriguing aspect of this study is that, although the secretaries generally feel both that they are producing more with computers and that they are not adequately compensated monetarily for this, they continue to work at CMU. Equity theory (Lawler, 1971) posits that in an exchange process a person's sense of equity or fairness (and therefore their job/pay satisfaction) is a function of the ratio of their perceived inputs and outcomes. People believe they are in an equitable situation if their ratio of inputs/outcomes is perceived as approximately equal to that of relevant others. Equity theory assumes that people are motivated to avoid or rectify inequitable situations. It is plausible to suggest that the positive changes the secretaries perceive in themselves and in their work relationships also function as outcomes or ''payment.'' Perhaps managers should note that the apparent economic benefits of advanced technology may result not just from machines that enable people to produce more. These benefits also result from new self-perceptions engendered by working with computers and from new work relationships in the office. These potential (and potentially positive) outcomes of introducing advanced technology in the office should not be ignored.

9 Automating a University Library: Some Effects on Work and Workers

Sara Kiesler, Scott Obrosky, and Felicia Pratto

This chapter is about the CMU library and what happened when computers were introduced to automate library work at CMU. A university library is a special unit in the university organization with unique kinds of workers, routines, and technologies. Library professionals have unique values and norms. Still, the library shares most of its structure, processes, and conditions with the larger university organization. For example, library procedures for budgeting resources, hiring personnel, and cleaning buildings are much the same as in all academic and administrative departments. Also, the library shares with these other units the same kinds of constituents – students, alumni, faculty, research workers, and administrators.

Because the library is a small distinct unit within the larger university, it is a good place to study technological change. Small numbers of people working in a bounded location make repeated interviews and observations practical. We can compare the effects of computer technologies used only for library work with general-purpose computer technologies used in offices across the campus as well as in the library. In this study, we collected data from library records and from library staff in 1983 and again in 1985. Our purpose was to learn about the effects of introducing special and general computing on library work and workers. For reasons to be explained shortly, we thought we would observe both intended and emergent effects of computing as we defined them in Chapter 3.

When we began this study, the library seemed on the verge of a technological revolution. The organizational conditions for change were auspicious. Slack resources existed in a healthy university budget and foundation grants had been offered to the library for new technology. Administrators were willing to release library professionals from time spent on day-to-day operations so they could learn about computing. Competence existed in the computing skills and interests of some of the library professionals and administrators. Also, library staff could (and did) call on expertise from the university at large. Zeal existed in the vision, and specific support of technological change, of central administrators, the library director, and librarians.

131

Computing was to be the solution to the library problem at CMU. At the close of the 1970s, CMU was changing from a regional to a national university. It was attracting more top students and faculty from across the country. The library, however, had a small and inadequate collection, and its services were too limited for a major research institution. Computers would turn a backwards CMU library into "the electronic library of the future" (University Libraries, 1982a). They would put CMU "in the forefront of library automation in the country" and "far ahead of any comparable library in the country" (University Libraries, 1982b). Within the library, people were told that computerizing library work would demonstrate to the world that the library was participating in the CMU electronic community. It would make the library more popular with students, because CMU students were predisposed to use computers. It would raise the status of library workers with faculty, who already used computers in their everyday work. It would generate more attention and financial support from the university administration. It would enhance the external prestige and job mobility of librarians. Finally, administrators hoped that by introducing the new technology across the whole library, the relatively autonomous departments would be brought closer together. One respondent remembers this excitement (numbers designate interviews):

When LS2000 was coming, before the on-line catalog came up, there was all this "Rah rah, hurrah." On-line catalog. Great stuff! Morale boosting meetings. And "You guys are great. You're doing a wonderful job, and everyone's doing their job and they're wonderful!" We're going to burn the card catalog! (78)

The sell was spectacularly successful. In 1982, when we began planning this study, everyone we met at the library talked about the desirability of computerizing the library. Everyone wanted to participate. The high enthusiasm and multiplicity of envisaged positive outcomes is one reason we expected emergent effects. That is, if an innovation consists of many good ideas, many enthusiastic people, and many supportive interactions, then many different things will be going on. If many different things are going on, the innovation is unlikely to be exactly the way it was defined initially. If the innovation changes, then the effects will move beyond those intended, and unanticipated consequences will emerge.

Another reason to expect emergent effects was that the special library technology, along with general office computing, was to be built as a multiplicitous resource – a technology used by different people for different tasks. This statement requires some prior explanation of library work and how it was expected to change. Library employees consist of three main categories. First, there are administrators, most of whom hold advanced degrees in library science work(6 in 1983). Next there are professional librarians (16 in 1983) who assist people and decide what to buy, and then support staff (34 in 1983). One kind of support staff, the technical processing staff, orders library materials, keeps accounts, and keeps the catalogs current. Another kind of support staff, circulation staff, maintains records of the circulation status of all library holdings. Before any computers were introduced, 5 separate paper technologies and routines were used to process library holdings. The holdings were recorded in a card catalog and in a shelf list. Circulation records were kept on file cards. Paper library cards were issued to borrowers. Acquisitions records were kept in accounting books and files. Also, general office work (such as preparing correspondence) was done by hand and using typewriters. People communicated from office to office by telephone and typed memoranda.

Computer technologies first began to enter the library in 1980, when support staff began keeping acquisitions records on a time-shared university computer. In 1981, librarians began to use the time-shared computers to do general computing, especially to exchange electronic mail. (When this study began in 1983, half of the library staff used electronic mail at least weekly.) The special library innovation was announced in 1982. The library director described plans to develop an automated library information system, now called LS2000, to support all record keeping in the library, including the card catalog. The new technology would consist of a computer data base of all the library holdings, software to use the data base in various ways, and terminals and light pens for reading and changing information in the data base. There would be different types of access to the data base for different staff members. Circulation staff would record the circulation status of books through one entry to the data base. Technical processing staff would update the bibliographic record of holdings through another entry. Library users and librarians would search the on-line catalog (that is, the record of library holdings preserved in the data base) using terminals rather than trays of cards. Through computer mail, employees would exchange information and messages, and librarians would answer questions of library users. The designation, "library patrons," was abandoned for the more modern, "library users."

New computer technology in the library was intended to have several technical effects: (1) Computers would be used for office work and for library work, which would reduce autonomy and isolation of tasks. (2) Everyone would use the same technology and data base, so people would learn to do others' work and become less specialized. (3) The number of records per library holding would change from five to one, eliminating such tedious tasks as typing revised catalog cards and copying overdue notices. (4) With tedious tasks eliminated, fewer technical processing staff would be needed.

In sum, the new technology, both general computing and LS2000 for dedicated library work, would be used for many different kinds of work in the library, including communication. This should produce emergent effects, in addition to the intended technical effects, because the more people use computers in many ways, the more likely computing might change how people think about library work or about themselves as library workers. The more people use computers, the more likely they would communicate electronically. Communication in organizations is typically regulated by organizational position or status (O'Reilly & Pondy, 1979). Electronic mail tends to deregulate communication across organizational boundaries (Sproull & Kiesler, 1986). Therefore, computerization of the library might lead to changes in communication patterns, such as more communication across organizational statuses or departments.

In this chapter we describe our study of intended and emergent effects of library automation. The next section describes the library organization and our survey samples. Then we describe how the library technology changed and its intended technical effects. Finally we describe the emergent effects. At the outset, we were able to observe effects only during a two-year period, so there is no way of knowing how transient or enduring these effects might be.

The Library and How We Studied It

The library at CMU is actually a system of three libraries, employing 61 people and housing 650,000 volumes. Hunt Library, the largest, houses the social sciences, humanities, fine arts, and music collections. The Engineering and Science Library houses the physics, engineering, statistics, computer science, and mathematics collections. Mellon Institute Library houses the biology and chemistry collections. The library system also includes the Technical Processing Department, the Special Collections Department, and Audio Visual Services.

We surveyed the library staff twice, first in 1983, two months prior to the anticipated arrival of LS2000, and again in 1985, 10 months after LS2000 became operational. The samples consisted of 40 of 58 employees in 1983, and 57 of 61 employees in 1985. There were 31 employees who participated in both years. These samples consisted of all employees who were on campus at the time of our surveys. The employees participated voluntarily, and they were assured their responses would be kept confidential. Each participant was interviewed individually and asked to complete a printed questionnaire, the entire transaction taking about one hour. A set of questions was repeated in both years. In addition, we made observations of equipment and library work to see how library technology and work changed, and reviewed records of budgets, grants, minutes of meetings, and memoranda about new library technology.

Intended Technical Effects

Technological change was the most important and riveting event in the CMU library during the early 1980s. As one respondent said: "I can't imagine what the CMU library would be like if it weren't for this automation project'' (30). In organizations generally, large technological change typically leads to proliferation of ideas, people and transactions over time, and with proliferation, to complexity (Van de Ven, 1986, p. 597). At CMU, the development and application of library computer resources depended upon a large and increasing number of people with different perspectives and skills, such as employees of the software vendors, CMU library staff involved in training, and special technical consultants hired to do programming. These people, though different, did not work in isolation; whatever they did influenced others working on the technology. This interdependence created two kinds of complexity: ongoing uncoordinated technical change and differentiating competency. Uncoordinated technical change happened as revisions made to one part of the library technology required other, unanticipated revisions. For example, the library's new minicomputer was discovered to have too little capacity to provide the intended campus-wide access to the on-line catalog. To solve the problem, CMU technicians installed a local area network and made it possible for LS2000 to run on a CMU all-campus computer. The network immediately enabled more people to communicate and to use the on-line catalog. This required library technologists to spend extra months training other library staff. Programmers also spent many months changing the system so that it would be usable by a wider clientele.

Differentiating competence happened as some library employees acquired extraordinary skill and competence with computers and the library technology. The competent group gained recognition, prestige and support within the library. This created a new social category of library technologists that did not fit within the traditional order of academic library professionals and skilled support staff.

How Library Technology Changed

General computing using the time-shared university computers was already being implemented in the library when the special library computing information system, LS2000, was first announced in 1982. The plans were for the integrated computer library system to be fully operational by 1985. But hardware failures and the sale of the software vendor to another firm caused delays in the introduction of LS2000. In the summer of 1985, when we took our second measures, the on-line catalog was operating, but the acquisitions, circulation, and serial check-in functions were still being developed. Table 9.1 shows when planned and actual implementation of LS2000 took place.

Although some of the planned new computer technology had not yet been introduced by 1985, some of it had been implemented much sooner than intended and some computer technology that was not planned had been introduced.

Table 9.1. *Planned and actual dates of the implementation of LS2000 functions*

LS2000 Plan (and intended users)	1982 target	Actual implementation	1985 target
E & S on-line catalog (librarians, patrons, reference support staff)	Sept. 1982	May 1984	
Hunt on-line catalog (librarians, patrons, reference support staff)	Jan. 1982	Sept. 1984	
M I on-line catalog (librarians, patrons, reference support staff)	Aug. 1983	Sept. 1984	
Remote access (patrons)	1985	Limited access 1984	Full access 1986 or 1987
Retire physical catalog (librarians, patrons)	July 1983	Not updated after July 1984	?
Circulation (circulation support staff)	Sept. 1984	—	May 1986
Serials check-in (circulation support staff)	July 1983	—	?
Acquisitions (technical processing staff)	July 1983	—	?

The major anticipated but early change was the implementation of multi-user remote access to the on-line catalog. In theory, the technology for multi-user access functions had been available since the on-line catalog started operation in 1984, but it was not advertised. Then a few faculty who asked were told how to reach the on-line catalog through the network, and students learned about it by word of mouth. As a groundswell of demand for remote access started building, it became obvious that the minicomputer on which LS2000 ran would grind to a halt if it had to support both internal operations, such as data base maintenance, circulation transactions (when brought up), and distributed access by people across the campus. This forced library technologists to rethink the problem of remote access. They solved the technical load problem by using LS2000 to produce a tape output of library records which they then converted to a format usable by the retrieval system on a campus IBM 3083 machine. The campus computer was designated as the one to run LS2000 and the library's own computer was designated as the one for all internal data base maintenance work. Solving the first technical problem then created the problems of improving the on-line catalog sufficiently so that anyone on campus could use it and creating both on-line and face-to-face training procedures. To solve these problems, several librarians were relieved of their regular duties and they were assigned to work almost exclusively on the new computer system.

There were two major unanticipated changes, one in general office computing and one in library computing. The major unanticipated change in general office computing was an influx of microcomputers and printers, which encouraged staff to use computers for text editing and document preparation. (See Chapter 4 for how this change took place across the whole campus.) According to our inventories, in fall of 1983, the library had 25 terminals, 6 printers, and 2 microcomputers. By the summer of 1985, the library had 35 terminals, 16 printers, and 22 microcomputers, excluding equipment in people's homes. This represents equipment increases of 40%, 166% and 1,000%, respectively. The biggest change, that is, the introduction of microcomputers, was never mentioned in the plans of 1983.

A major unanticipated change in special library computing was the addition of access to national computer data bases (e.g., Dialog, Search helper, BRS, Willsearch, Easynet, Infotract), which enlarged the scope of electronic information search and retrieval possible at CMU. The accessibility of the library information system via the campus network and mainframe computers made it possible for faculty and students, in their offices, to do searches on these national data bases.

In sum, the process of technology development in the library was one of ongoing additions and revisions of technology which unexpectedly affected other parts of it, and resulted in both planned and unplanned technological change. People experienced this as an absence of coordination:

And then the on-line catalog came up and it's like we're all in this free-roll down hill.... It just seems like every department is sort of going on its own, and has been for the entire year. We're all just sort of taking over and blundering through our own part.... (76)

In addition to technical changes in hardware, software, and resources, technological change consists of changes in behavior and attitudes. The most immediate change in the CMU library was differentiation of library staff competence between those who worked intimately with the new technology project and those who did not. Involvement with the technology project created a group of approximately 20 "library technologists" who gained special influence within the library. Library technologists tended to be high in organizational status – that is, they were most likely to be administrators and next most likely to be professionals. High status influenced access to computers and computing, and therefore the opportunity to develop competence. This differential access according to status is described by one respondent.

There was even an incident last week where a support staff wanted to take a break. She was at a terminal. She left for a couple of minutes, and a librarian sat down and pulled up a record ... The support staff person came back and the librarian started yelling at her and everything. And it was the support staff's time. If she was a librarian, then she wouldn't have been yelled at and her time [on the computer] wouldn't have been stolen. The librarian apologized later on, but the incident still happened.

The statistics bear out this respondent's impression of uneven access. Computer hardware was distributed unequally across organizational status. Administrators were the best equipped with terminals and microcomputers in 1983, followed by librarians and then support staff (see Figure 9.1). All groups had more equipment in 1985, but the relative distribution of equipment among groups remained the same. Administrators still had much more equipment on average than did librarians and support staff, and they acquired new equipment (i.e., microcomputers and printers), while librarians and support staff also acquired the more old-fashioned terminals.

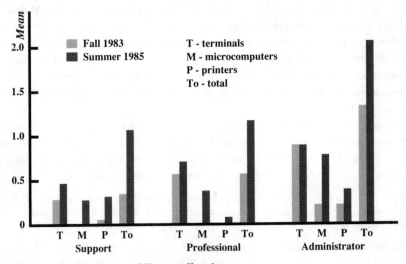

Figure 9.1. Computer equipment of library staff workers.

The number of staff who had computer accounts on the university time-shared computer system increased 68% from 1983 to 1985. However, as was the case with equipment, access to the university computer system was not equal across status. In 1983, professionals had the highest proportion of computer accounts (88%), followed by administrators (75%), and support staff (13%). In 1985, 100% of professionals and administrators had computer accounts, and many more support staff had accounts (52%). Because of their greater number, support staff had the largest proportion of the total accounts in 1985, that is, 41% (versus 16% in 1983). But still, access was correlated positively with organizational status.

One possible reason for allocating computer access by status is that status is a credible criterion for allocating scarce resources. The library director explained his view of this:

As a few got [computers], others came along and asked for them, sometimes simply because Sally had one. In time, as new systems came on stream, everyone would have some need to use computers. One problem was in keeping people interested and convincing them their time would come... We took a top-down approach. Department heads, supervisors, and librarians needed to be comfortable with computing to identify applications and provide support and training to support staff...

In addition to the status effect, interest and chance led some employees within status positions to have a greater involvement with computing and the new technology. Although advertising for new staff stated, "We are seeking librarians willing to share in the development of computing technologies," only two of the library technologists came to CMU as computer experts. All the remaining library technologists gained their competence in computing in the CMU library. New (and usually young) employees were more likely to be in the group of library technologists. One administrator, a library technologist himself, talks about the selection of new people, equating technological competence with commitment to library work and youth.

There are the older ones, who have been here 10 years or more, and the younger. And those groups are oriented toward different goals. The older group, they see library work as something to do between break and lunch. We who have been hired since [the director] came in, are much more oriented toward computing and *library* positions and less toward social interactions (81).

A clerk who had worked at the library nearly 20 years reflected the same belief about age and technology: "The trend is toward younger people. They haven't hired anyone that's older in a long time. I think that younger people are more in tune with computers. We older ones don't catch on as fast" (80). Differentiation of competence in the library created a new social division that competed with the traditional library order. That is, rewards and recognition, as well as power to influence the development of new technology, accrued to the library technologists:

The people here who seem to be the happiest, maybe they're not better at automation, but they really express an interest in it, they seem to get a lot of things. And the other people tend to, I think, not get those things. Like nice raises, and lots of committee memberships and praise and that kind of stuff. They tend to form these little cliques that are hard to deal with (11, librarian).

I want to reemphasize about the polarization among librarians. Some people get to do fun things and some of us have to sweat in order to get anywhere. If you don't do a technology project, you're not valued as much (30, librarian).

I think the range of people in the library is broader. There are people working here that are from the old school of librarianship, and new people who come in who have a different philosophy of how libraries should be run – using computers (78, support staff).

The library technologists influenced which technical changes took place in the new computing systems. More computer applications were made in departments having more library technologists, such as in the main reference department. In the audio-visual department, where library technologists did not work, potential computer applications were ignored:

There hasn't been much moving in developing a strong media department. Because other things have taken priority and I don't know, I'm not saying it shouldn't. But the computing system is one priority. So much time, so much money, personnel, going on-line, developing that consistently with academic departments. I don't think too much time has been put into seriously undertaking a strong non-print media collection in the library or anything else.

Audio-visual isn't really a big part of the computerization. In most commercial firms, the computer plays a central role ... but in this place people don't recognize us as being able to produce things for their departments they could use for promotional reasons, or as a tool. We don't use the computer. It's never been there so they live without. Once they did, they would be using it more and more and we would be recognized. First increase the awareness and need (96).

Despite chaos and excitement, unplanned and planned technology changes (which required changes in people's work, which we describe below), and creation of a new in-group of library technologists, people in the library held as strongly positive attitudes about new technology and library work in 1985 as they did in 1983. We measured job attitudes in 7 questionnaire items and attitudes about technology in 17 items. All of the ratings were highly positive, and none of the ratings changed from 1983 to 1985. Everyone, even those who did not use computers, thought people should learn computing and not ''resist'' technological change:

A perfect example is Beverly, who has been doing on-line searching for 20 years and who is not afraid of computers to the best of my knowledge. But she's never figured out TOPS [the campus computer system running the computer mail program]. She has been shown over and over and over and over and *over* how to read a message and send it. She'll go weeks without reading her mail. It's as if she has a deliberate resistance. And she's been shown over and over. It's been said the only reason she hasn't been fired is to keep Sue here (30).

Positive support of new computer technology in the library cannot be explained by ignorance or non-use of computers on the part of the majority of employees, the nontechnologists. As we shall show, nearly everyone in the library used the new technology. People also acquired knowledge. For example, in response to the interview question, "Could you describe LS2000?" employees were able to describe an average of only two technical attributes or effects in 1983. By 1985, they described four. In response to this question in 1983, 56% volunteered that they did not know much about the system, while only 19% said this in 1985 ($z = 8, p < .01$).

Use of Computer Technology

We asked our respondents to examine a list of ways to use computers in the library, to check those that applied to them, and to indicate how frequently they used a computer for those purposes. We categorized the uses as either general office work using the general computing system or specialized library work using the dedicated library computer system. General computing includes text editing, sending computer mail, and making signs. Specialized computing includes using the on-line catalog and national library data bases. We analyzed these data on computing use for the staff as a whole and also for the 31 people who were in the sample in both years. The first set of data shows *organizational change* in computer behavior from 1983 to 1985, but this change can be attributed to new people entering the sample in 1985 as well as to changes of behavior in the people who were there in both years. The second set of data shows how the same people changed their behavior, that is, *individual change*. From these analyses, we found that individual change was virtually the same in quantity and direction as organizational change. For simplifying this presentation, we will talk about organizational change, which is shown in Table 9.2.

In general, library employees used a computer for more tasks, and more of them used a computer, in 1985 than in 1983. If we compare the percentage of people who never or hardly ever used the computer for any purpose versus those who used it daily or weekly, the percentage of nonusers dropped from 28% in 1983 to 4% in 1985 ($z = 3.4, p < .01$). The biggest changes occurred in the specialized library computing category.

Table 9.2 shows how computer use varied as a function of people's organizational position and how that behavior changed from 1983 to 1985. The data show that change occurred in all groups, but most of all in support staff positions. In 1983, 45% of the support staff did not use a computer at all. By 1985, 48% used a computer for office work and 78% used a computer for library searches and other library work, leaving only 7% nonusers.

We carried out chi square analyses of the interaction of organizational position and frequency of computing. The larger the chi square value, the stronger is the

Table 9.2. *Percentage of library employees who use a computer for different purposes as a function of their organizational status*

Status position	(n)	Frequency of use in 1983			(n)	Frequency of use in 1985		
		Daily	Weekly	Never		Daily	Weekly	Never
Any computer use								
Administrators	(6)	67	17	17	(10)	90	10	0
Professionals	(14)	86	7	7	(16)	81	19	0
Support staff	(20)	55	0	45	(31)	77	16	13
General office computing								
Administrators	(6)	67	0	33	(10)	80	10	10
Professionals	(14)	86	7	7	(16)	81	19	0
Support staff	(20)	15	20	65	(31)	32	16	52
Specialized library computing								
Administrators	(6)	17	50	33	(10)	40	40	20
Professionals	(14)	57	29	14	(16)	75	13	13
Support staff	(20)	45	0	55	(31)	71	7	23

Note: Percentages in rows may not sum to 100 due to rounding.

association between status position and the frequency of computer use. We found that the influence of status on computer use decreased from 1983 to 1985. For all computing, the status by frequency χ^2 is 8.5 (n.s.) in 1983 and 2.1 (n.s.) in 1985. For library computing, the status by frequency χ^2 is 13.3 (df = 4, $p <$ .05) in 1983 and 8.0 (n.s.) in 1985. However, for general office computing, the status by frequency χ^2 is 18.2 (df = 4, $p < .01$) in 1983 and 17.4 (df = 4, $p < .01$), still significant, in 1985. These last statistics reflect the fact that in both 1983 and 1985 many more administrators and professionals than support staff used a computer to do general office work; this status effect did not change over time. The absence of change in this category is explained in part by the greater access to computer accounts and equipment of administrators and professionals compared with support staff. Where access was less constrained (the library's terminals to do on-line searches were located in public places), support staff used the computer more.

In summary, we found that computer use by the entire staff increased from 1983 to 1985. One intended effect of the new technology was that computers would be used for office work. Our data show that this change did take place, although more so for administrators and professionals than for support staff. The status effect confirms the findings of others that valuable resources tend to be dominated by people who have more status or authority in organizations. Despite this top-down effect, the amount of computing resources accessible to, and used by, CMU library support staff was very significant.

Another intended effect of the new technology was that specialized library computer technology would be used by everyone, and library work would become less differentiated. Our data show a substantial increase of computing by support staff and even by administrators to do special library work such as on-line searches. We also observed informally that many faculty and students started doing computer searches using the on-line catalog and national data bases. Much as reference librarians used to do library searches using their special knowledge of the library and of library information sources, this change is one of "deskilling" (see Chapter 2). That is, the librarian's craft turned into a task anyone could do using a computer.

Distribution of Staff and Tasks

In addition to intended technical changes in tasks, new library technology was intended to make the library more efficient overall by eliminating duplication of records. This would permit a reduction of the clerical work force. Because the LS2000 data base system was not fully implemented by 1985, we cannot examine the full effects of computerizing all library records. In fact, library prosperity and full-time clerical staff did not change by much. The operating budget of the library increased 25% from 1983 to 1985, no more than the university budget as a whole, which increased 28%. The capital budget is harder to trace, because some capital expenditures (as for modernization) were part of general university capital expenditures. The library won some special university capital funds: $333,000 for automation itself, $300,000 for new acquisitions, and $40,000 for study facilities. In addition, the library received larger and larger allocations for computing on the university mainframe computers and for printing on the laser printers. The library also won a large Mellon Foundation award which supported staff and patron computer training, research, and computer software development in addition to some capital costs. The available data suggest that expenditures per patron were about the same from 1983 to 1985.

Between 1983 and 1985, there was moderate turnover of library staff. Three administrators, three professional librarians, and five support staff left library employment. One librarian was promoted into an administrative position as head of a technology project. The library hired 14 new employees: 3 administrators, 3 librarians, and 8 support staff members. The net increase of the full-time work force was only 3 people (58 to 61 total).

The biggest change in staffing was completely unanticipated: a 50% increase in (full-time equivalent) student help. Students were assigned many routine and some nonroutine tasks in the library. In some cases they did tasks that librarians used to do. For example, students were employed to teach people to use LS2000. Students had never been employed to teach people to use the card catalog; librarians did that. A greater relative reliance on nonprofessional, inexperienced and part-time help is a deskilling effect observed by many employees. Most of them thought part-time employees displaced the tasks (and potential job positions) of experienced, full-time support staff who in turn did tasks formerly done by librarians:

More and more what they're asking people to do here doesn't really require, doesn't benefit that much, from experience. Yuppies [i.e., students] are much more expendable. I think lately you could run the system paying the minimum amount for yuppies, and have them come for a two or three year period and then letting them leave for some other job, which is going to be hard to stop anyway. Not building a real solid support staff that stays a long time and has good benefits, good pay and that kind of thing. The university only pushes the professional staff. They want them to come in and change things. Help create new ideas, add new things. Not run the place. The support staff, they're running more and more the day-to-day operations of this place (90).

As support staff and students took over more of the routine library work, librarians' work underwent a kind of "upskilling" in that they used their newly acquired computer competence to do new kinds of tasks. Some of these were:

1. *Library instruction.* Librarians created instructional materials on library information resources in the form of tours, orientation sessions, subject classes, and increased publications. Two librarians began to take formal classes.
2. *Liaison with academic departments.* All the reference librarians were assigned to specific departments to work with faculty to develop collections, instruction, and data base searching.
3. *Data base searching.* Librarians not only searched the literature for students and faculty, they taught students and faculty to use the on-line catalog and developed methods for training them to do searches in national data bases.
4. *Library information services.* Librarians wrote the text for the Library Information computer files, and worked on screen displays for the on-line catalog.
5. *Research and publication.* Librarians undertook much more research and were encouraged to publish it.

Two new jobs were created for librarians: Electronic Information Systems Project Director (EISPD) and the Librarian for Educational Computing. Both of these jobs involved planning and acquiring computer software for the library and starting new computer services, such as electronic publishing and an educational software library.

In summary, along with technical effects on office work and library work, we found an effect on the distribution of tasks and skills in the library. Even though the new technology was incomplete, some tedious tasks (e.g., typing catalog cards) had been eliminated. Other tasks (e.g., teaching people how to search the catalog) required lesser skills. There was an increase in part-time help and, generally, in the average library experience and professional training of people doing library work. At the same time, many of the librarians were doing technical computing development, administration, research, and training using new computing skills. Hence the overall effect was one of "reskilling."

Emergent Effects

Attentional Effects

In addition to reskilling, which has both intended and emergent properties, we found two kinds of unanticipated secondary social consequences of new technology in the library – attentional and social contact effects. The principal attentional effect of new computing technology in the library was a marked increase in the popularity and prestige of the library and librarians, and within that group, of library technologists. Within CMU, more people used the library. From the academic year 1983–84 to 1984–85, traffic into and out of the library increased by 31%. The university population of students and employees increased only 16% during this period.

Librarians gained prestige. Within the library itself, we asked people, "Is a prestige distinction made between librarians and nonlibrarians in the library?" In 1983, 67% said yes, and in 1985, 94% said yes. Librarians who were also library technologists were thought to have the highest status of all. Librarians also gained prestige outside of CMU. We illustrate this in Table 9.3, which lists the external activities of the library's professionals. Library computer technology was the subject of the large majority of these activities, and was the topic of all but one of the papers published in each year.

Social Contact Effects

We thought communication among staff members might increase because of the greater numbers who shared the same (computer) work technology and because of the availability of computer mail. To study communication, we showed employees a list of everyone who worked in the library and asked them to indicate which of the people on the list they knew, which people they talked with at work, and which people they talked with socially. We used the number of people that respondents talked with about work as our measure of the communication network. Table 9.4 shows how people in the library communicated with colleagues in their own status position and with people at other status levels.

First we can look at which groups seem to communicate among themselves the most. In both years, administrators followed by professional and support staff

Table 9.3. *Professional activities of library staff members*

Activity	1983	1984	Jan – June 1985
Papers published	1	4	7
Papers presented	1	8	5
Professional orgs.	11	27	20
Editorships	0	2	2
Grant proposals	0	3	0
Manuals written	0	1	1
Courses taught	2	1	2
Total activities	15	46	37

communicate with the highest proportion of other members in their own status category. This may be indicative of the relative size of the three groups or of administrators' need to coordinate the activities of the library among themselves. Demands for coordination as reflected in communication with others may decrease with status.

In 1983, the professionals talked to the highest average proportion of staff members in each status category. In 1985, administrators took the lead. This shift can be traced to an increase of communication between administrators and support staff, offset by a decrease in communication of professionals. That is, the change in the communications pattern suggests greater direct contact between administrators and support staff and reduced contact between professionals and the other groups. Based on our interviews and observations, a likely explanation for this change is that professionals were performing fewer supervisory and routine library functions and working on more isolated projects using computer information technology. Meanwhile, support staff and students took over library routines, and were supervised by administrators. The communication pattern follows the status hierarchy in both years. Staff members in general communicated with a higher proportion of administrators than professionals, and with a higher proportion of professionals than support staff.

In previous research we have argued that electronic mail reduces constraints from organizational status (Sproull & Kiesler, 1986). Hence, if the library increasingly enables people to communicate using computer mail, then communication across status boundaries should increase for those people who use the technology. Mindful of the fact that half of the support staff still did not have good access to computer mail in 1985 (i.e., they did not have computer

Table 9.4. *Percentage of library employees of different status with whom library employees communicate, as a function of their own status*

Status position of communicators		Status of recipients of communication:						
		1983				1985		
	(n)	Adm.	Prof.	Supp.	*(n)*	Adm.	Prof.	Supp.
Administrators	(6)	87	70	47	(10)	90	76	64
Professionals	(14)	81	76	64	(16)	78	65	51
Support staff	(20)	39	40	42	(31)	49	46	47

accounts whereas all of the administrators and professionals did), we examined communication in 1983 and in 1985 as a function of computer mail use. Table 9.5 shows the most important pattern: People who used computer mail communicated with many more people, by far, than did people who did not use computer mail; the multivariate Wilks Lambda F-test was F (3,91) = 15.2, $p <$ .01. These data may indicate that communication in the library increased among people who participated in the new technology introduction, or that people who use computer mail have some other quality that increases communication.

Discussion

In most field research on new technology, the investigator has access to only one set of direct observations (usually in the midst of technological change or soon after the technology has become routine). In order to infer what is changing, the investigator must rely on retrospective, often biased evidence about the past or on projections of the future. The longitudinal method used in this study, however, employed direct observations of events repeated twice and separated by two years. Therefore, we can talk more confidently about actual change in resources, behavior, and attitudes.

The technological changes that took place in the CMU library consisted of two kinds of new technology and two kinds of intended technical effects. The two kinds of new technology introduced in the library are the planned technology, such as installation of LS2000, the on-line library catalog, and unplanned technology such as the influx of microcomputers and subscriptions to national data bases. The two kinds of technical effects are office work effects and library work effects. The office work effects consist of modest increases in general office computing, such as text processing and exchanging of computer mail. Office computing was used much more by administrators and professionals than by support staff. All of the administrators and professionals had good access to

Table 9.5. *Percentage of library employees of different status with whom library employees communicate, as a function of using computer mail*

Computer mail used by communicators?	(n)	Status of recipients of communication[a] 1983			(n)	1985		
		Adm.	Prof.	Supp.		Adm.	Prof.	Supp.
Yes (at least weekly)[b]	(20)	78	76	62	(34)	76	66	54
No (monthly or never)	(20)	44	39	39	(23)	47	42	46

[a] Adm. = administrators; Prof. = professionals; Supp. = support staff.
[b] All but three employees who use computer mail do so one or more times each day.

office computers and computer accounts whereas only half of the support staff did. These results accord with the theory that computers support the people who have the most power, but perhaps the status effects will disappear as the technology saturates the library. The library work effects are somewhat different. These effects consist of very large increases in library computing work, which includes using LS2000 as well as using national data-bases. And the effects are seen throughout the library organization, across all status levels, even among clerks and part-time student workers. Outside the library people are starting to use the on-line catalog remotely. Because library computing enables many people to do what librarians alone once did, the technology has had a democratizing (and deskilling) effect in the workplace. This is born out by the large increase of student employees, some of whom do important library work. It has also created the opportunity for librarians to do new kinds of work.

The social effects of technology most apparent from our data are both attentional and social contact effects of the kinds we described in Chapter 3. The attentional effect consists of increased prestige and status of professionals and administrators in the academic library community. The social contact effect is more communication across status boundaries, and more communication by people who use the technology of computer mail. Librarians became a little more isolated and support staff a little less so. Are these really enduring social effects or are they simply transient effects that will go away when the technology is more firmly entrenched? We believe (but will have to test these beliefs against the evidence) that the attentional effects on prestige may decline as computers become more familiar in libraries, and the comparative advantage of this library grows smaller. However, the role of the librarian and of libraries is likely to continue changing as librarians and library administrators take further advantage of computers as "information machines." New attentional effects may take place, especially people's views of information and how one acquires information. The social contact effects in the library might be enduring as more people share the same technology and do overlapping kinds of work. Further, as computer mail spreads through the organization, communication across organizational and status boundaries might become even more prevalent than it is today.

10   Instrumental and Symbolic Aspects of an Executive Information System

Suzanne Penn Weisband

Computers are proliferating in executive offices, not just in universities but in other kinds of organizations as well. Why is computer office technology so popular among managers? Some writers – the "technology optimists" described in Part I – argue that computerization is the outcome of rational decision making. As computers become increasingly affordable and friendly, they can become a management tool, instrumental to achieving greater managerial efficiency and productivity (e.g., Ellul, 1964; Anderson, Hassen, Johnson, & Klassen, 1979). Others argue that computerization is the outcome of symbolic decision making. That is, computing is imbued with the positive cultural meaning that western societies attach to technology and information (Anderson et al., 1979; Bikson, Gutek, & Mankin, 1981; Mowshowitz, 1981). Computers foster organizational legitimacy (e.g., Kling & Scacchi, 1982), and support political power (e.g., Downs, 1967; Danziger, Dutton, Kling, & Kraemer, 1982; Dutton, 1981; Kraemer, 1982; Robey & Markus, 1984). Hence, not just attributes of the technology, but also social values in the organization and larger society must be considered to understand why managers acquire computers.

Probably, computers have both instrumental and symbolic significance for managers. Computers can speed up managers' report preparation, expand their communication horizons, and improve their access to organizational data, such as personnel statistics. But computers also represent rational thinking, innovation, and productivity, independent of any direct impact on managerial tasks (Markus, 1983). This chapter, about the introduction of an executive information system (EIS) to university administrators, illustrates instrumental and symbolic aspects of managerial computing.

Instrumental and Symbolic Aspects of Computing

Managers who use computers do so in four main ways: to write and edit text (such as reports), to communicate using electronic mail, to do accounting tasks using spreadsheets, and to organize information (such as personnel data) using data base management programs. Our own and others' evidence (e.g., Chapters

150

5 and 6 of this book; Sheposh, Hulton, Ramras-Berlin, & Trinh, 1985), show that the first two uses dominate by a very wide margin, but much of the literature on executive computing focuses on data base information systems and computer "decision aids" (e.g., McFarlan & McKenney, 1983; *Wall Street Journal*, 1983). In this literature, the rational basis for using computers is to produce more, better, and faster information, which will increase efficiency and productivity. In the popular press, too, one sees pictures of managers examining computer screens on which graphs or charts are depicted, implying that the manager is receiving decision-relevant, clear, accessible, reliable information.

If it is sensible that managers use computer information systems, certain assumptions can be made about their implementation. First, there are likely to be financial and technical barriers to adoption (Franz & Robey, 1984; McFarlan & McKenney, 1983). Second, these problems might be overcome with technical solutions such as more efficient programs. One approach to implementation is the system life cycle approach, which is intended to ensure success by monitoring system development as it passes through a predetermined sequence of stages, or life cycles (Lucas, 1982). The stages might include a study of project feasibility, the design of specification requirements, training programs, installation, maintenance, and evaluation. Steering committees might be formed to direct the life cycle phases, to review proposed systems, and to administer information system policy. This strategy assumes the existence of coherent managerial goals which, once discovered, can be mapped onto the attributes of the information system (Kling and Scacchi, 1980).

The instrumental significance of computing can be important in all organizations, including universities, that trade in information. University administrators use statistical data, if only to help in their negotiations with faculty (Pfeffer, 1981). Computers could make these data more accessible. Even more useful might be such mundane applications as electronic mail, which makes possible faster information exchange among people. However, values and activities other than information processing are important to managers. For example, in universities, administrators must protect and enhance the institution's reputation. Administrators must create conditions that nourish the organizational culture, and that are conducive to socialization of people to that culture. It is possible that computing has as much to do with these other symbolic activities as with the performance of information-processing tasks.

A symbolic perspective on computing differs from the instrumental perspective in that it deemphasizes the technical attributes of the computer. A symbolic perspective focuses on the meanings or ideas of computers and computing inside and outside the organization. When ideas about computing are shared, they frequently become norms for perceiving, believing, evaluating, communicating, and acting within the organization (Goodenough, 1970). Norms provide a way of justifying how things are being done and what people want done. Sometimes these justifications are institutionalized, that is, formalized in organizational activities or offices. For instance, in organizations where people value the rational basis of computing (e.g., its instrumental value for greater productivity), administrators will establish computer planning committees (Pfeffer, 1981). Zucker has argued that "social knowledge once institutionalized exists as a fact, as part of objective reality, and can be transmitted directly on that basis. For highly institutionalized acts, it is sufficient for one person simply to tell another that this is how things are done" (Zucker, 1977: 726). Hence, the existence of a computer planning committee, perhaps one that espouses the "life cycle" approach, turns hopes for computing into fact.

One function of computers as an organizational symbol is to enhance organizational legitimacy independent of their effects on efficiency and task productivity (Meyer & Rowan, 1977). Because more, better, and faster information is associated with rationality, the introduction of computer information systems for managers can represent an organization's commitment to rational practices. As such, computing enhances managerial status and prestige, and the reputation of the organization as forward looking and forward moving. The mere appearance of computerized information processing can justify the decision to adopt executive computing even when it is unclear how computer data will be used to improve decisions or even that the data will be used (Danziger et al., 1982; Feldman & March, 1981; Wildavsky, 1983).

Another function of computers as an organizational symbol is to socialize people to organizational culture. Some organizations that value new technology sponsor workshops where computer novices learn to log on and to use simple programs, such as games, electronic mail, or spreadsheets. Some organizations let people take home personal computers. Some encourage family members to participate in computer training. These experiences are not just a matter of learning new skills; they also serve as a "foot in the door" for technology and technology advocates (Crawford, 1982; Nyce & Groppa, 1983). When people begin to enjoy sending electronic mail, or using a spreadsheet, they are acquiring the readiness to accept new computer technology, to attend to organizational decisions and events surrounding computers, to feel similar to other computer users, and to overlook problems caused by computers (Beniger, 1983). In the absence of symbolic socializing experiences, computing attitudes will be more difficult to predict (Caporael, 1985).

What makes computers especially effective as symbols is that they can function as cultural artifacts independent of how they are used. High-status hardware and computer-printed reports prove managers' commitment to new technology. Not everyone is eager to use computers, and those who are not may find computers appealing as simply a status-increasing technology (King &

Kraemer, 1984). Computer sales talk and computer jargon are symbolic also. Expressions such as "office of the future" and "management information system" help convince managers that computing is desirable, even those who have never logged on to a computer. Computer artifacts and language are a way to generate organizational enthusiasm for computing, well before computers can prove themselves useful in performing specific tasks.

Instrumental and symbolic aspects of computing and computer-based information systems need not be mutually exclusive. People respond to instrumental and to symbolic opportunities (Kling, 1980). In this study we examined the introduction of one information system and variations in managers' statements about computing to see how their attitudes and behavior might reflect instrumental and symbolic aspects of computing.

The Setting and the System

During the summer of 1982, CMU introduced a management information system for its top administrators: the president, vice-presidents, heads of major business units and institutes, and academic deans, a total of 25 people. A few of these administrators were computer experts, and every one of them supervised at least one secretary who used a computer. Four of the administrators had never used a computer when we conducted this study, and almost half did not use a computer interactively. As a group, top administrators used computers less than any other group of people on campus.

In October 1981, a university provost proposed the idea of an information system for administrative personnel "to provide greater involvement of senior administrators in the [university's] computing environment." This proposal was met with positive enthusiasm by most of the senior administrators, and they encouraged the provost to pursue the idea of an executive information system. The provost allocated $50,000 in the Computation Center budget to the project. The office systems coordinator and her superior in the Computation Center were given the task of developing and implementing the system. It was to be called the Executive Information System, or "EIS." In June 1982, EIS was introduced to the 25 top-level university administrators and deans. It was described as "a high-quality information environment." The campus computer newsletter praised EIS as "another step toward widespread computer use" on campus: "With EIS, the gap is closing between traditional computer users and non-users. University executives can benefit from information processing, but they needn't become full-time CRT operators to do it."

Introducing EIS involved three steps. The first step was obtaining and installing two computer terminals for each of the participants who did not already have them, one terminal for the office and a second, with a dial-up modem, for home.

The second step was to choose software for EIS. Perhaps because of limited resources, or perhaps because one-third of the administrators were novices, the Computation Center staff did not design any special software programs for EIS. Instead the EIS software was chosen from existing, popular, and reliable programs already available on the mainframe computers used by most of the CMU community. Many of the EIS participants already had computer accounts on one of these mainframes. For EIS, every administrator received an account, if he or she did not already have one, on the same mainframe, which would make communication among them simpler and faster than communication across the network. The administrators were to be encouraged to use communication and text processing functions available on that mainframe. EIS had no data bases or data base management programs, though a budget planning data base was promised for the near future. The third step involved designing and distributing an EIS users' manual. The manual was clearly written and attractively formatted, and it was bound in leather notebooks. On the cover of each notebook, the participant's name was embossed in gold lettering. Inside, the manual began with a list of the 25 administrators who were members of EIS and their computer addresses, and instructions for obtaining help directly from the office coordinator. The rest of the manual contained tutorials on basic skills such as logging on, sending and receiving mail, and creating and editing texts.

In summary, EIS was not a formal data base system or a management information system. In the technical sense, EIS simply added computer accounts to an existing mainframe in a time-shared system with good programs for text editing and communicating by electronic mail. But EIS also created a formal computer user group of top administrators expected to engage in computing and computer communication. In short, EIS institutionalized computing for administrators.

Hypotheses

Based on our consideration of instrumental and symbolic aspects of institutionalized computing, we formulated some hypotheses about the effects of EIS on individual administrators. As an instrumental tool, EIS might change how administrators used their time. Administrators might use new sources of information, or they might exchange more information. As a symbol, EIS might improve the organizational legitimacy of computing. EIS might help socialize administrators and others to computing.

Theories of instrumental and of symbolic processes make some different predictions about the causes of differences in individuals' behavior, that is, the conditions for people behaving differently when confronted with the same situation. Instrumental theories assume or assert that individuals act differently

because their preferences are different. Preferences differ because real consequences differ. Hence, if Administrator A uses a computer and Administrator
B doesn't, Administrator A, but not Administrator B, should believe that computing is useful to him (his preference) and will lead to more productivity (his
consequences). This idea leads to the theory that individual attitudes about
personal consequences will predict individual behavior (Ajzen & Fishbein,
1980). To predict whether an administrator uses a computer, one ought to be
able to ask the administrator what he or she thinks of computers.

Studies have shown repeatedly that attitudes and behaviors are frequently in-
consistent (e.g., Abelson, 1982; Fazio & Zanna, 1978; Snyder & Swann, 1976).
Snyder and Swann (1976) demonstrated low attitude-behavior correlations
among people who had not thought about an issue before filling out an attitude
scale (prior thought resulted in a higher correlation). These results cast doubt on
a simple instrumental model of attitudes and behavior, that is, a model that says
if people think computers are useful they will use them.

One explanation of low attitude-behavior correlations is the existence of symbolic attitudes (Abelson, 1982; Sears, Hensler & Speer, 1979), which we first
mentioned in Chapter 3. A symbolic attitude is a "cluster of value orientations
which are not usually well articulated in terms of the instrumentalities of real-
world policies, but rather in terms of the shared feelings of a social group"
(Abelson, 1982:139). Members of a group might express positive attitudes
about computing as a reflection of the values of the group, regardless of variation among group members in their real need for, or use of, computers. Whereas
the instrumental model predicts behavior will follow from expected personal
consequences, the symbolic model predicts behavior will follow from group
norms and values. The instrumental model predicts marked individual differences in computing based on individual circumstances. The symbolic model
predicts that individual differences will be small. Rather, there should be
marked group differences in computing based on group values.

In this research, we tried to evaluate the instrumental theory by asking administrators how computers influenced the use of their time. This measure
pertains to a very specific behavior (i.e., does the computer help to perform
tasks), and it should predict computing behavior if computing is an instrumental
activity of administrators. This measure should not predict computing behavior
across individuals if computing is a symbolic activity of all administrators.
Rather, all attitudes should be positive (if computers are a positive symbol) and
unrelated to actual computer use.

One way to infer the existence of symbolic processes is to examine group
attitude differences where one might expect group values to differ. For analysis,
we grouped respondents along four dimensions to examine some ways that
group values might affect attitudes. The dimensions were (1) computer exper-

Administrators did not seem to be bothered by the fact that computing reorganized their time.

tise (experts versus novices), (2) hierarchical position (top-level administrators versus other EIS participants), (3) organizational position (college deans versus administrators in central administrative units), and (4) EIS involvement (implementers versus other EIS participants).

Respondents were classified as experts if they reported themselves as having expertise, used some EIS facilities, and previously worked from a terminal at home. The rest of the administrators were classified as "novices." We examined the idea that the novices would be even more positive about computing than the experts. These novices were introduced to computing in a sheltered environment and in a situation where they did not have to depend on computing to do their jobs. Hence they might adopt highly favorable, but somewhat unrealistic, attitudes about computing and the future of computers at CMU. We thought top administrators and administrators in central positions also would show very high optimism about computing and computers at CMU. These administrators, as a group, must be concerned about organizational legitimacy as leaders of the institution's internal constituents (students, staff, and faculty), and as representatives of the institution to its external constituents (alumni, trustees, prospective students, public and private financial supporters, and parents). The higher the authority and the more central an administrator's organizational position, the more critical it is to the administrator's effectiveness that computing at CMU "take." Hence the higher and more central the administrator's position, the more positive the attitudes that an administrator will express about computing. Finally, the implementors of EIS were expected to express favorable attitudes about EIS and computing since they were responsible for introducing EIS, and their reputations might suffer if EIS were perceived as a failure.

Method

The 25 EIS participants were 10 top-level executives, 6 academic deans, 1 nonacademic dean, 1 research institute president, 3 staff directors, and 4 directors who were responsible for developing and implementing EIS. The chart on Figure 10.1 indicates the organizational location of the EIS participants within the university and the composition of the groups used in the analyses.

Interviews were conducted with 24 of the 25 EIS participants two to three months after they were supposed to have received their manuals and terminals. (One vice president was out of the country during the interviews.) The interview lasted 30 to 45 minutes and asked about participants' jobs, computing generally, and EIS in particular. We tape-recorded each interview and carried out content analyses of the transcripts to measure attitudes.

We measured computer use by counting the number of different software packages or programs respondents said they used. Based on their answers to questions about specific software, administrators' computer use could be grouped into four categories: communication, text processing, data analysis and statistics, and programming. The respondents were given a score of "1" if they mentioned using any program within a category, and a score of "0" if they mentioned no program within a category. We also counted the number of different categories managers said they used. For example, a score of "1" means that the manager used the computer only one way. The largest score is "4," indicating the administrator used the computer to do all four kinds of computing. From answers to the question about time expenditures, we obtained administrators' beliefs about how computers improve work, and we correlated these answers with the computer use self-reports.

From the interview transcripts, attitude or opinion statements could be coded as positive and negative evaluations about EIS or computing in general, and expectancy statements about EIS or computing. Also the participants rated the value of EIS on a four-point scale. In the content analysis, positive statements about computing were statements in the first person that described computing favorably (e.g., "I think computers are very useful."). Negative statements were statements in the first person that described computing unfavorably (e.g.,

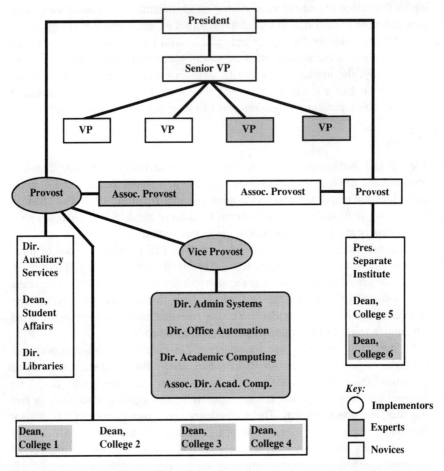

Figure 10.1. Organization chart of EIS participants.

"The computer gives me nothing but one big headache."). Expectancy statements were statements referring to respondents' intentions of future use, and their ideas about increased computer resources of the future (e.g., "There should be more computing on campus"). All of the expectancy statements were positive.

Results

By the time we conducted the interviews, 8 of the 12 novices, most of whom had never previously used interactive computing, were using EIS. None of the novice administrators had an easy time starting, as the following quotations illustrate:

...and I said, "Karen, I did it at 2 in the morning and it didn't work." "Well what's your password?" I said, "Well originally, they told me...that my password was Desk, but I've never logged into it, and haven't been able to log in." She said she would check it. And she came back and said, "Desk. Try it again." I went home that night, couldn't get it to work. I called in the next day and said I tried Desk; I tried my social security number; I tried everything I could think of, but apparently the password that they had inserted was "Desks," the plural of desk. (E)

I've gone through it all. It took me about a month and a half. But I've gotten through it all. I just have to force myself to do it step by step. (K)

Table 10.1 summarizes how administrators described their use of computers and EIS in 1982. Everyone who now used a computer, that is, 20 (83%) of the 24 respondents, reported using it for electronic communication with other people. More than half of the users (and 46% of the total group of administrators) used the computer to do text processing. Only a few users (17% of the administrators) carried out computer data analyses or programming. On average, the respondents said they used the computer for two different purposes, communications and text processing.

Some of the answers to interview questions revealed how administrators reacted to EIS in particular. Though everyone received the manual, four respondents did not look at it and another four had not yet used any of the EIS programs. Of those who did report scanning the manual, most respondents said it was useful; only a few said it was confusing.

Instrumental Uses of Computing

EIS designers believed that one goal of EIS should be to provide a uniform environment for organizational decision making by having all administrators use the same computer system. This goal would seem instrumental to the managerial function. If administrators use the same system and the same sources of data, their information environment should be more reliable and more efficiently distributed. As it turned out, although there was no formal information system, all of the 20 administrators who used the computer used electronic mail to communicate with one another. As more administrators learned to use the system, more of them exchanged electronic mail with other administrators. Hence EIS provided more information by enhancing direct interaction among people rather than by providing statistical data.

I know faculty have their own terminals and they're on regularly. I have to start sending them mail when they know I'm on. It's a way for them to send me mail. A lot of them (this is really a very important concept), they don't want to bother me about small issues, and they feel they don't want to show up [in my office] to ask me about this or that frustration, but by being able to send me a private electronic message they know they're not showing up in my office but I'll read it. And in fact I can reply to it quickly or forward it to somebody else. It lowers the barrier. One faculty member I rarely talk to,

Table 10.1. *How administrators reported using computers and EIS in 1982*

Interview questions	Administrators who answered "Yes" (%) (N = 24)	Computer users who answered "Yes" (%) (N = 20)
Computing		
Have you ever [interactively] used a computer?	83.3	100
Do you have a computer at home?	62.5	75
Does the computer influence your time?	58.3	70
Does your work at home differ from your work at the office?	20.8	25
Do you have any problems using computers?	70.8	85
What do you use the computer for at the office (at home)?		
Communication	83.3	100
Text processing	45.8	55
Data analysis	16.7	20
Programming	16.7	20
EIS		
Have you received the EIS manual?	100.0	100
Have you scanned the manual yet?	83.3	100
Were there useful sections?	62.5	75
Were there confusing sections?	12.5	15
Have you used EIS?	83.3	100

once we started communication on this [computer], we just kind of communicated much more than we ever did face to face. (R)

Novices were surprised at what they had been missing:

This to me is the funny part. When I logged in, there were about 25 letters that people had sent me over the last year...that I knew nothing about. (E)

Most of the administrators gave instrumental explanations of their computing. When they were asked if computers influenced how they used their time, 14 of the 20 administrators who used computers described ways that computers helped them do their work; 6 said that the computer did not influence their time. The 14 administrators who said the computer influenced their time described 39 different ways computers did so; 30 of the comments addressed the efficiency and flexibility of computer communication and computer text editing.

We don't have to play telephone tag. (D)

People respond by electronic mail or they call me on the phone. That's one of the revelations of [the computer] – people respond. (A)

[Electronic mail] has made me much more effective. (S)

I spend less time in meetings because the little issues get solved with electronic mail. (D)

If people need me, they'll get a hold of me that way [electronic mail] (G).

Administrators did not seem to be bothered by the fact that computing reorganized their time.

Having it available 100% of the time has influenced the way I schedule my time. (L)

I have to use it at night or in the early mornings because things are so congested here [in the office]. (J)

I work at home because it's relatively easy to get on [the computer]. (T)

It's somewhat like a new toy. You play with it, and you add time that way. If you're not careful it can take more time than it should. (K)

None of the administrators said that computers made them inefficient, not even those who complained about congestion on the computer system or those who implied they were working more hours by spending time at home using the computer.

Symbolic Uses of Computing

The symbolic perspective on computing helps one understand some of the peculiarities of EIS, such as why it was called an executive information system. The symbolic perspective emphasizes the usefulness of symbols and symbolic acts to socialize people and to reinforce organizational legitimacy. CMU had committed itself to becoming a fully saturated computing community and a leader in educational computing. Yet before EIS, fewer than half of CMU's administrators were regular computer users, and some had never even logged on to a computer. EIS was symbolically significant at CMU because it suggested a new and useful way for administrators to use computers. With a fancy system title, new terminals, and gold-embossed manual as enticements, all administrators might be recruited into the computer-oriented culture of CMU. One EIS member said, "What I like best of all about [the manual] is that they put your name in gold" (X). Another thought, "… there is an enormous degree of status involved in these executive manuals" (B). EIS focused busy administrators' attention on computing, and it induced the novices among them to learn to use a computer. EIS created an identifiable group of computer users, the EIS group of top administrators. They communicated with each other using the computer system. These activities seem to have reinforced administrators' commitment to computing personally and their belief in computer technology for administrators and CMU more generally.

I was not a user. Although I had accounts on [one machine], I did not use it because I was relying mainly on the students and operators in the Robotics Institute to do my programming ... I thought it was going to be cumbersome, and I found it extremely easy, very, very inviting and enticing. (A)

I personally use [the computer] just for the mail system and for the BBoard. We have in mind to implement a number of on-line accounting systems where we can get up-to-date financial information from it, so it's a management information type thing from my point of view. (H)

I think that, first of all, EIS emphasizes management to the university administrators. It makes them think about management, and how they manage their own time, how they manage the activities of their colleges or of their organizations. I think, second, it exposes them to the technology, and it makes them think about using computing as part of their own lives. Its very important in that respect. And I guess, third, I believe that when its fully developed – and I think it's not anywhere near fully developed now, I think we're still at a fairly infant stage – but I think when it's fully developed it will turn out to be a very useful management tool, and we already see some of that now. I mean, I can't get to [name of top administrator] for love nor money. And the way I get to [him] is I send him electronic mail. And that way I can always, within a 24-hour period, I can always communicate with him. But I can call him for, you know, weeks at end, and he's never there, and he never answers my calls but if I send him an electronic mail message, I get an instant response from him. And that's really true of all of us. All of us are in and out enough that it makes it very hard to really rely on most of the standard procedures. (S)

EIS was a quiet event at CMU. Few outside of the select group of participant administrators knew of it. Although the campus computing newsletter described EIS once, no mention of EIS was ever made in either the student newspaper or the faculty – staff newspaper. This is congruent with viewing EIS as a socializing and legitimizing mechanism for administrators, rather than as a vehicle for directly enhancing the legitimacy of computing across all of CMU's constituencies.

Individual Attitudes About Computing

Administrators' positive attitudes about computing were significantly correlated with the number of different ways they used the computer (scored $0 – 4$; $r = .46$, $p < .05$). Those who enumerated ways that computers influenced their time reported using twice as many kinds of computer programs as did respondents who did not think computers influenced their time $F(1, 22) = 5.91$, $p < .05$. These results support an instrumental model of computing in that reported computing behavior fits beliefs about the personal usefulness of computing.

Heavy and expert computer users were also enthusiastic about computing in a different way. The experts liked computing now, but non-users and novices were more positive about the idea of computing in the future. These data are shown in the first two columns of Table 10.2.

Table 10.3 presents data for all administrators. It shows the correlations between positive and negative statements and the type of computer programs, if

Table 10.2. *Average number of attitude statements by administrators*

| | | | Categories of administrators[a] | | | | | |
| | | | Imple- | | Top- | | | |
Attitudes	Experts (N = 13)	Novices[b] (N = 11)	mentors (N = 6)	Others (N = 18)	level (N = 10)	Others (N = 14)	Central (N = 18)	Deans (N = 6)
Positive statements	5.1	3.0	5.0	3.9	2.9	5.1	3.6	5.3
Negative statements	3.9	3.7	1.8	4.5[*]	2.1	5.1[+]	3.1	6.2
Expectancy statements	1.7	4.3[**]	1.0	3.5[*]	3.3	2.6	2.9	2.7
EIS rating[c]	3.6	3.2	3.8	3.3	3.3	3.5	3.4	3.5

[+]$p < .10$ [*]$p < .05$ [**]$p < .01$
[a]Significance tests are based on t-tests with 22 degrees of freedom.
[b]These are EIS novices. Four of the 11 are also novices to computing in general.
[c]Significance test is based on a t-test with 19 degrees of freedom.

any, respondents said they used. The data show that managers and administrators who used the computer for communication talked more positively about EIS and computing ($r = .38$) than non-users. Those who did data analysis and programming, or those who used the computer in more ways, talked more negatively about EIS and computing. These negative statements reflected criticisms of EIS rather than of computing in general.

I guess my perception is that there really isn't an EIS. What there are is 24 people who are being taught how to log on to the computer. But there's really not a system that supports those people and that does anything significant. (F)

I think EIS is far too grand a term, since we can't get any accounting information or anything else. It's not even remotely constituting of a management information tool. It's a joke. (N)

This is not an executive information system; it's an executive mail system. (J)

The ratings of EIS are telling, however. *Everyone* gave it a high rating, including the four who had not used any of the EIS facilities (one person had not even received his terminal). Of the four non-users, three of them gave EIS its highest rating of 4 points, including the individual who did not yet have his terminal.

Table 10.3. *Correlations of attitudes and computer uses.*

	Computer uses			
Attitudes	Communication (0–1)	Text processing (0–1)	Data analysis/ Programming (0–1)	Number of uses (0–4)
All administrators (N = 24)				
Positive statements	0.38*	0.08	- 0.14	0.06
Negative statements	0.29	0.25	0.36*	0.46**
Positive minus negative	0.03	- 0.14	- 0.36*	- 0.30
Expectancy statements	- 0.12	- 0.24	0.03	- 0.08
EIS rating (N = 21)	- 0.05	0.35	- 0.05	0.13
Computer users (N = 20)				
Positive statements	—[a]	- 0.09	- 0.25	- 0.25
Negative statements	—	0.15	0.32	0.37*
Positive minus negative	—	- 0.16	- 0.38*	- 0.42*
Expectancy statements	—	0.22	0.06	- 0.01
EIS rating (N = 17)	—	0.46*	- 0.07	0.24

* $p < .05$, ** $p < .01$
[a] Correlations cannot be computed because all computer users communicate electronically.

Group Attitudes About Computing

One indication of the symbolic aspects of computing is the degree to which attitudes about computing were expressed as a function of organizational position. These data are shown in the right-hand columns of Table 10.2. At the outset, practically everyone made positive remarks about EIS and computing at CMU. But, top-level executives, EIS implementors, and administrators in central positions tended to make fewer negative statements about EIS and computing. These findings support the idea that administrators who are required to justify organizational actions are unlikely to talk negatively about the ideas surrounding them.

Discussion

This study shows that instrumental and symbolic aspects of computing can coexist in an organization. In this study, administrators found computers useful, especially for communication and text processing. But, consistent with organizational values, they liked computers whether or not they used them.

Administrators at CMU were eager to use computers, and if they had not done so before, the administrators we studied enthusiastically tried to learn how. The administrators believed that computers are instrumental and useful in their jobs. All of them appreciated using the computer for communication, and most for text processing. Administrators who already used the computer when EIS was introduced did not view EIS as a technical improvement. The experts wanted data base information systems and were disappointed, but these same people were optimistic about the future. We think EIS was never actually intended to be a formal information system designed for administrators, but rather an enticement for putting all administrators on the computer. The people who planned EIS knew they must first initiate administrators to computing before they could successfully introduce a shared computer data base.

Surrounding new computer users with the symbols of EIS but sheltering them from the complexities of a real data base management information system seems to have been a smart idea. The information-system symbols were motivating; the simple activities promoted confidence. As we will show in Chapter 11, student novices at CMU experienced just the opposite kind of initial encounter with computers (that is, few positive symbols and unsheltered, confusing experiences), an initiation that resulted in anger and withdrawal for a significant minority. Imagine the ire of senior administrators if their first encounters with computing consisted of interactions with a new, untested data base information program on a heavily loaded time-sharing system. Given that it was important to bring all the senior administrators into the computer age early in the 1980s (before friendly, reliable, and useful information systems were available on campus), introducing novice administrators to electronic mail and text processing gave them positive feedback immediately. It also made them members of CMU's computing community and participants in the wave of the future. It put them in closer contact with other administrators. These administrators were being made ready to use computers and formal management information systems in the future. These symbolic processes were probably as instrumental, ultimately, as learning specific computer skills in that they indirectly promoted the development and actual use of computers at CMU.

Epilogue

What happened to EIS? In the spring of 1986 we conducted a telephone survey of the original members of the EIS group. Its purpose was to find out if EIS still functioned, if the data bases that were being planned in 1982 were available, whether administrators used computers as much as they had, and whether they still held positive attitudes about computing. Of the 24 EIS members we interviewed in 1982, we contacted all but 2 (both of whom were traveling abroad). Thus the 1986 sample consisted of 22 people. All of the interviewed sample, except one former dean, were still administrators. Six members of the group had left CMU for positions at other universities.

When they were reminded about a survey on EIS in 1982, all of the administrators remembered it but at the same time nearly all of the administrators (77%) said that EIS no longer existed. Administrators remembered EIS in three ways. Two thought it had been an "information system." The majority (50%) thought it had been a tool for communicating with other administrators and part of the university's time-sharing system.

I think the function that EIS served [was] primarily associated with communication functions. (E)

I would argue that what was the original part of the Executive Information System was trying to get everyone on mail. (X)

EIS is part of the whole electronic mail system. (S)

I used [EIS] primarily to receive messages. I also sent messages through it frequently. It was mainly a mail system as I used it. (T)

The next most frequent recollection of EIS was that it was a socializing mechanism for novice administrators (23%).

The idea of EIS was to get documentation into the hands of the executives, and to that degree it was an event that happened and was successful. (K)

EIS to me was a pair of binders that were tutorials. (D)

EIS was a collection of little 'how to use the system' manuals. I don't think it ever really became a functional system. I'm not even sure if it was a system. (U)

With respect to the current situation, however:

The concept of EIS, to provide tools for computer literacy and computer access for deans and [administrators], served its purpose. I don't think there is anything formally operating like that [EIS] now. (M)

Hence in 1986, although EIS had not been abolished formally, it had no important social or technical reality. No new members had been added to the EIS group since it was first formed. No technical functions had been added. Members of the original group moved away or to different jobs, and some used different computer systems, so EIS, as a communications group, had fragmented. The manual was no longer used to introduce administrators to computing.

Independent of EIS, the administrators were computing more than ever. More of them had computers at home, and fewer reported problems using a computer. A summary of these findings is in Table 10.4. The table shows results for six different samples: the original 1982 sample, the 1982 sample interviewed in 1986, the 1986 sample broken down by administrators remaining at CMU and by those who left CMU, and the 1986 sample of former novices.

In addition to an increase in the amount of computing administrators reported doing, there were changes in the technology administrators used and in the ways they used computers. The most striking technology change was that nobody at CMU used terminals. (One administrator who left CMU still used a terminal in his new university.) All of the administrators remaining at CMU had personal computers in their offices (primarily IBM and Apple); some also had workstations. Another technology change was that five administrators (23%), through job relocation ($N = 3$) or organization changes within CMU ($N = 2$), lost their connection to a university network. These administrators tended to stop using computers to communicate.

The changes in how administrators used computers are shown at the bottom of Table 10.4. In 1982 the administrators used computers largely for communication and text processing. In 1986 administrators were using computers for more purposes – to analyze numerical data (including using spreadsheet programs) and even to access data base information systems. Nearly half of the administrators (48%) reported that they used these facilities of the computer to "help them make decisions" whereas in 1982 they rarely said that.

The lingering effects of EIS as a socializing mechanism are shown in the responses of former novices and of administrators who left CMU. The principal discovery about novices is that the computing gap between them and (former) experts had nearly disappeared. One former novice said, "EIS was very good, with comfort level and ease, to do communication (that was how I mainly used it). At that time, it was both fun and useful, and it made it easy to get hooked" (E). And when talking about computing in general, a former novice said, "I am much more pro-computing. I honestly think it could be a terrific benefit. I'm really sold on it" (N).

Administrators who left CMU also talked enthusiastically about computing at CMU and their experience in the EIS group.

[EIS] certainly raised my level of expectation. I'm hoping that eventually we will have the same level of sophistication that currently is at Carnegie Mellon, and that existed back in 1982 ... The longer I'm away from Carnegie Mellon, the higher I rate [EIS]. We have nothing like it. The system here is absolutely chaotic. (T)

Another administrator who left CMU said he was going to implement a system

Table 10.4. *How administrators reported using computers in 1982 and in 1986*

Interview questions	Percent who answered "Yes"					
	1982 Sample (N = 24)	1982 Sample retested in 1986 (N = 22)	1986 Sample (N = 22)	1986 Sample at CMU (N = 16)	1986 Sample left CMU (N = 6)	1986 Former novices (N = 10)
Computer at home?	71	59	91	94	83	90
Problems with computer?	67	68	23	31	0	30
What do you use the computer for? Communication	83	82	68[a]	75	50	50
Text processing	46	46	91	88	100	80
Data analyses	17	9	77	69	100	70
Programming	17	14	32	25	50	30
Data base IS	—	—	73	69	83	60

[a] The result of omitting administrators whose computers were stand-alone rather than connected to a network is that 88% used a computer for communication, an increase of 5% since 1982.

with "many of the same features that EIS had" where he worked currently. "I thought EIS was a good model for the way things should happen" (W).

But EIS was not a perfect socializing mechanism. Two administrators had withdrawn from computing entirely:

Computing and I do not get along well at all … I don't know how to program, the system has changed three times, and I don't know how to get from one thing to the next. I don't know how to use it. It's terrible to be one of the major administrators of the university and not know how to turn the machine on, but I don't. (B)

EIS got to the point where I could never get on it anymore. I just quit using it, I haven't turned the thing on in months. (A)

In summary, a retrospective view of EIS indicates that it succeeded in introducing novice administrators to computing and contributed to their enthusiasm and competence to undergo further socialization to computing. EIS also supported the positive attitudes and behavior of the expert members of the same project. In all, eighteen of the administrators said they used computers as much as or more than they did in 1982 (82%), two used them less often, and two did not use them. Former novices said: "I am a great advocate of computing now" (X); "I'm convinced it [computing] is the wave of the future"(T); "I was always very high on it [computing]"(S). This illustrates the positive symbolic attitudes about computing that administrators continue to express.

Part IV

Students and the Social Environment of Computing

Part IV focuses on students. While earlier chapters described what computer resources students use, the chapters in this part emphasize a socialization view of computing. By this we mean not simply how do students learn some computing skills, but also how do they develop the ability and willingness to use computers in their lives. Computers have affected students' self-esteem, intellectual life, and social life.

[Computing] has given me the sense that I can do more things and I am not nearly as intimidated by new challenges now. (Senior interview, 1985)

The amount of more intelligent people I've met down there [in the terminal room]. . . . What I did on the computer seems so amazing to me. . . . Then I thought that some of the people around me were doing such more complicated things and how smart they must be. (Freshman interview, 1982)

Hello, my name is Kevin Blake. I have no plans for Spring Break. Would anyone like to take a trip with me? I like hiking, camping, and old movies. (Post on a computer bulletin board, 1983)

Chapters 11 and 12 look at freshmen; Chapter 13 looks at seniors. Chapter 11 describes how 1982 liberal arts freshmen reacted to their programming course. We did not measure how well or poorly students could program after taking that course. Our interest is in students' experiences with the computing environment, their reactions to those experiences, and their willingness and interest to be further socialized into computing. In socialization terms the experience of these novices seems to have been generally a negative one. A majority of them end up like the student who admits she has become "kind of leery" of computing. By comparing student reactions to their computing course with reactions to their other freshman year courses, we can net-out the effects of reactions to college courses in general. This is an important research strategy. Too often, analysts report people's reactions to computing in a vacuum. They don't provide any answer to the question, "Compared to what?"

While Chapter 11 describes attitudes at the end of the freshman year, Chapter 12 tracks how attitudes about computing change over the course of the freshman year. Chapter 12 also looks at science and engineering freshmen as well as liberal arts freshmen. Expected differences between technical and non-technical students are found and noted. This chapter also reports differences between men and women, with men more positive toward computing than are women. But the difference between men and women is much narrower at the end of the freshman year than at the beginning, suggesting a "leveling-up" process.

Chapter 13 is based on a series of interviews with seniors in 1985 – the same students who were interviewed as freshmen in 1982 for Chapter 11. In contrast with their views as freshmen, these seniors were overwhelmingly positive about computing. As earlier chapters have indicated, CMU was a different computing place in 1985 than it was in 1982. There were vastly more computers, more computer experts, and more students and faculty with computer experience. Computers had become a general-purpose tool for all kinds of students, not just a specialized tool for future computer scientists. The computer culture was becoming integrated with the general culture of the university, and vice versa. These technological and social changes at CMU seem to have made a positive difference in students' socialization to computing. Because ours is a case study, we cannot say definitively that change in the social environment made a difference. Studies at other universities and other kinds of organizations will help us understand the role of the social environment in people's socialization to computing.

11   Encountering an Alien Culture

Lee Sproull, Sara Kiesler, and David Zubrow

Many organizations today are faced with the problem of introducing managers, secretaries, and other nontechnical people to computing. Previous investigations of this problem have generally not focused on organizational settings but have used a technical, instructional, or individual abilities perspective. Technical analyses usually investigate the relative ease or difficulty with which new users learn particular computer operations as a function of equipment or software variables (e.g., Bury, Boyle, Evey, & Neal, 1982; Black & Moran, 1982). Often these users are not new to computing itself, but rather are simply new to the particular operations being studied (e.g., Schneider, Nudelman, & Hirsh-Pasek, 1982; DeYoung, Kampen, & Topolski, 1982). Instructional analyses usually measure the accuracy with which people learn certain material, perhaps as a function of alternative instructional techniques (e.g., Taylor, 1980). Analyses of individual abilities assume that more able students will have better experiences (e.g., Arndt, Feltes, & Hanak, 1983). In none of these perspectives does the investigator consider what the new person learns about such issues as: the context in which computing occurs, the status positions for those who compute, the kinds of people who compute, the social organization of computing, and the values placed on computing. These are cultural lessons and they constitute an important part of the newcomer's learning.

In this chapter we use a cultural perspective to try to understand people's initial encounters with computing. We begin by exploring some of the ways in which computing is embedded in a larger social order and suggest some of the ways in which it will be alien to newcomers. We then draw upon work in organizational socialization to suggest how newcomers will respond to it. Finally, we present a two-part study that investigates initial encounters with computing at CMU. The results of this study reveal that newcomers do indeed learn powerful cultural lessons about computing.

Computing as Culture

Cultural Context

In the early days of computing, few people outside the scientists and engineers directly involved in producing and using the new machines had any contact with

173

computers (McCorduck, 1979). But today, ideas about computers, if not actual experience with them, permeate our society. Thus, in 1982 *Time* magazine named the computer, "Man of the Year"; computer magazines are found on newsstands; managerial publications such as *Fortune* and the *Harvard Business Review* publish numerous articles on managing computing; consultants are offering advice on how to overcome "fear of computing." Schools and universities are requiring their students to take programming courses or purchase microcomputers. Sales of machines to households are burgeoning. Computer camps are oversubscribed.

Cultural components of these phenomena include generally shared beliefs such as "everyone can benefit from computers," "anyone can use a computer," and "the more powerful the computer, the better" (e.g., Ogdin, 1982). The use of terms like "novice," "user," and "wizard" signal cultural roles and values. *The Hackers Dictionary* (Steele et al., 1983) offers an irreverent description of the culture through definitions of many of its terms and phrases. The prevailing high evaluations of computing and its "ways of life," despite problems inevitably connected to the technology and its introduction into organizations and everyday life, indicates that norms of the culture are uncritically accepted by many people (Kling, 1980). Although a cultural perspective on computing is not commonly found in the scientific literature (see Turkle, 1980, & Kling, 1980, for two exceptions), the popular press frequently describes computing subcultures. See Zimbardo (1980) and Levy (1982) for a description of the hacker subculture at Stanford University. Kidder (1981) describes a similar culture in an industrial setting.

It would be difficult for a novice to sit down at a computer or terminal today without encountering the culture that surrounds computing. The novice will confront not merely neutral stimuli to which he may respond as desired, which he may regard as good or bad, right or wrong as immediate experience instructs. Most of the stimuli – hardware, software, manuals, the social and physical context – have already been judged by the social order and the novice's predecessors. In this sense any particular machine is an artifact of and embedded in the culture that produced it. Encounters with that artifact are also encounters with the culture and will lead to cultural lessons as well as to learning more narrowly focused on particular machines.

Certain organizational features found in research, development, and engineering divisions within the computer industry itself and college campuses foster development of a computer culture. One is that computers are used for many different purposes. On a typical college campus, for example, the same machine or machines may be used for research, administration, accounting, teaching, and text processing. Thus these machines tend to have operating systems and programming tools that make them relatively easy to use. Second, because these machines serve many purposes, many kinds of people have access to them. And furthermore, this access is relatively direct. That is, people have their own accounts; there need be no intermediaries between them and the machine. Third, many of the people with direct access are relatively smart, young, and they don't have enough to do. That is, they are students. They have few family or economic responsibilities, flexible schedules, and the stamina to stay up all night. Fourth, these organizations tend to be less bureaucratic and formal than most government, commercial, or manufacturing settings. In these cases, where smart understimulated people have direct access to flexible machines in non-bureaucratic settings, the culture of computing is nurtured and can flourish.

Every culture has values and norms, a status hierarchy, membership signs and boundaries to distinguish members from nonmembers, a language, and its own artifacts (Gamst & Horbeck, 1976). Although their specifics will differ from campus to campus, some of the general features of the culture of computing are quite widely shared. The culture is an adolescent one. Pranks, tricks, and games are benignly tolerated when not actually encouraged. People are often impolite and irreverent. Mild larceny is also tolerated, if not encouraged, through faking accounts, stealing time, copying proprietary software, and breaking codes. The culture is individualistic and idiosyncratic. Social cooperation or coordination is rarely necessary. There is competition to write the best, fastest, biggest program or to build the best, fastest, smallest hardware. The status hierarchy is revealed through assigning people to such categories as wizards, wheels, hackers, users, and losers. True members of the culture can be found at the terminal room or computer center at all hours of the day and night.

The Alien Nature of Computing

Despite its rapid intrusion into many areas of life, computing currently is not just something new. It is also strange. Its spatial and temporal characteristics, controllability, and nature of feedback are unlike those of other technologies. Consider a college student encountering a time-sharing system and some of the ways in which academic computing differs from all other course work. Computing differs in time and space characteristics from other academic activities. Whereas in other courses students are free to choose the time and space that suit them best to do their homework, students of computing are tied to a terminal room and a time at which a terminal is available. Computing also differs in reliability and controllability. When a student is reading a history book, the page never goes blank. When a student is writing a paper, if his pencil breaks he can sharpen it. But computer tools are not under a student's control. Computing also differs in speed and nature of feedback. If a student is doing a physics assignment, the first wrong digit he writes on the page does not generate an immediate cascade of error messages. In other courses, a student may stop after his exertions and imagine that the essay is good enough, or that he has worked enough math problems to demonstrate competence. In computing, there is no stopping until the program works – it either does or it doesn't.

In order for a novice actually to use a computer system, he must make his way through a host of arbitrary conventions that are unrelated to the science or theory of computing. New students are thrown into a sea of syntax, I/O devices, priority classes, programs, and system quirks with no conceptual life vest to keep them afloat. The stylized nature of person/computer interaction can be particularly alienating to these students. All new disciplines involve learning conventions, but it is humiliating to be at the mercy of so many seemingly trivial arbitrary ones. These problems are compounded because computing is a scarce resource on almost every college campus; thus students can be forced to wait long periods of time just to gain access to the potentially frustrating machine.

As strange as these experiences may be, their strangeness is exacerbated by the fact that they occur within a social context with which other people are quite comfortable. This embedding of computing in the larger life of the organization distinguishes students' computing encounters from those of say, the physics laboratory. While the physics laboratory may also lead students to feel out of control, it is a very sheltered and isolated environment apart from the real business of physics or anything else. By contrast, the newly computing student must compete for terminal time and cycles with administrators who are managing accounting, secretaries who are typing manuscripts, faculty members who are doing research, students who are doing assignments, and "hackers."

Processes of Encountering

One learns a culture through socialization into it. vanMaanen and Schein (1979) describe organizational socialization as the "process by which an individual acquires the social knowledge and skills necessary to assume an organizational role" (p. 211). In the case of computing, the organizational role is that of "computer user." Once a person acquires that role in any organization, one then occupies a different status in all subsequent organizations.

If the culture is an alien one, then socialization will occur under conditions of strangeness. Strangeness or unfamiliarity means that the novices' habitual and therefore efficient models and means for learning will be neither useful nor appropriate. As a result, novices must learn how to learn as well as what to learn. They must develop new ways of assimilating information and a new framework for it. They must learn how to recognize and interpret cues, and whom to rely upon as informants. They must learn how to organize new bits and pieces of knowledge into coherent theories. In these processes the novice brings capabilities, prior experiences, and expectations to the new setting.

The initial interaction between a novice and a new culture inevitably produces reality shock for the novice. Reality shock is composed of changes, contrasts, and surprises (Louis, 1980). Changes are simply objective differences from the novice's prior situation, for example in title, workload, compensation, location, food preferences, social customs, and even facial expressions. Contrasts are differences in what is subjectively salient from that in the novice's former situation, for example in images of surroundings, pace, ethos and language (e.g., Smalley, 1963). Both changes and contrasts can be anticipated by the novice preparing to enter a new culture; through anticipatory socialization (Merton & Rossi, 1968), a novice can ease his transition to a new culture. Surprises, on the other hand, are unanticipated differences between expectations and reality. For example, technical assistants and management personnel sent overseas often experience role ambiguity and loss of personal status that are not at all what they anticipated (Byrnes, 1966; Higbee, 1969). Reality shock is important to the novice because it signals that prior instrumental behaviors are no longer appropriate and new ones must be learned. It is also important because it colors the early lessons learned in the new culture. The nature of the reality shock and how it is managed by the novice and the organization do much to define the process and outcomes of socialization (David, 1971; Church, 1982).

Reality shock leads the novice to experience confusion, both about self and the external environment (Oberg, 1966). Confusion about self leads the novice to feel overwhelmed and to question aspects of his or her self-identity or self-image. These questions can be of the form, "What am I doing?" and "Do I look foolish?" or "Maybe I'm not the person I thought I was." Confusion about the external environment leads the novice to question the capabilities and motivations of those around him. These questions can be of the form, "Do those people really know what they're doing?" or "Why can't they communicate clearly?"

Reality shock and confusion lead novices to try to establish control over the situation. In attempting to control the situation (for example, by explaining surprises) the individuals try to reduce discrepancies between the current state and reference values or standards in the situation (Kanfer & Hagerman, 1981; Bandura, 1977; Thompson, 1981; Carver & Scheier, 1982). These attempts can entail mental activity alone, for example constructing satisfying interpretations of the confusing events. They can also entail actions such as increased effort or talking with other people about the situation. In either case, aspects of the culture will play a part in the control attempts. They will provide sources of information for constructing interpretations and people who function as comparators or standards against which the novices can judge their behavior. If the control attempts are successful, the individual will be able to learn the values and skills necessary for the new role (i.e., to become socialized).

The initial interaction between a novice and a new culture inevitably produces reality shock for the novice. Cartoon from the student newspaper.

If the control attempts are not successful, anger or withdrawal will arise (Carver, Blaney, & Scheier, 1979; Brockner, 1979). Anger leads to intransigence – active rejection of the values of the socializing or enculturating agents (Goffman, 1961). Intransigence guarantees that the novice will remain an outsider but it allows the novice to maintain a positive self-image. The intransigent novice might say, "These people are so crazy that only an idiot would want to act like them." Withdrawal also precludes positive socialization, but does not contribute to a positive self-image. The withdrawing novice might say, "I'm no good at this and there's no sense in trying."

If computing does represent an alien culture, then we would expect that novices' first computing encounters would engender high reality shock caused by changes in amount of work, kind of work, place of work, timing of work, and surprises (differences between expectations and reality). Reality shock leads to confusion. We would expect that novices would be confused about their own capability and roles and that of the experts in their environment. The most likely responses to reality shock and confusion are attempts to exert control by using resources in the cultural setting. These resources might include other students or teachers who provide ideas and behavioral examples of control responses. If control attempts are successful, the person has gained the potential of becoming further socialized and a cultural recruit. If control attempts are unsuccessful, anger or withdrawal will ensue and the person is likely to become a cultural dropout.

In organizations, most novices will ultimately come to terms with the culture of computing. At an elementary level they will learn to work with computers, and some will become experts. But if the above framework is meaningful, novices will also learn much more in their initial encounters with computing. They will develop an image of "the computer," of the social organization surrounding it, and of their own degree of cultural competence. For the organization, these understandings are probably more important than any technical details of writing or using programs that can be conveyed to its nontechnical people in an introductory encounter because they determine a person's willingness to undergo further socialization.

Overview of Empirical Work

In the spring of 1982, we conducted a two-part study to explore the cultural perspective on computing and some hypotheses derived from the model described above. In part one, we conducted a survey of liberal arts freshmen to explore how their first encounters with computing might have differed from their first encounters with college generally (Feldman & Newcomb, 1969). This survey allowed us to rule out the possibility that college, not computing, was the alien culture by testing the predictions that reality shock and confusion will be stronger in computer programming courses than in other courses, and that there will be more control attempts and more failures of control attempts in computer-programming courses than in other courses. Thus:

1. For nontechnical students, the computer programming course will be different from, and will violate expectations of, college work to a greater degree than other courses. This reality shock will be experienced as confusion about self and the environment.
2. Students will exert more control attempts in computer programming courses than they will in other courses by, for example, seeking out others and seeking explanation.
3. Students will have more difficulty finding constructive ways to exert control in programming courses than in other courses; they will exert more unconstructive control; and they will experience more unsuccessful outcomes as indicated by withdrawal and anger.

Part two of the study used interview data to explore these processes. We asked a group of liberal arts freshmen to talk with us about their initial experiences with computing to see if their descriptions revealed elements of the process we have described above. In addition, we were interested in whether the students' descriptions would reveal aspects of the culture of computing, its alien nature, and the cultural lessons learned that were not measured in the survey.

Part One

Method and Analysis

In order to compare computing to other kinds of college experiences, we administered a fixed-response questionnaire to 268 liberal arts freshmen during their required social science class in the spring of 1982. (This represents 95% of the freshman liberal arts class.) Students were asked to assess one of their English, social science, mathematics, and computer science (computer programming) courses on a number of dimensions using the scale:

1. false; not at all true
2. neither true nor false
3. true or very true of this course

   The conceptual dependent variables were reality shock, confusion, control attempts, and outcomes (academic success, anger, and withdrawal). They were measured using the questionnaire items listed in Table 11.1. Statistical comparisons were made across courses to evaluate how similarly the students rated each course. These comparisons were conducted using repeated measures analyses of variance and *t* tests comparing courses and items within each factor. A "true or very true" response was set equal to "1" and any other response was set equal to "0". (When comparisons are made such that 1 = false or very false, 2 = neither true nor false, and 3 = true or very true, then the findings are stronger statistically but harder to interpret.)

   The findings are based upon the responses of the 208 students who answered questions about one course in each of the four categories of courses we listed (English, social science, mathematics, computer programming). The typical student in our sample was enrolled in a computer programming course at the time of the survey (nearly the end of second semester, freshman year), and was also enrolled in a literature course, an interdisciplinary social science course, and in calculus.

   Approximately 60 students were excluded from the analysis because they had not yet taken a computing course (a few others were not freshmen or had not taken a course in one of the other categories). This introduces bias in our sample; however, we believe it is a bias that works against our hypotheses. According to some of the students in question, they postpone computer science because they have heard it is "terrible" and they want to have the summer (or the following year) to concentrate on it. Hence the students not included in the analyses are likely to be especially negative about the computing course.

Results

Computing versus Other Courses. Table 11.1 presents the percentages of students who answered "true or very true" to questions about each course. These data indicate that students' experiences with computing are quite different from their encounters with other disciplines. For the three items related to reality shock, an average 79% of the students answered "true or very true" for computing. In contrast, the average for the other three courses ranged from 20% to 27%. Confusion also was greater in the computing course, with three of the five variables having values at least three times the averages of the other courses. (The second most confusing course was English, which belies the idea that nontechnical students are generally more confused by quantitative courses.)

The control attempts that we investigated were talking with others about the course and making causal attributions about their good and poor performance in the course. Generally, more students in computer programming talked with others about the course. More than in other courses, they talked with friends, past students in the course, and counselors. The item "class members help one another" yielded a 71% true response in computing, but averaged only 47% in the other courses.

Overall, fewer students in the computing course made constructive attributions of performance (the greatest number were in English and mathematics). On three out of six positive attribution items, computing was lowest. Although students in computing just as frequently claimed to desire understanding and to be motivated as they did in other courses, they tended not to attribute their good performance to their ability. In addition, they made more unconstructive attributions. The data suggest that, when they were explaining their performance in their computing course, students externalized their successes and internalized their failures. Especially significant are the relatively high frequencies of, "When I did well it was because I had good luck" and "When I did poorly it was because I had poor ability."

The outcomes of the students' encounters with computing and other freshman courses, as reflected in our survey, were mixed. There were no overall statistical differences across courses in the percentages of students who indicated that academic success was being or had been achieved. Mathematics scored highest overall in numbers of students saying they performed "better than I expected." Social science was most frequently given credit for "acquiring knowledge." Computer science was most frequently cited for "learning valuable skills." On the other hand, the percentages of students who experienced anger and withdrawal were much greater in the computer programming course than in other courses. Forty-one percent said they wanted to "do just enough to get by" in computing versus an average of 14% in the other courses.

Comparing computer science to mathematics (usually calculus) tells us something about whether the problems students had with computing were due to its quantitative nature. Table 11.2 shows, contrary to that idea, that computing was a more shocking and confusing experience than mathematics was, that it

Table 11.1. *Percentage of students answering "True or very true" to question-naire items, by course*

Questions about socialization processes	My English course	My Social Science course	My Math course	My Computer Science course
Reality shock				
This course:				
Takes more time than I expected	28	19	17	78
Very different from other courses	22	40	19	82
My work habits in the course are				
very different	20	23	23	76
Confusion				
I feel I don't know what I am doing	11	8	20	59
I worry that I might look foolish	9	4	6	20
The course has a clear division of tasks	44	65	48	44
I feel like a different person when				
I am in class	14	11	12	24
I feel overwhelmed by the work	23	13	17	76
Control attempts:				
1. Talking to people:				
I talk to friends about this course	68	66	61	87
I talk to my instructor	60	33	28	59
I talk to students who took the				
course in the past	38	45	41	70
I talk to other faculty about				
this course	9	5	9	21
I have talked to a counselor about this				
course	17	10	17	43
Class members help one another	32	52	57	71
2. Constructive attribution:				
I am highly motivated	29	28	29	24
I really want to understand	64	68	78	65
When I do well it is because				
I worked hard	72	69	65	72
When I do well it is because				
I had good ability	57	47	59	30
When I do well it is because				
the instructor was good	42	50	34	16
When I do poorly it is because				
I didn't work hard	52	50	51	44

continued

Table 11.1 *(cont.)*

Questions about socialization processes	My English course	My Social Science course	My Math course	My Computer Science course
3. Unconstructive attribution				
When I do well it is because				
I had good luck	32	27	27	41
When I do well it is because				
the task was easy	26	30	40	27
When I do poorly it is because of				
poor ability	18	13	24	37
Outcomes:				
1. Academic success				
My performance is better than I expected	19	15	27	21
I am learning valuable skills	36	44	46	50
I am acquiring knowledge	66	77	71	56
2. Anger				
I get the feeling my instructors don't				
know what they're doing	16	11	33	59
This course makes me angry	27	15	28	72
I complain	40	25	40	79
3. Withdrawal				
I want to do just enough to get by	16	10	16	41

Note: Repeated measures (courses by items) analyses of variance were performed on these data. All course main effects were significant $p = .05$ or better (F ranged from 3.6 to 123, $df = 3$ and 276 to 312). Degrees of freedom varied because subjects who did not answer an item for four courses were dropped. A few course-by-item interactions were significant. We assume this to mean that some items discriminated among courses better than others, an essentially trivial finding.

precipitated more talking to others as well as more unconstructive attributions, and that negative outcomes – anger and withdrawal – were significantly higher.

Some effects of background. We investigated the influence of previous experience with computing and of gender on responses to the courses. Fewer students who had taken a previous course in computing (probably a high school course) experienced reality shock ($F = 3.0$, $p < .05$), but there were no other differences attributable to prior experience.

Gender differences were found for reality shock, confusion, and talking with others. Male students were more likely to experience reality shock in courses than were female students ($F = 4.34$, $p < .05$). However, female students were

Table 11.2. *Comparison of computing with mathematics and with other courses*

	t	df
Reality shock		
Computing vs. mathematics	15.60	114
Computing vs. other courses	16.03	101
Confusion		
Computing vs. mathematics	9.44	113
Computing vs. other courses	9.49	100
Talking to people		
Computing vs. mathematics	10.31	115
Computing vs. other courses	10.46	102
Constructive attribution		
Computing vs. mathematics	-3.60	105
Computing vs. other courses	-2.28	92
Unconstructive attribution		
Computing vs. mathematics	1.30	104
Computing vs. other courses	2.66	92
Academic success		
Computing vs. mathematics	-1.10	113
Computing vs. other courses	0.23	100
Anger		
Computing vs. mathematics	10.43	111
Computing vs. other courses	12.62	99
Withdrawal		
Computing vs. mathematics	4.95	117
Computing vs. other courses	4.61	104

Note: The above statistical t tests were performed on the data presented in Table 11.1. For example, the first row shows that, for the three Reality Shock items, the mean frequency of "true or very true" answers was greater when students evaluated their computer science course than when they evaluated their mathematics course. "Other courses" refers to the mean frequency of "true or very true" answers for English, Social Science, and Mathematics. The critical value for this table is 2.10 ($\alpha = .05$, $k = 4$, $df = 60$) based on the adjustment recommended by Winer (1971, p. 202) for a set of comparisons sharing a common treatment (hence correlated responses).

more confused by computer programming whereas the male students were more confused by mathematics, social science, and English ($F = 2.88$, $p < .05$). Consistent with these results, female students were more likely to talk with others about their computer-programming course whereas the male students were more likely to talk with others about their courses in mathematics, social science, and English ($F = 4.94, p < .01$).

Classification of Students by Outcomes. We classified students as potential cultural recruits or dropouts according to their answers on the survey, and compared the resulting distributions for each course. This analysis, presented in Table 11.3, is consistent with our prediction that computer programming will produce more cultural dropouts and fewer cultural recruits than other freshman courses will. By our count, over one-third of the students in computer programming were potential cultural dropouts in that they reported no academic success at all (i.e., none of the three success items was checked as true). Only 8% of the students were potential cultural recruits who reported at least one academic success item as true and no anger or withdrawal. By contrast, the percentages of potential cultural recruits in other courses was much higher and, in those courses, potential recruits were a higher percentage than were potential dropouts.

Part Two

Method

Twenty-five students, randomly selected from the liberal arts freshman class, were invited to talk with us about their experience with computing. This procedure yielded 23 interview subjects (two could not be found). Each interview, consisting of twenty-nine open-ended questions and lasting about half an hour, was conducted by one of three trained interviewers during two three-day periods in the spring of 1982. The questions (in addition to general background questions) centered on students' expectations about computing, their experiences with it, and their evaluation of it. For example: "Describe your first encounter with the computer [here]." "Where do (did) you do your computer work?" "Please describe some occasion when you felt especially proud (unusually discouraged) about something that happened to you in relation to the computer." All interviews were tape recorded; tape transcriptions were entered into computer text files for purposes of content analysis (Sproull & Sproull, 1982).

The data reported below are of two types: frequency data that suggest trends and direct quotations from students that illustrate the nature of those trends. Because of the open ended nature of many of the questions, it is not always appropriate to use the question as the unit of analysis in reporting frequencies; groups of questions, or even the interview as a whole, is sometimes the more

Table 11.3. *Classification of students according to potential cultural outcomes*

Course	Potential dropouts: no academic success items reported (%)	Mixed case: one or more success, and anger/withdrawal, items reported (%)	Potential recruits: one or more success, and no anger/withdrawal, items reported (%)
English	28.3	34.0	37.7
Social Science	20.7	24.5	54.9
Mathematics	24.3	40.1	35.5
Computer Science	35.1	56.8	8.1

appropriate unit. Unless otherwise noted, the quotations illustrate dominant or modal responses. At a minimum, the data demonstrate the existence of the phenomena we are interested in. More usefully, we believe, they can be viewed as a first step in specifying the determinants and consequences of the process of encountering an alien culture.

The Sample

The sample consisted of 12 males and 11 females. The two factors that predominated in their decision to come to this college were its general reputation (59%) and its liberal/professional and business majors (36%). Almost all of the students framed at least one of their principle objectives for this year in terms of grades (86%). But their stance toward grades was sharply differentiated: 54% said they want to "do well"; 41% said they want to "pass." An additional important objective is intellectual growth with 64% of the sample mentioning learning and discovering interests. Going into business (64%) or to professional school (34%) are the most prevalent post-graduation plans.

Half the students had some experience with computing before coming to the university; 36% had a course in high school. No student believed that his or her high school experience was directly relevant to computing at college; half of them acknowledged that it gave them some general familiarity. Sixty-eight percent of the sample took a computer science course (Pascal) during their freshman year. This compares with 77% for the freshman class as a whole. Students who had taken a high school course were more likely to take computing during their freshman year than were those who had no previous course. Students whose academic goal was to do well were no more or less likely to take computing during their freshman year than were those whose goal was to pass. For students who took computing, this course figured heavily in all of their comments about computing, as we shall see below. All of the remaining students had at least some direct encounter with computing during the year as in, for example: using a document formatting program to prepare letters, participating in a psychology experiment in which stimulus materials were presented on a computer terminal, doing logic problems in their philosophy course, and testing hypotheses about the French Revolution in their history course.

Prominent in student descriptions of their experiences were comments about how different computing is from other things they are used to and how it makes them feel out of control. These students did not dwell on how they attempted to regain control, but they did reveal some interesting lessons they learned as a result of their attempts.

Results

Describing their Experience. Four elements predominated in students' descriptions of their experiences with computing and can be viewed as components of reality shock: time, the terminal room, actually working on the computer, and course-related factors such as lectures, homework, and exams.

Many students (68%) reported computing to be much more time-consuming than they had expected. They reported having to spend long hours at the computer center, often late at night, and having to schedule the rest of their life around the availability of computer time. As one student said (codes in parentheses are unique student identifiers),

If a computer program is due that week, then the computer sign-up times range all over my entire schedule. I have to arrange everything else around that computer time. If I get computer time at 6:00, then I have to have everything else arranged around that. It just rearranges everything. If you work from 11:00 until 3:00 or from 1:00 until 2:00 or however you work, it arranges your time. It just totally re-does your schedule. (P16)

Another student explained that late at night is the only time for uninterrupted work.

Last semester more than a couple times I got up at four o'clock to go to the computer room so you could get on the terminal and not be crowded out because there're so many people there. (R18)

Of the 8 students who did not find the time demands of computing remarkable, 4 had no course experience with computing, 3 still acknowledged having to schedule around the computer, and 1 had a terminal in his room. But this student is the exception. Late hours, long hours, and constrained scheduling characterize most students' encounters with computing and constitute one component of reality shock. The terminal room itself is a second component of reality shock. Most students (77%) find it somehow unpleasant, with the major complaints being about crowding and lack of privacy.

There's so many people who want to use them. There're enough terminals but it's just that there's rush hours and you just can't get on at all and then it will crash during that time and it takes even longer because people will wait for it to come back up. Plus privacy. It's kind of crowded and you can't set your books down cause there's not enough space between terminals. (I9)

Another student said about the terminal room:

I was surprised, really surprised at the people set up along the benches. There's no privacy. Where I was [in the Computer Science department], they had little stalls for each terminal. I thought that was a much better idea, just because I would think that working at a bench like that would be really distracting. It reminded me of a horse at a trough. (X24)

Four students had no complaints about the terminal room, but an equal number had extremely negative reactions. One student said:

I feel like I'm in 1984, cells right next to each other. It's like Russia. You've got to just get as many people as you can, crammed in there ... They're all white. And all they have are computer information on them. Maybe they could have a picture of Picasso. Anything just to break the monotony ... All you see are computer geeks and computers and the xerox machines and white on the walls ... (Q17)

Only 6 students had used a terminal anywhere other than the main terminal room. They all appreciated the quiet and privacy of terminal rooms in other campus buildings. One student occasionally worked in a fraternity house:

I was there until 4 o'clock in the morning. It was nice because the guys ... I had a little tape on. There weren't all these people around bugging you ... It was just nice to be away from everything and everybody. (K11)

Working on the computer itself produces a third component of reality shock. A striking instance of this is seen in how students described their first encounter with the computer at college. For example:

I sat down at this computer and started hitting the buttons and it started making all this noise and people kept looking at me. I didn't know what I was doing. I didn't even know if it was on. (C3)

And another student said,

And the first time it's like, "Wow, a computer! I've never used one of these before. I wonder how it works? ... You didn't know what you were doing. I mean, you knew because the teacher told you what to do but you were just like, 'Oh, well, I type this, then I type that and I hope it works. Here goes ...' (R18)

The fourth major component of student descriptions of their experiences with computing is course work – lectures, assignments, exams. During the fall

"All you see are computer geeks and computers..."

semester computing course, students' final grade was based entirely on a five-hour programming exam – the mastery exam – taken at the end of the semester. Although programming assignments were offered as homework, they were optional. During the spring semester, homework was mandatory and the mastery exam carried less weight.

Students' perceptions of the lectures had two features relevant to reality shock. The first had to do with their content; the second, with their relationship to homework and exams. A small number of students had expected the lectures would include more emphasis on the range of computer functions and applications. As one said:

I did not expect I'd have to write out programs. I expected [to learn] here's how to use it to our advantage with economics and all sorts of fun courses like that. (Q17)

More students were surprised that the lectures seemed to have very little to do with writing programs or the mastery exam.

I get the feeling from my computing teacher that he's just telling me half the story. That's all he is telling me because when I get to the computer I still don't know what I'm doing, even after listening to him in class ... He explains procedures and functions and major things but he doesn't show us how to write a program. (L12)

Apparently there is a common tension in introductory programming courses between the principles of programming and the specifics of any programming assignment; it is common for professors to want to teach general principles and for students to want to be taught specific techniques. For the students in our sample, this tension manifests itself in beliefs that the lectures are irrelevant or not helpful. Three-quarters (73%) of the students who had taken or were taking a computing course evaluated the lectures negatively.

The fact that all (for fall semester) or a large part (for spring semester) of the student's final grade was based on a mastery exam was clearly an important way in which students were surprised by this course. Two-thirds (67%) of the students with course experience commented negatively on this feature of the course.

That was the biggest change, when they told you everything was based on this one big final. All of a sudden, all of the pressure was on that one five hour test. (M13)

Reactions to Their Experience. Students described several ways that they feel out of control in their encounters with computing. Seventy-seven percent of the students reported such an experience. One common catalyst is ignorance:

It's frightening when everyone else is around you just typing in as fast as they can, and you don't even know what to do. (E5)

Another is system crashes:

I was almost finished with a program and it crashed. I didn't have a save. I didn't put save on. I had to start over. It was heartbreaking. (O15)

And a third is experts whose "help" simply emphasizes these students' fragile positions:

I was on the computer and something happened. I didn't know what was going on. I saw a guy sitting over there who looked like a real hacker. So I asked him, and he got up, and he started doing all of this stuff with my account without telling me what he was doing. He started messing around, 'You need this. Let's see, I'll give you this file.' It's like, what are you doing? He wouldn't tell me. (W23)

These experiences appear to be engendered in part by students' comparing themselves with others more expert than they and in part by feeling victimized by others as well as by the machine.

In attempting to gain control over their situation, all but one of the students who had taken computing experienced some success. One-third were proud of their performance on the mastery; two-thirds were proud of getting a program to run, often after a great deal of work.

I was just euphoric. I was just ... I was so glad. I remember that night I went running home and there were some kids in my room. I was just going crazy and they didn't know what for. It was probably just the most basic program, but I was just so psyched-up that I couldn't sit still. (C3)

Over half the students who hadn't yet taken a computing course also had found occasion for pride in an encounter with computing. The student who used text editing to type a letter thought it looked "very nice" (X24). One student took pride in logging in without help (N14). Another was proud of error free output in a history assignment:

It took me 20 minutes one night not to do a program but to get data from a program and run it. It came right out with no errors. It was perfect. I thought I did a good job. (O15)

Students also found occasion for discouragement; 82% reported some discouragement. Of those who had taken computing, one-third mentioned their performance on the mastery; almost two-thirds mentioned difficulty with trying to get a program to run. Other students reported discouragement with system crashes and a screen that scrolled too rapidly. On the whole, particularly for those students who took a computing course, the negative experiences outweighed the positive ones. The combination of long hours, an unpleasant terminal room, confusing interactions with the machine, seemingly irrelevant lectures, a difficult mastery exam, discouraging times, and feeling out of control was oppressive.

Cultural Learning. In the aftermath of reality shock, confusion, and control attempts, students emerged having learned some cultural lessons. Newcomers commonly have a relatively undifferentiated view of a culture's social organization; these students were no exception. The students had only a rough idea of how the formal responsibility for computing on campus is managed. When asked to describe the major activities of the computation center, half the students had difficulty with the question. No single activity was mentioned by more than half the students. (Nine students said the computation center gives help; 5 said it maintains equipment; 3 said it writes programs.) One student, while admitting she had never thought of the computation center as an organization, was able to produce a helpful analogy for the computation center:

I just thought of it more like a library: a place where you use things that you can't use anywhere else. And they're there to help you with your classes. If you stretch it a little, you can think of the user consultant as a librarian, someone who advises you when you don't know what to do. (K11)

192	L. Sproull, S. Kiesler, and D. Zubrow

Only one other student was able to provide an analogy for the computation center, an analogy of a very different sort:

They have little gnomes and they sit down in the basement ... in bug hot rooms, like the devil, and mess around with students and put errors in their programs. (J10)

The students' perceptions of the social organization of computing at the university were dominated by a we/they distinction: there are people who are competent in and committed to computing and there is the rest of the world. From the students' perspectives, people who use the terminal room are divided into two categories: "we" who do not know what we are doing and "they" who do. "They" are also differentiated by special names, characteristics, and behaviors. Two-thirds (68%) of the students made this distinction in their comments.

Within this dichotomous view of the world, students made both positive and negative assessments of "them," although people making negative assessments outweighed those making positive ones five to one. Positively, "they" are viewed as very smart and competent:

The amount of more intelligent people I've met down there ... What I did on the computer seems so amazing to me ... Then I thought that some of the people around me were doing such more complicated things and how smart they must be. (C3)

Negatively, "they" are viewed as having strange personal habits and being very difficult to talk to.

Some people just live and die with computers. They sleep there. They don't get any sleep because they sleep with computers ... They can't relate to anything but the computer. They can't talk to a normal guy. Even when they talk, they talk computer language. It's like they've turned into a computer. (Q17)

In addition to learning the rudiments of role and subculture differentiation, students began to learn about the computer itself as a cultural artifact. This learning took the form of being able to use terminology properly, understanding that there are multiple computer functions and uses (and that this generality is valued), and not anthropomorphizing the computer. Employing terminology in their conversation is a sign of cultural learning. For example, one student, in describing an occasion that made him feel proud, said,

I would say the first time I had a program actually work on the computer. It had taken some work to get through all the debugging. I call it debugging now. It's just correcting errors ... (A1)

Some students demonstrated an understanding that there are multiple computer uses by distinguishing writing programs from using tools:

It depends if I think about programming or if I think about using a computer. I don't like programming too much but when it comes to using a computer like the Minitab system that manipulates stuff for you, I like that kind of stuff where you use the computer to do stuff for you. But I don't like programming the computer to do the stuff. (K11)

Complexity in thinking about computers was, however, not typical of these students; only five students exhibited some sense of differentiated function in their comments about computers. Some students still anthropomorphized the machine. Five students said something like the following:

I mean, sometimes I feel like the computer is out after me. You know, everybody gets that feeling that the computer's after them sometimes. (Q17)

Personal Outcomes. In forming their overall assessment of the effects of computers and computing, students distinguished between effects on themselves and effects on society. They are impressed with the capability and versatility of computers for society as a whole, believing they are the "wave of the future" (J10). But they were less positive about the effects of computers on themselves personally. In assessing the effects of the computer on their activities as students, 13 students listed more negative effects, 6 students listed more positive effects, 2 students listed equal numbers of positive and negative effects. One student who characterized the entire experience as "a fight," exemplifies an outcome of anger.

The whole fact that you have to fight to get on, you – the whole computer theory, everything about computing here is a fight to do it. It's something you don't want to do and you have to fight to get in there to do it. And you have to fight to sit down and do it. And you have to fight the system to stay up. And you have to fight your program to make it work. And the whole time you're fighting the clock. (J10)

Another student, exemplifying withdrawal, said:

Looking back, I'm really not afraid of computers, but I'm going to try to stay away from computers. I know I shouldn't, because it's probably the thing of the future. But I'm really kind of leery to get into any type of computing again. (C3)

This student of course does not speak for all freshmen. An opposite, but less common, view was offered by another student, who exemplifies success in her willingness for further socialization. When she learned that she would have to do a history assignment on the computer the semester following her computing course, she said,

I was glad that we were doing it on the computer. I don't know why. I just thought, 'Oh neat, we get to use the computer again.' (K11)

Discussion

We speculated that novice encounters with computing could be interpreted by considering computing as culture rather than simply as tool. In a series of open-ended interviews novices revealed reactions to computing which seem to have been influenced in part by the social order surrounding computing: by the attitudes and behaviors of people who are good at it, by the management of computing resources, and by the general perceived importance of computing in society and the organization. They also revealed different ways of trying to cope with the strangeness of computing, each associated with more or less success. We believe these interviews reveal reasons for the differences found in the first part of our study. There is nothing in the way electrons flow, operating systems work, or Pascal procedures are written that explains the reactions to computing and computer science courses we discovered. We believe they are explained, instead, by novice attempts to operate in and make sense of an alien culture.

People who know how rapidly computing technology is changing may claim that this research studies a non-problem in that soon the particular artifacts present in our study will be replaced by different computer systems or will be improved by better human factors engineering. Indeed by 1985, three years after the data reported in this chapter were collected, freshmen were less dependent on large mainframes and were using PCs much more. But the questions that we ask about culture, socialization, and control are independent of any particular computer system and are more tied to particular organizational settings. It is true that computer systems are always changing, but the social settings remain relatively stable. Indeed freshmen in 1985 found computing still to be different from their other courses, although the differences were somewhat diminished from 1982 (Sproull, 1986). Furthermore, the belief that things will get better in the future does not relieve us of the responsibility to understand them as they are today. This is not to deny that computers may serve long-term educational and organizational goals. The point is that whatever computer systems we happen to have now do result in short-run problems and it is precisely about the short run that people express concern.

This work highlights a nice irony in organizational socialization. CMU clearly values computing quite highly. But in their enthusiasm for computing, its managers and experts have created situations in which it is hard for novices to be enthusiastic. Like the overzealous tour guide who forces his charges to climb endless sets of steps for the perfect view, to eat sheep's eyeballs for the perfect culinary experience, and to sit through a five-hour native poetry reading, this organization can produce more cultural dropouts than recruits.

12 How Computing Attitudes Change During the Freshman Year

David Zubrow

One social issue arising from an increased dependency on computers is whether the distribution of computing skill and knowledge may create or exacerbate group status differences (Chen, 1986; Marvin & Winther, 1983; Papert, 1979). That is, will some groups tend to dominate the technology while others are isolated from it? Certainly individuals will differ in their ability and motives to use computers. But optimally differences in competence will not be determined by ascribed group membership, such as gender. Nor should achieved group membership, such as academic background, prevent one from obtaining the necessary skills to be technically and socially competent in computing. Yet the potential exists for such differences to occur if only select groups are given opportunities to compute or if students are treated differentially as a function of their group membership in their initial computer training (Kiesler, Sproull, & Eccles, 1985; Lepper, 1985; Linn, 1985).

Gender differences in computing skills and attitudes have been reported. Hawkins, Sheingold, Gearhart, and Berger (1982) found that boys were considered by their teachers and classmates to be more knowledgeable about computers within an elementary classroom. Felter (1985) reported that sixth and twelfth grade boys generally had greater achievement, more confidence, and more positive attitudes toward computing than did the girls in these grades. Neither Hawkins et al. nor Felter controlled for the varying amounts of computer experience among their subjects. It is well established that girls have less computer experience, on average, than boys do. It could be that this difference in experience accounts for the difference in computing attitudes.

Among studies controlling for varying levels of experience, the results are mixed. Some researchers found gender differences between males and females with comparable levels of experience. For instance, Lockheed, Nielsen, and Stone (1983) reported that among students with similar levels of computer experience, males tended to have greater gains in computer literacy than did females. Chen (1985) found experienced males to have greater confidence in their computing skills and less anxiety towards computing than did experienced females. Similarly, Wilder, Mackie, and Cooper (1985) found gender differences among college freshmen in attitudes reflecting familiarity and

195

confidence with computers to persist even after experience was controlled. Alternatively, Chen (1985) also reported that significant attitudinal differences between male and female high school students disappeared when the amount of computing experience was controlled. Loyd and Gressard (1984) also found computing experience to be a prime explanatory factor of computing attitudes. In a study of undergraduates, Shields (1986) found experience to be significantly related to positive attitudes towards computing. Gender did not account for a significant amount of variance beyond that already explained by experience.

Another group difference that has concerned people is the differences between technical or science-oriented students and liberal arts students. Few researchers have studied performance or attitudinal differences in computing among students in different curricula. Computing at the university level is still taught primarily from the viewpoint of computer science, and emphasizes programming. This approach to introducing students to computing favors technically oriented students. Sproull, Zubrow, and Kiesler (1985) found that technical students tended to have more positive attitudes and better computing skills than did their liberal arts counterparts. These results, however, did not control for differential levels of prior computing experience among the students in these curriculum groups. The question remains as to whether differences exist in attitudes toward computing among academic disciplines beyond those accounted for by varying levels of computer use or experience.

Chapter 11 describes the attitudes of liberal arts students toward computing at the end of their freshman year in 1982. This chapter explores attitudinal differences among college students over the course of their freshman year, 2 years later, in 1984, and tracks how their attitudes changed over their entire freshman year. It focussed particularly on the effects of two kinds of group membership, gender and academic major. And it also investigated the effects of prior computing experience on attitudes toward computing.

Method

The Data

Attitudinal data were collected by Cohen, Sherrod, and Clark (1985), who surveyed a random sample of about 200 CMU freshmen four times during the 1983–1984 academic year to study the development of social support and social relations. They asked questions about computing once in the fall and once in the spring. In addition, I obtained data from the university registrar on academic background (e.g., SAT scores and size of high school) and college courses and grades, and from the university health service on its utilization and students' medical histories. These data were merged with the questionnaire data.

The first survey in the fall produced full responses to the computing items from 149 subjects, but attrition left only 84 subjects with complete data by the end of the year. Since our research questions focussed in part on change over the year, this set of 84 subjects was the most appropriate for analysis. To investigate the possibility of selective attrition, I compared the fall scores for spring responders and nonresponders. No significant differences appeared between means or variances for the dependent variables under consideration here. Also, there was no association between remaining in the study and level of computer experience prior to college ($\chi^2(1) = .18$, $p = .67$). The students who stayed in the study had a significantly higher mean SAT mathematics score, 679 versus 647. However, SAT mathematics scores were confounded with the other explanatory variables and had no significant contribution to the amount of variance explained in the dependent measures beyond that accounted for by the other explanatory variables. The students who dropped out of the study were academically more heterogeneous than the group who stayed in the study, as reflected by their larger variances on the academic data (i.e., number of units taken, SAT scores, and mathematics and computing QPA's), but their mean scores are similar to those who stayed in the study.

Of particular interest to this study were 12 attitude questions about computing. From a factor analysis of these items, three factors were extracted: confidence, positive affect, and game playing. Together these account for 60% of the variance in the original data. Since the first two factors seem most significant and interesting for policy and theoretical purposes, I used only these factors as the bases for the dependent variables. (See Figure 12.1.) They account for 54% of the original variance. On the basis of the factor analysis, I assigned each item to the one factor on which it loaded most highly. An internal reliability analysis of the items constituting the factors yielded alphas of .85 for the confidence items and .84 for the positive affect items. To compute the factor score for each student I reversed the coding for the negatively worded items, summed the assigned variables (i.e., an implicit unit weighting scheme), and divided by the number of items. The resulting factor scores retained the 0 – 4 scale. Self-reports of confidence in computing ability and positive affect toward computing constitute the dependent variables for this study.

The explanatory variables explored in this chapter are gender, academic major, and computing frequency. Information about gender and academic major came from the registrar's data and the information concerning pre-college and college computing frequency was reported on the questionnaire. Gender is a dichotomous variable. Academic major was dichotomized into technical and nontechnical majors. Engineering and science majors were coded as technical majors and liberal arts and fine arts majors were coded as nontechnical majors. Unlike gender and academic major which remained constant for the subjects over the course of the year, the measure of computing frequency could vary

Factor	Item
Confidence	• Do you think it will be difficult to learn the computer skills you will need to get along at CMU?
	• Does the idea of being required to use a computer in your college work make you feel anxious or uncomfortable?
	• Are you skilled at computer programming?
	• Do you consider yourself a "hacker" (i.e., an expert at programming who spends a lot of time "hacking away" in order to discover what can be done on the computer)?
	• Compared to other people entering CMU, how much do you think you know about computers?
Positive Evaluations	• If you have some experience using a computer for work or school, how much have you enjoyed it?
	• How much are you looking forward to using computers in college?
	• If you had a personal computer or computer terminal in your room, how often do you think you would use it for work and play?
	• Are you considering buying your own personal computer?
	• How did CMU's computer reputation affect your feelings about enrolling at CMU?

Figure 12.1. Assignment of items to computing attitude factors. The items are the questions asked in the fall of the academic year. They were rephrased appropriately for the spring data collection. One item from the "positive affect" factor, "looking forward to using computers in college," was not asked in the spring.

from the fall to the spring. How frequently students computed was measured on 5-point scales ranging from ''none'' to ''very much.'' The fall questionnaire asked students to rate their frequency of using computers prior to college. The spring questionnaire asked the students to rate their frequency of computer use during the freshman year. Thus, these measures refer to different time periods and rely on the students' own reports of computer use. The computing frequency scales were dichotomized, the lower 3 values were labelled ''none/some'' and the two upper values were labelled ''much.'' Collapsing the scales in this fashion facilitated the analysis by allowing the computer-use measure to be included in regression analyses as a dummy variable. This procedure is a more conservative approach to the use of this type of data than treating the scale as an interval-level measure.

Research Questions

The analyses presented below chart respondents' changes in attitudes toward computing over time and test for associations among computing attitudes, group memberships, and levels of computing frequency. Computing attitudes are viewed as a function of students' academic major, gender, and use of computers. Academic major and gender serve as proxies for interests and orientations that might predispose students to have more or less favorable attitudes toward computing. Frequency of computing is conceptualized as directly influencing attitudes. The timing of the questionnaires and the phrasing of the questions makes this a reasonable choice. Furthermore, this model is the most prevalent in the literature and facilitates the comparison of these results with those of other studies. Admittedly, attitudes and behaviors probably influence each other, but this investigation was not designed to explore or resolve this issue.

The analyses address the following set of questions. First: When freshmen enter college, what are their initial levels of (1) confidence about their ability to use computers and (2) positive affect towards computing? Do groups of students categorized by gender (male, female) or major (technical, non-technical) differ in this respect? How does pre-college computing frequency influence these levels and differences? Second: What are the levels of confidence and positive evaluations at the end of the freshman year? How much have they changed over the course of the year? Does change occur differentially among groups? Third: Does the amount of pre-college computing frequency have any relation to the end-of-year results? Does the amount of pre-college computing frequency vary from one group of students to another?

Results

Initial Computing Attitudes

Upon entering college, students on average had only a modicum of confidence in their computing ability (M = 1.92 on a 0–4 scale), but they felt rather favorably towards computing (M = 2.70 on a 0–4 scale). The same relationship held true for each of the student subgroups, as may be seen by inspection of Table 12.1.

Significant differences between men and women were found for both of these measures. On the computing confidence measure, men (M = 2.24) reported greater confidence on average than women did (M = 1.25; t (82) = 4.72, p < .01). Likewise, men (M = 2.89) were more positive toward computing than were women (M = 2.33, t (82) = 2.94, p < .01).

The results of comparisons between students in technical and nontechnical majors were similar to those for gender. Technical students (M = 2.13) reported

Table 12.1. *Means for confidence and positive affect of freshmen in the fall and spring*

Freshmen	Confidence		Positive affect		
	Mean	S.D.	Mean	S.D.	N
Fall					
All	1.92	1.020	2.70	0.863	84
Gender					
Men	2.24	0.932	2.89	0.802	56
Women	1.25	0.857	2.33	0.874	28
College					
Technical	2.13	1.000	2.83	0.788	64
Nontechnical	1.22	0.725	2.30	0.989	20
Computing frequency					
None/some	1.34	0.685	2.26	0.677	52
Much	2.84	0.744	3.35	0.579	32
Spring					
All	2.01	0.915	2.36	0.766	84
Gender					
Men	2.24	0.879	2.47	0.712	56
Women	1.56	0.829	2.15	0.837	28
College					
Technical	2.22	0.901	2.50	0.737	64
Nontechnical	1.34	0.584	1.93	0.703	20
Computing frequency					
None/some	1.68	0.818	2.13	0.641	44
Much	2.38	0.883	2.63	0.813	40

significantly higher confidence in their computing abilities than did nontechnical students ($M = 1.22$, $t(82) = 3.75$, $p < .01$). Technical students also were more positive toward computing ($M = 2.83$) than their nontechnical counterparts ($M = 2.30$, $t(82) = 2.45$, $p < .02$).

Confidence was significantly related to pre-college computing frequency. Students with "none/some" experience ($M = 1.34$) showed less confidence than those with "much" experience ($M = 2.84$; $t(82) = 9.46$, $p < .001$). Positive affect and pre-college computing frequency were also significantly associated ($t(82) = 7.12$, $p < .001$). Students reporting that they computed relatively more frequently prior to college had greater positive affect toward computing ($M = 1.66$) upon entry to college than those who had less pre-college computing experience ($M = 1.05$).

When considered in isolation, each of the independent variables demonstrated explanatory power with respect to both confidence and positive evaluations. Two questions were then pursued: How much variance do the independent variables explain together? What is the relative importance of each independent variable in a multivariate context? These questions were addressed using regression analysis and commonality analysis (Kerlinger & Pedhazur, 1973).

To assess the simultaneous explanatory power of gender, academic major, and computer frequency on freshmen attitudes in the fall, a series of dummy variable regressions were estimated for confidence and positive affect. The fall and spring data were analyzed separately, using hierarchical models with all possible orders of entry for the main effects of the independent variables. The hierarchical approach permitted assessing of the amount of variance (R^2) accounted for by a particular set of variables as well as the importance of each explanatory variable as indicated by its unique contribution (i.e., semi-partial correlation squared) to explaining the variance in each equation. Additionally, change in R^2 was evaluated to determine whether the addition of more variables to the equation significantly improved the amount of explained variance. Table 12.2 reports the results for both the fall and spring although this section presents only the fall results.

The equations containing all the main effects accounted for 60% and 37% of the variance in confidence and positive affect, respectively. For confidence, all three explanatory variables made significant contributions to the amount of variance explained. Comparison of the semi-partial correlation coefficients showed that pre-college computing frequency uniquely accounted for half of the explained variance. The unique contributions to explained variance by gender and academic major totalled 12%. The remaining 38% of explained variance cannot be unambiguously attributed to any of the independent variables due to their confounding. For positive affect only the pre-college computing frequency variable made a significant contribution to explained variance. Academic major and gender did not significantly improve upon the amount of variance accounted for by pre-college computing frequency. Clearly the amount of pre-college computing frequency is the most powerful variable for explaining confidence and positive affect among students in the fall of their freshman year.

Confounding among the independent variables can be considered to be the amount of variance in the dependent variable explained jointly by the independent variables. To determine the degree of confounding among the independent measures, the R^2 and sum of the squared semi-partial correlations can be compared. This comparison is reported in Table 12.2 as the percent of explained variance that was shared among the independent variables. It was computed by dividing the sum of the squared semi-partial correlations for all independent variables in an equation by the R^2, subtracting this figure from 1,

Table 12.2. *Regression and commonality analysis results: confidence and positive affect on computing frequency, academic major, and gender*

Model	R^2	df Reg	df Reg	Sig Reg	%Shared variance	Change R^2	P-value for change
Confidence in the fall							
AM*	.146	1	82	.00	—	—	—
G*	.214	1	82	.00	—	—	—
G*, AM*	.302	2	81	.00	19.24	—	—
PFreq*	.522	1	82	.00	—	—	—
PFreq*, G*	.573	2	81	.00	28.41	.051	.01
PFreq*, G*, AM*	.602	3	80	.00	38.25	.030	.05
Positive affect in the fall							
AM*	.068	1	82	.02	—	—	—
G*	.095	1	82	.00	—	—	—
G*, AM*	.137	2	81	.00	19.36	—	—
PFreq*	.352	1	82	.00	—	—	—
PFreq*, G	.364	2	81	.00	22.85	.012	n.s.
PFreq*, G, AM	.373	3	80	.00	31.72	.009	n.s.
Confidence in the spring							
AM*	.171	1	82	.00	—	—	—
G*	.121	1	82	.00	—	—	—
G*, AM*	.244	2	81	.00	19.34	—	—
FConf*	.521	1	82	.00	—	—	—
FConf*, FFreq*	.567	2	81	.00	18.25	.046	.00
FConf*, FFreq*, PFreq	.583	3	80	.00	66.84	.016	n.s.
FConf*, FFreq*, PFreq, AM	.594	4	79	.00	72.24	.011	n.s.
FConf*, FFreq*, PFreq, AM, G	.594	5	78	.00	73.94	.000	n.s.
Positive affect in the spring							
AM*	.104	1	82	.00	—	—	—
G*	.039	1	82	.07	—	—	—
G, AM*	.122	2	81	.01	16.58	—	—
FPosA*	.295	1	82	.00	—	—	—
FPosA*, FFreq*	.331	2	81	.00	21.47	.036	.04
FPosA*, FFreq*, PFreq	.335	3	80	.00	50.76	.004	n.s.
FPosA*, FFreq*, PFreq, AM	.353	4	79	.00	55.04	.018	n.s.
FPosA*, FFreq*, PFreq, AM, G	.353	5	78	.00	55.10	.000	n.s.

Notes: G indicates gender; AM indicates academic major; PFreq indicates pre-college computing frequency; FFreq indicates freshman year computing frequency; FConf indicates confidence in the fall; FPosA indicates positive affect in the fall; Dashes indicate results not computed.
* $p < .05$ for that effect.

and multiplying the result by 100. This figure represents the amount of explained variance that could be attributed to any of the independent variables had they been analyzed in isolation. As can be seen, a moderate amount of confounding exists among the independent variables with respect to both confidence and positive evaluations. The degree of confounding among the independent variables was not troublesome from a theoretical or inferential viewpoint given their rather rough grained level of measurement.

End of Freshman Year Computing Attitudes

At the end of the year the average confidence score was 2.01 and for positive evaluations it was 2.39. These scores reflect an insignificant upward shift in confidence $(M = .10, t (83) = 1.26$, n.s.) among the students, but a significant downward shift in their positive affect toward computing $(M = -.34, t (83) = -3.96, p < .001)$.

Analyses like those done on the fall data were also carried out using the spring survey data. (See Table 12.1 again.) Men $(M = 2.24)$ still had greater confidence than women $(M = 1.56, t (82) = 3.36, p < .01)$. The difference between the two means, however, was reduced by 31% due to an increase in the average score of women and virtually no change in the average score of men. The results for positive affect show the difference between men and women to have become insignificant $(t (82) = 1.81, p = .07)$. This change was driven by a relatively large decrease in the mean positive affect score for men coupled with only a slight decrease among the women.

Technical and nontechnical students continued to differ in their degree of confidence $(t (49) = 5.11, p < .001)$. As in the fall, technical students $(M = 2.50)$ reported greater positive affect toward computing than did nontechnical students $(M = 1.93, t (82) = 3.08, p < .01)$. Also, those students reporting more frequent computing during the freshman year had greater confidence $(t (82) = 3.77, p < .001)$ and more positive affect $(t (82) = 3.14, p < .001)$ toward computing than those who used computers less frequently.

Again, to assess the simultaneous explanatory power of the independent variables a regression analysis like the one conducted on the fall data was also carried out on the spring data. However, the set of variables included in the analysis was expanded. To control for each student's initial attitude level, their fall scores for confidence and positive affect were included (Feldman, 1972). The pre-college computing frequency variable was also included to test for any enduring effects of earlier exposure that were not reflected in the students' fall attitude scores. Freshman year computing frequency represented the students' most recent level of experience with computing. Gender and academic major completed the set of variables for the analysis.

The models were estimated using stepwise regression with no constraints on the order of entry. The selection process for both confidence and positive affect was the same: fall attitude scores entered first followed by the measure of frequency of computing during the freshman year. The fall attitude measures accounted for a significant amount of variance in the spring attitude scores (R^2 equalled .52 and .30 for confidence and positive affect, respectively) as might be expected. The increment to explained variance accounted for by the freshman year computing frequency variable was .05 for confidence and .04 for positive affect. (See Table 12.2.) The coefficients for their effects were positive in both instances, as expected. None of the other explanatory variables met the statistical criteria for inclusion in the analysis subsequent to entry of the fall attitude and recent computing frequency variables. However, regressions were run adding each of the remaining variables one at a time to complete the table. As can be seen from the table, pre-college computing frequency, academic major, and gender make only minimal improvements in the amount of variance explained. Consistent with the results reported, the semi-partial and partial correlations of fall computing attitudes and freshman year computing experience dominate those of the other variables. The results are similar to those found for the fall data in that most recent computing frequency, that is computing during the freshman year, accounted for the majority of explained variance for both confidence and positive evaluations that is not accounted for by the fall attitude measures.

Analysis of the confounding among the independent variables showed the fall computing attitudes and the frequency of computing during the freshman year to be fairly independent. The amount of explained variance shared by these two variables was 18% for confidence and 21% for positive affect. When pre-college computing frequency enters the equation, the amount of explained variance shared by the independent variables soars. This increase is driven by the high correlation between fall computing attitudes and pre-college computing frequency. The fall findings foreshadowed this result. Recall that pre-college computing frequency showed a significant relationship to both fall computing attitudes.

Change in Computing Confidence, Positive Affect, and Computing Frequency

Because the data as a whole suggest computing frequency influences students' levels of confidence and positive affect toward computing, an interesting question is how change in level of computing frequency relates to change in confidence and positive affect. A crosstabulation of students' reported pre-college and freshman year computing frequency revealed that 24% of the students reported more frequent computing during their freshman year than during their pre-college period while 14% reported computing less frequently during their freshman year than during their pre-college period. To carry out the analysis, change scores were created by subtracting fall attitude scores from spring attitude scores. To represent change in computing frequency reports, a three-level categorical variable (increased, decreased, and no change) was created. Since gender and academic major failed to make any significant contribution to explained variance in the earlier analyses, they were omitted from this current analysis of change. A one-way ANOVA using change in reported computing frequency as the independent variable showed a significant, positive association with both confidence ($F(2,81) = 4.85$, $p = .01$) and positive affect ($F(2,81) = 3.55$, $p < .05$). Table 12.3 shows the mean changes in confidence and positive affect as they were related to change in reported computing frequency. If reported computing frequency stayed the same or increased, confidence increased. However, if reported computing frequency declined, so did confidence. For positive affect, a similar pattern occurred given the overall downward trend in this measure. Those students whose reported computing frequency remained the same or increased showed smaller declines in their positive affect toward computing than did those whose computing frequency reportedly decreased. However, this variable only accounts for a fraction of the variance in the change scores (11% and 6% for change in confidence and positive affect, respectively).

Computing Frequency of Student Groups

When they entered college, technical males reported the highest frequency of pre-college computing. (See Table 12.4.) Over half of these students reported computing frequently prior to college, while only 18% of the technical females reported this level of pre-college computing. At the other end of the spectrum, 30% of the nontechnical women reported no prior experience with computing. By the end of the freshman year, almost all of the technical men and women reported they had acquired much computing experience. Given the initial differences, the distribution for technical men remained virtually the same while that for the women shifted upward. For nontechnical students the picture is less clear. The elimination of the 30% of nontechnical women reporting no computing experience and the doubling of the percentage of women with a high frequency of computing might suggest that this group is moving toward parity with the other groups of students. However, other factors must be kept in mind which caution against this interpretation. The university strongly encourages all students to take computing during their freshman year so the elimination of those with no experience is to be expected. Also, the small N for nontechnical women prohibits any meaningful interpretation of the change in percentage of women in the more frequently computing category.

Table 12.3. *Mean changes of confidence and positive evaluations as a function of change in computing experience*

Attitude	Up	Change in computing experience Same	Down
Confidence	0.32	0.14	-0.45
Positive evaluations	-0.17	-0.28	-0.87
N	20	52	12

Discussion

This research explored the attitudes of freshmen toward computing before and after one year of living in a highly computerized academic environment. It took a step toward understanding attitude differences among groups of students and how college computing experience might influence these attitudes. Before discussing the results, two cautions regarding interpretation and generalization of the findings need to be mentioned. First, the set of students sampled for this research is not representative of the population at large. Probably, the sample is biased in the direction of being more accepting of computing than the general public given that they chose to enroll in this institution. This bias should reduce the likelihood of negative attitudes. Caution must be exercised when generalizing the results beyond the individuals self-selecting themselves into this setting. Second, the dynamic relationship between attitudes and behaviors was simplified and some critics might take issue with the conceptualizations applied in this work. In particular, it is easy to imagine that attitudes might be powerful influences on students' initial decisions to get involved with computing. From this perspective, those who are favorably disposed toward computing would do it more often than those who are not. Attitudes lead behaviors. Of course, attitudes are not static and it seems reasonable, even within this framework, that behaviors might then play a role in reinforcing existing attitudes or causing them to change.

The primary finding of this study was a positive relationship between computing frequency and computing attitudes. The frequency that students' computed prior to college predicted their attitudes at the beginning of their freshman year. As expected, the more students computed, the more confident and positive were their attitudes toward computing. Then, after controlling for their attitudes in the fall, computing frequency during the freshman year related positively to their

Table 12.4. *Percentage of students with "much" pre-college and freshman year computing experience by group*

| | | Experience time period | | |
| | | | Freshman | Change |
Group	N	Pre-college	year	over time
All	84	38	48	10
Gender				
Male	56	50	54	4
Female	28	14	36	22
Academic major				
Technical	64	45	56	11
Nontechnical	20	15	20	5
Two-way classification				
Technical males	46	57	61	4
Technical females	18	18	44	26
Nontechnical males	10	20	20	0
Nontechnical females	10	10	20	10

attitudes toward computing in the spring. If the frequency of their computing decreased, they tended to become less confident and more negative toward computing. The extent of recent contact with computing influenced and changed attitudes toward computing.

One finding of some interest is that positive affect declined over the freshman year. A somewhat related finding was reported by Wilder, Mackie, and Cooper (1985). They noted in their survey of students in grades K-12 that there was a significant decline in liking computing by grade. Among the students in the current research, the decline was most pronounced among those entering college with the greatest amounts of computing experience. The decline in attitudes may have resulted from the failure of their computing experience to meet their initial expectations. At the moment, this is just speculation. Future research might investigate the reason for this decline in attitudes over time and elucidate the expectations of novices with respect to computing.

The results of this study do not support a claim of gender differences for confidence and positive affect toward computing. Variation in confidence and positive affect was most strongly related to the frequency with which these students computed. Only at the beginning of college did gender make a significant improvement in the explanation of students' confidence. This result suggested that prior to college women felt less confident about their computing abilities than did men with similar levels of computing experience. This effect

disappeared by the end of freshman year. Gender played no role in the explanation of positive affect. Note that the differences in the means on both the
confidence and positive affect measures shrink from the fall to the spring suggesting women's attitudes were converging with those of men. This change can
be attributed to the increase in the amount of computing experience gained by
the women as a group. Overall, the data do not support the notion of gender
differences with regard to attitudes toward computing.

This finding is similar to that of Chen (1985), but contrasts with that found by
Wilder, Mackie, and Cooper (1985). Outside of the computing domain, Boli,
Allen, and Payne (1985) found that experience factors accounted for much of
the differential performance and perceptions of performance in a sample of
high-ability men and women in undergraduate mathematics and chemistry
courses. Gender had little direct effect. The results reported here suggest a
similar process.

Academic major yielded results like those of gender. In the fall, technical
students reported greater confidence in their computing abilities than did the
nontechnical students. This effect persisted even after controlling for the varying levels of prior computer experience. Like gender, this was the only
significant effect of academic major in the multivariate context.

A final observation regarding the analysis of the computing attitudes is that a
large amount of the variance in positive affect of computing remains to be
explained. By far, computing experience was the most powerful explanatory
variable considered here. Although not reported, interactions among the independent variables, several general measures of social support and personality
and mathematics SAT score were also tested. None of these made any
significant contributions to explained variance beyond that obtained by computing experience. Alternatively, the variables considered here did quite well at
explaining the variance in confidence.

Environments like the one these students experienced will quite likely become
more common in colleges and universities as computing is incorporated into
more functions in the academic workplace. As a result, many students might
have computing experiences like those of the students in this study. Additionally, as computing further penetrates our society, more college students are
likely to believe it is in their own interest to develop computing skills: computing may be a necessary part of their professional development. It is safe to
assume that in the future the set of students learning to compute will be increasingly heterogeneous.

What do these findings suggest about promoting the development of positive
attitudes toward computing? Based on the relationship between computing frequency, attitude levels, and attitude change, the primary implication of this
research is that curricula should be structured to provide students with ongoing

opportunities to compute. During each year, courses should be offered that include computing. Note that these need not be computer science courses. The findings of this study address contact with the technology, not the nature of the contact.

The data on rates of pre-college computing experience and the relation of this experience to computing attitudes suggest that educators may need to encourage some groups of students to take the initial step into the world of computing. But some specific policies will have to follow from that general advice. In the first place, students differentially place themselves in environments where they will get computer experience. For example, girls are less likely than boys to enter computer camps, computer game arcades, and technical universities (Kiesler, Sproull & Eccles, 1986; Hess & Miura, 1985; Kotlowitz, 1985). Characteristics of those environments, or of the computer experiences they offer, are less attractive to girls than to boys. Educators have offered different solutions to the self-selection problem (Rouvalis, 1986). Some believe software should be tailored for girls. Some believe the context in which computing experiences occur needs to be tailored. They argue girls will like the same software as boys do if only they do not have to compete for access and if they are encouraged to learn computing to the same degree boys are. Similarly, different strategies have been offered to alleviate the differential selection of nontechnical and technical people into computer experience environments. Since our knowledge of the problem is limited, these ideas are worth pursuing as empirical questions.

A second policy domain concerns the design of curricula. In the current study, college freshmen learned a programming language, usually Pascal. They also learned how to use a command-driven text processing program, a document production program, and electronic mail and network communication programs. Many learned other applications, such as statistical packages and graphics programs. We do not know which of these experiences were most useful in giving students computer skill and confidence. We do not know the influence of the difficulty of the curriculum or of its diversity. Equally, we do not know what computer experiences were detrimental. The previous chapter indicates that the introduction to computer science at this university overwhelms and repels a significant minority of students. But also, some of the students who reported a devastatingly harsh initiation to computing as freshmen eventually learned to love computers, as the next chapter will describe. We should try to learn how difficult, how diverse, and how sheltered a good computer curriculum needs to be.

One aspect of curriculum policy has to do with with the content of computer literacy courses. Some writers have argued that learning programming algorithms and theory is important to introducing computer concepts (Sheil, 1981). But there is another view that students need only learn to use those applications, such as electronic mail and computer conferencing, text and document production, graphics, and computer art, design or music composition, that are relevant to their functional needs. They argue that these competencies are not only useful, fun and confidence-boosting, but all that most people need to know about computers.

The technical capabilities of computing are tremendous. But, we must be careful that the social effects of computing work for a more equitable society and do not create or exacerbate gaps between social groups.

Appendix. Comparison on selected measures between students with missing and valid responses for the computer items in the spring

	Missing in the spring			Valid in the spring			Tests for equal varience		Test for equal means	
	Mean	Variance	N	Mean	Varience	N	F-Stat	p	T-Stat	p
Confidence (fall)	1.870	1.151	65	1.910	1.036	84	1.11	0.648	-0.26	0.798
Positive affect (fall)	2.720	0.799	67	2.701	0.745	84	1.07	0.761	0.13	0.761
Pre-college computing frequency (% high)	0.348	0.230	69	0.381	0.239	84	1.04	0.882	-0.42	0.674
Total courses (fall)	5.736	1.685	87	5.732	0.542	101	3.11	0.000	0.08	0.935
Total units (fall)	45.851	17.314	87	45.069	11.827	101	1.46	0.066	1.41	0.160
Math units (fall)	8.023	15.840	87	9.465	6.750	101	2.35	0.000	-2.89	0.004
Math QPA (fall)	2.729	1.418	70	2.921	1.092	95	1.30	0.238	-1.10	0.272
Computer QPA (fall)	2.765	2.972	34	3.140	2.170	43	1.37	0.333	-1.03	0.307
Total courses (spring)	4.976	1.348	84	4.980	0.360	101	3.75	0.000	-0.03	0.977
Total units (spring)	45.536	23.290	84	46.188	15.896	101	1.47	0.068	-1.01	0.315
Math units (spring)	9.202	42.471	84	11.416	26.225	101	1.62	0.021	-2.53	0.012
Math QPA (spring)	2.893	1.175	63	3.057	0.677	94	1.73	0.016	-1.02	0.310
Computer QPA (spring)	3.444	1.796	36	2.826	2.634	46	1.47	0.243	1.84	0.069
SAT verbal	579.081	9178.215	87	571.818	5704.781	99	1.61	0.023	0.57	0.570
SAT math	646.897	10330.893	87	678.990	4960.244	99	2.08	0.000	-2.47	0.015
Age	18.840	0.650	75	18.636	0.303	88	2.14	0.001	1.08	0.067
Total health visits	1.533	4.306	75	1.511	4.897	88	1.14	0.572	0.07	0.948
Tangible support	8.382	5.579	87	7.981	5.327	100	1.05	0.820	1.17	0.242
Belonging support	6.676	5.005	87	6.442	6.812	100	1.15	0.512	0.59	0.554
Self-esteem support	8.314	5.094	86	8.033	5.180	100	1.02	0.940	0.84	0.401
Appraisal support	7.785	13.184	86	7.276	13.712	99	1.04	0.855	0.94	0.348
Depression (CESD)	17.990	121.352	86	16.261	118.353	100	1.03	0.901	1.07	0.284
Physical symptoms	20.464	243.859	86	16.581	142.707	100	1.71	0.010	1.88	0.062
Perceived stress	30.333	72.352	86	29.466	68.178	100	1.06	0.772	0.70	0.482
Social anxiety	14.907	21.800	86	15.010	21.455	99	1.02	0.936	-0.15	0.881
Social competence	25.292	110.670	47	24.303	116.122	81	1.05	0.874	0.50	0.615

13   Learning to Like Computing

Lee Sproull and Tony O'Dea

In 1982 we discovered that CMU liberal arts freshmen found computing to be difficult, confusing, strange, frustrating, and alienating, particularly in comparison with other academic experiences. Chapter 11 describes these findings in detail. What happened to those students during their remaining years at CMU? Did their negative attitudes persist or did continued exposure to the CMU computing environment lead ultimately to the positive socialization that had not occurred during freshman year? This chapter describes how some of the same students we had studied as freshmen in 1982 felt about computing in the spring of 1985 just before their graduation.

Procedure

We had interviewed a random sample of 23 students in the spring of 1982 and wanted to reinterview them all in the spring of 1985. We were able to locate 18 of them; the remaining five had left college or transferred at the end of their freshman year. Of the 18 remaining on campus, we were able to complete interviews with 14. The other 4 could not be interviewed because of scheduling conflicts. Thus these interviews represent 60% of those interviewed as freshmen and 78% of those remaining on campus from the original freshman sample. The students who had left at the end of their freshman year had been unenthusiastic about computing, but they were no more so than those who remained. Hence attitudinal differences we find between freshman year and senior year are probably not attributable to attrition in the sample. We interviewed 9 males and 5 females. Seventy percent of our respondents had a professional major, either industrial management (35%), public policy and management (24%), or information systems (12%). This is somewhat larger than the proportion of professional majors (55%) and males (54%) in the graduating class as a whole.

The interview consisted of open-ended questions about computing experiences during the freshman year, computing experiences from the sophomore to senior year, the culture of computing on campus, and future expectations about computing. In addition, all the respondents filled out 38 7-point Likert scale items measuring attitudes about computing. All interviews were conducted by the second author. Transcriptions were entered into computer files for text analysis.

Findings

Memories of Freshman Year Computing

Students' memories of their freshman year computing experience are quite consonant with their descriptions at the time as we described in Chapter 11. Their overall general memory is that the experience was a negative one. In response to the question, "In general, what was your freshman computing experience like?" students made 10 positive statements (e.g., "It was kind of worth it"), 62 neutral statements (e.g., "I worked with the Philosophy tutorial program"), and 52 negative statements (e.g., "It was a disaster"). A similar general question had elicited 9 positive comments, 20 neutral comments, and 30 negative comments in 1982. Below, we quote our respondents directly, with the letter in parentheses identifying the respondent. The first quotation in each pair is from the 1982 interviews; the second is from the 1985 ones.

1982: I hate them.

1985: I hated it. (L)

1982: Frustration … I don't know what I'm doing yet.

1985: I was very turned off. (P)

1982: I don't really have good thoughts of computers at the moment.

1985: It was terrible. (J)

1982: I get really kind of tense inside, because computers really make me uneasy.

1985: It was bad. (C)

Their specific negative memories included late nights at the terminal room, not knowing how to log on, not being able to get a program to run, and feeling that everyone else knew more than they did.

Everyone around you [in the terminal room] is making you nervous. When you're a freshman you think everybody else knows what they're doing, and you try to cover up your unfamiliarity. (S)

Two Likert scales measuring students' experience with and perceptions of computing summarize much of their evaluation: the extent to which computing is or is not *confusing* and the extent to which it is or is not *worthwhile*. The Likert scales were of the form "My freshman experience with computing was…" on a 7-pt. scale where 1 = very strongly disagree and 7 = very strongly agree. (Values of 1 to 4 were recoded as "not agree," and 5 to 7 were recoded as "agree.") Eighty-four percent agreed that their freshman experience was confusing; 61% agreed that it was not worthwhile. (See Figure 13.1.)

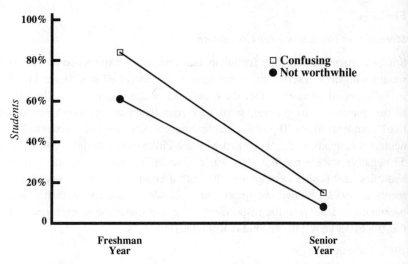

Figure 13.1. Students' evaluations of computing at end of freshman and senior years.

Computing at Graduation

By the end of their senior year, students had become much more positive about computing. They reported that their attitudes were positive, that they had learned skills, and that they were eager to learn even more.

Attitudes. In contrast with their memories of freshman year computing and their descriptions of it at the time, students' current attitudes were quite positive. Ninety-two percent said their attitude toward computing had become more positive than it was during freshman year.

I think computers are useful. (L)

Using the computer makes things a lot easier. (P)

It's a good tool. (J)

I think they're great. (C)

In describing their present attitudes about computing, students made 32 positive statements (e.g., "I appreciate the help computers give people"), 18 neutral statements (e.g., "I use it for writing papers"), and 8 negative statements (e.g., "I don't like to program"). By the end of their senior year only 15% of the students found computing to be confusing and only 8% found computing to be not worthwhile. (See Figure 13.1 again.)

Skills. Ninety-three percent reported that they had acquired specific skills and abilities with respect to computing. Seventy-eight percent had developed skills using applications software, primarily text processing and document preparation software (64%) and data management and analysis applications such as Lotus or statistical packages (43%). Fifty percent reported that they had acquired programming skills, typically in Pascal or FORTRAN. Note that all of the students had been required to take at least one programming course. Thirty-six percent took at least one additional course. There is a positive association between taking at least one additional programming course and reporting programming skills ($r = .45$, $p = .05$). Most students who took only one programming course (62%) did not report that they had acquired programming skills. But there is no association between taking an additional programming course and reporting skills in using applications software.

Seventy-eight percent believed they had acquired more general skills as well as specific ones, principally being able to use more than one computer system and being able to think more logically. Fifty percent had learned to use more than one computing system and felt comfortable moving from one system to another.

For every machine procedures will basically be different, but I have gained a clear grasp of what an operating system is. I have learned more about the fundamentals of computing and the way to apply those fundamentals to whatever system one is using. (C)

And 50% believed that their experiences with computing had made them think more logically.

The computer has helped me be more procedural about how I perform a task. Now I try to break tasks down more logically. (F)

Since I've learned Pascal, I've learned to break down problems more than I did before. I do this for non-computer-related problems. (U)

One might suspect that the students who took more than one programming course were also the ones who reported acquiring more general skills. There is a positive association between taking at least one additional programming course and the perception of thinking more logically ($r = .44$, $p = .04$). But there is no association between taking at least one additional programming course and using more than one computer system.

Students believed that the skills they had acquired have adequately equipped them for the future (85%) and that they will indeed use those skills in jobs they will hold (71%).

I won't be able to write programs with computers, but I won't need adjustment time to get used to being around computers. I'll only need brushup time. There are seniors at other universities who've never touched a computer. (Q)

I have learned a lot. My skills are not endemic to just one machine. I have tried to get an overall understanding of computing systems. I am prepared to go into a job and have some understanding once given basic commands. (C)

Not only do seniors believe they have acquired important computing skills and abilities, but every one of them would like to learn even more about computing. Seventy percent would like to learn more about applications software such as spreadsheet or text-processing programs. Forty-six percent of students would like to learn more programming skills. Fifteen percent wanted to learn more about PCs.

In sum, by the end of their senior year students had become positively socialized to computing as indicated by positive attitudes about computing, the acquisition of specific and general computing skills, and desire to learn even more about computing. Some of our findings help highlight the difference between a socialization view of computing and an instructional one. All of the students reported that they wanted to know more about computing, yet only 36% of them had taken an additional programming course. An instructional view emphasizes performance in courses, taking them and doing well in them. In this view the fact that only 36% of students had taken more than the introductory programming course might be viewed as a negative outcome. By contrast, a socialization view emphasizes the importance and pervasiveness of computing in the entire organizational environment, not just in the classroom. In this view the classroom is only one place to learn about computing. Other places and occasions are just as legitimate.

Lessons About the Culture

During their freshman year students learned some simple and mostly negative "lessons" about the computer culture, which we described in Chapter 11. By the end of their senior year, some students' views of that culture had become more complex. We asked students if there were a computer culture at CMU and, if so, to describe it.

All of them believed that there is a computer culture at CMU. And some (35%) still held the simple, relatively negative image:

They have long, uncombed, unwashed hair and spend all of their time talking about and working on the computer. (L)

If you are asking how I or others perceive the culture, a stereotype would be an extremely bright individual ... with an extreme communication problem and a lack of good writing skills. I also think these people have an oral communication problem, and their conversations suggest tunnel vision since their speech is filled with computer jargon. In the business world, they will do "well" financially, if well is defined in monetary terms, but if well means reaching top management, I don't think they will do as well as others. They focus too much on computers. (H)

But more students (65%) had developed a more positive and a more complex view of the culture.

The culture is positive. Many people are enthusiastic about computing ... young, enthusiastic, inquisitive, friendly. (F)

I think there's a tri-level culture. There are people who interact with the computer daily, hourly, all the time. There's a second culture that uses it to their advantage whenever they can. They don't go overboard like the first group I mentioned. There's also a third group who interacts with the computer when they're told to or when they have to or when they feel it's absolutely necessary. (S)

What Caused the Change?

We asked students how, if at all, their freshman computing experience had influenced their subsequent computing experiences. And we also asked them to describe the experiences that were "most important" in shaping their current attitudes toward computing, no matter in what year they occurred. Social scientists recognize many difficulties in asking people to infer the causes of their own attitudes and behavior (e.g., Dawes & Smith, 1985). Their inferences may be self-serving, may underestimate the effects of environmental features, may overestimate the effects of dramatic events, or may be stereotyped. In experimental research one can test for some of these inferential biases by varying question order or type or by using a variety of different data collection techniques, strategies not open to us in this study because of the small sample size. Yet people do commonly offer explanations for their attitudes and behaviors. This subsection reports some such commonly offered explanations with the caution that they may not be entirely accurate or complete. Nonetheless they represent a plausible account of important change factors.

The Role of Freshman Experiences. Sixty-two percent believed that their freshman year computing experiences were a negative factor in their coming to understand and appreciate computing.

I think it pushed me away from programming applications because of my difficulty getting through Pascal. (A)

I never wanted to touch the computer again. (J)

Twenty-three percent believed those experiences had no effect. And 15% believed that their freshman year experiences had a positive effect on their subsequent view of computing.

My freshman experiences made me want to learn more about the computer and be able to hop on the band wagon. As I saw how much the computer could do, I wanted to learn more about the future and learn what I could do. (I)

Using the Computer. All students used computers after their freshman year. The major classes of use were in programming courses, in applications programs for specific courses, in text editing, and in part-time and summer jobs. Some, but not all, of these experiences contributed to students' becoming more positive about computing.

All students used computing in course work past the freshman year, although, as we reported above, fewer than half of them (36%) took any additional programming or computer science course. Non-programming courses in which students used computing included statistics, computers in organizations, econometrics, marketing, optimization, and American history. Fifty percent of students nominated course-related computing as their most successful computing experiences. These experiences ranged from passing the mastery exam in the introductory programming course (which the student had failed as a freshman) to building a computer interface for handicapped children as part of a senior honors thesis in psychology. Although half the students found course-related computing to be their most successful computing experience, none reported that course-related computing contributed to making their attitudes toward computing more positive.

Text processing (writing, editing, and document creation) was an important use of computing for 93% of students. Thirty-six percent nominated text-processing as their most successful computing experience: these experiences ranged from spending three or four weeks getting a résumé "to look the way I wanted it to" (I) to "getting a 25-page paper with footnotes and bibliography to successfully compile and look good" (A). And 58% of students believed that text processing had contributed to making their attitudes more positive.

Just seeing how nicely the papers turned out was an important contributor. (B)

Being successful at text editing was the experience. (V)

In addition to course-related and text-processing experiences, 64% of students had part-time or summer jobs that entailed computing. For example, one student used text processing while working for the dean's office; another sold software in a computer store; another was a program analyst for a major computer manufacturer.

Living in the CMU Environment. The previous subsection focused on students' own actions and explicit beliefs about why they had changed – taking courses, creating documents, and holding jobs. But an equally important factor in contributing to students' changes was simply continuing to live in the CMU environment for three more years. As we noted in Chapter 4, those years saw a significant change in the computing resources available to students. One of students' big frustrations as freshmen was that computing resources for them were in short supply. By their senior year access was easier because there were many more computers on campus. Furthermore, freshmen in 1982 had no choice about the kind of computer they would use. The increase in computing resources was one of variety as well as quantity. Thus students now had more choice over what kind of computer to use for what project. Another big frustration for freshmen was that even when they did gain access to a computer, it would often crash. The big increase in personal computers meant that students not only had access to more computing but had access to what they perceived to be more reliable machines.

The social environment of computing also became much more hospitable for these students. As freshmen, they felt they didn't know where to turn for help. But by their senior year they believed that both the formal and the informal support systems had improved. Support services, such as help provided by user consultants, were better.

The user consultants are helpful. Since freshman year, they're a lot more knowledgeable. (K)

Students also became members of informal peer networks that provided help and support.

Now I have more of a network of friends who are doing computer things. We may talk about how someone's going to do their paper. In addition to the people in the computer center, I have friends as information sources. (I)

Another student commented that *everyone* had become more knowledgeable about computing.

My roommate and fraternity brothers were helpful. Now, user consultants are a lot different. They're helpful, and so are professors. It seems that now there are more professors who know what they are doing, particularly humanities and social sciences professors have learned a lot about computing and relate to students better ... before it seemed that many others were just as confused as those seeking help. When I was a freshman, it seemed that only the computer elite knew what was going on. Now it is different ... For example, someone asked another person for help during my freshman year. The helper ended up deleting all of the person's files. Now that more people know about computing, there is a diffusion of knowledge and power. People seem to be more willing to help. (C)

Thus, the CMU computing environment had become a richer and more supportive one for students during their sophomore to senior years.

Discussion

We found that students who had been alienated by computing during their freshman year had become much more positive toward computing by the end of their senior year. Almost all of them displayed attributes of positive socialization: positive attitudes, acquisition of specific and general skills, and desire to learn more. Furthermore, a majority of the students had developed a more positive and differentiated view of the culture of computing on campus.

Although we discovered that students had become more positive, we were not able to isolate factors that caused the change or to estimate how much various factors contributed to the change. Based on our interviews and on previous research on socialization and attitude change, we believe that five factors probably contributed in some manner to students' view of computing by the end of their senior year in college: freshman computing experiences, post-freshman-year experiences, adequate computing resources, supportive social environment, and general maturation. These factors should be investigated in future studies.

According to the students themselves, freshman year experiences in general did not contribute directly to seniors' positive orientation toward computing. But they may have contributed indirectly through what is known as the "severe initiation effect." Investigators ranging from anthropologists studying pubertal rites of passage to psychologists studying willingness to join groups in laboratory experiments have discovered that people are more committed to groups or situations that impose severe initiation requirements than they are to ones that do not. As one social psychologist remarked, "People come to love that for which they have suffered" (Festinger, 1961).

In contrast to their freshman year experiences, students' post-freshman-year computing experiences seem to have contributed more obviously to their positive orientation toward computing. In their course work and in text processing, students used computing as a tool in the service of their own goals. And they found that it could be a helpful tool indeed. In the process, these students developed a very pragmatic orientation toward computing. They did not come to value computing as an intellectual abstraction or as a means for understanding the nature of intelligence; they came to value it as a helpful tool.

I think the computer is a very useful tool. (A)

I appreciate the help computers give people and how they make life easier. (F)

It's an aid to people... The more people use it, the more they see what it can do. (I)

The third important factor was students' having adequate computing resources available to them. Undoubtedly students' post-freshman-year experiences would not have been so positive if students had continued to experience the aversive freshman-year conditions of not enough computers, overcrowded terminal rooms, and unreliable machines.

The fourth important factor was that students found the entire social environment surrounding computing to have become a much more supportive one. Earlier chapters in this book demonstrate some of the real changes in the social environment between these students' freshman and senior years. But it must also be the case that the students themselves learned how to better negotiate within that environment. They developed their own support systems and learned how to operate comfortably within the large environment.

Students' increased sophistication in dealing with their computing environment is related to the fifth factor contributing to seniors' positive orientation toward computing. That is a general maturational factor. In general, twenty-one-year-olds who are about to graduate from college are more competent and confident than are eighteen-year-olds at the end of their freshman year. There is no reason to expect the students we studied to be an exception. Over the course of their four years in college, these students developed and matured intellectually and socially. Computing offered one occasion for that process to be played out. And computing maturation was, in part, simply a function of that larger process.

Part V

Conclusion

14   General and Practical Implications

Sara Kiesler and Lee Sproull

In this chapter, we talk about the generality and the practicality of our research. What have we learned about the process of change? What can we say, as an extension of our ideas and research on CMU, about technology change in other organizations? How can we advise people who are managing the introduction of computing into their organizations? Although the previous chapters represent many research projects, they sum to a case study of one organization ($N = 1$). Therefore we properly offer generalizations and advice as hypotheses, not conclusions. Another caveat: We omitted or slighted many interesting problems in this research. Some were projects for which we could not find financial support, such as how computers affect student dormitory life and students' social and intellectual development. Some were projects we started too late to be in this book, such as how computers change classroom communication and a study of teachers pioneering in educational uses of computing. Some were projects we didn't think to do, such as how computers change the status of students in the university. Naturally, what we say can't take into account what we might have learned had we not omitted those studies.

Generalizing About Technological Change in Organizations

To talk about what we have learned and the implications of our study for other organizations we first have to talk about the theoretical domain of our study. Theories of change in organizations are primarily different ways of explaining adaptive responses to demographic, economic, social, and political forces (March, 1981, p. 563). Organizational change can be studied as an evolutionary process whereby organizations react routinely to environmental forces such as changes in the economy or population (Nelson & Winter, 1974). Alternatively, organizational change can be studied from inside the organization, where people participate in change. In some of these studies, organizational participants are seen as active problem solvers (Lindblom, 1958; Cyert & March, 1963). In some they are seen as consumers of good ideas (Rogers & Shoemaker, 1971). Most of the literature on computer technology, which we have characterized as produced by "technology optimists," emphasizes one or both of the two latter perspectives. Still other studies see organizational participants as a mix of intentions,

225

competencies, and actions. This is our own perspective. We think much organizational change is conditional on, and influenced by, the selection and socialization of organizational participants. We then try to understand how intentions, competencies, and actions arise in the process of organizational change.

What We Learned

The focus of this book has been technological change, which some authors view as one variant of organizational change or innovation (Daft & Becker, 1978). However, technological change also includes new procedures, new products, reorganizations, and administrative changes and therefore cannot be separated conceptually from nontechnical organizational change (see also Van de Ven, 1986). We have observed that certain conditions, particularly zeal, expertise, and slack, foster change. That is, these conditions produce organizational participants willing and able to undergo technological change. What is the nature of this change? We find that technological change consists of three basic components: resources, behavior, and attitudes. Resources include not only technical things, like computers, but also facilities, policies, procedures, and services which form the infrastructure that make it possible for organizational participants to use the technology. Behavior and attitudes are equivalent to those competencies, intentions, and actions of organizational participants that comprise using (and fostering use of) new technology. Technological change does not happen in isolation, but in a cultural and organizational context. This means that culture and organization are both cause and consequence of technological change. One of the most surprising findings in our research was the many mutual transformations of university, computing culture, and computing that occurred as the institution underwent further computerization. Chapters 4, 9, 10, and 13 contain the most explicit descriptions of these transformations.

We began this research with the purpose of studying both intended and emergent effects of new technology. One important observation we made is that many planned and unplanned technical changes happened at once. The biggest technical changes during the early 1980s – the tremendous use of microcomputers and of communication on the existing networks – were unanticipated. These changes had both technical and social aspects. Technological change at CMU created opportunities to experiment even further with technological innovation. New technology had symbolic importance and had symbolic effects on both private and public behavior (e.g., Chapter 7). New technology was also an occasion to enact ongoing social processes, such as socialization (e.g., Chapter 11). We have organized the social consequences conceptually as attentional and social contact effects.

Attentional effects. In Chapter 1, Herbert Simon talked about how computer models of thinking might change the way we see ourselves in relation to nature – not as above it, but as part of it. Such change would constitute a profound attentional effect in that we might have less justification for valuing human life apart from other elements of nature. At present, attentional effects of computers seem to be more modest. Computers make it possible for ordinary people to learn new skills and to do tasks that were virtually impossible a few years ago. Librarians, for example, are creating important innovations in information search capabilities (Chapter 9). Computers also make it possible for people to do tasks that only highly skilled people did before. In the library, students and clerical workers are performing library tasks that librarians used to do exclusively. Taken alone, this effect is one of deskilling. However, "deskilling" sounds as though people are losing competence. Actually, librarians at CMU, especially the "library technologists," are learning and using new skills. Since the overall effect is a redistribution of competencies, we call it reskilling as well as deskilling. Another example of reskilling at CMU is that both male and female students are attaining competence in computing and forming new career goals as a result (Chapters 12 and 13). In addition to the direct effects on work and competence, there are symbolic effects which rebound to work and competence. People place a high symbolic value on computing skills and computer use. Hence those who gain computing competence also gain self-esteem and the prestige of others. We saw this impact on workers and managers in Part III and on students in Part IV.

One predicted attentional effect of computers is an increase in the importance for decisions and actions of quantitative, technical criteria (Danziger, 1985, p. 14). Our research shows that recently a significant number of administrators have been using computers to evaluate budgets and other quantitative information, and they report that computers influence their decisions (Chapter 10). Computers might also influence collective decisions in the organization in that quantitative data and analyses, rather than values and goals, become the focus of policy debates and decision making. Computers help make numbers understandable and they appeal to the idea of rational management. This appeal is illustrated by part of an interview given to us by an administrator at CMU who was talking about trying to hire a dean:

...one of our candidates was worried about his government pension and if he stayed at the government, how would that be compared to coming to CMU. One of the other administrators was trying to explain about this very long, complicated issue. It's a present-value discounting problem. I said, you know, look, it's too complicated, but I'll write you a program which will look at all these cash flows over time, and I'll make a series of different assumptions about how his salary will increase, and what will happen, and I said I'll give you back an analysis of which way he's better off. And it turned out that over the next 15 years, which we figured was a reasonable career for this particular person, he was approximately half a million dollars better off by coming to CMU than if he stayed at the government, where he thought he was going to actually lose money if he left the government. I mean we really printed out what would happen to him. I'd never thought about using a computer analysis as a way of enticing a candidate to come to CMU. He didn't come. Even after my analysis. He decided he wanted to stay in the government. We were probably better off without him I guess.

Social Contact Effects. Computers at CMU have changed social contact patterns. Only a few years ago, social scientists and technologists were warning that computing tends to isolate individuals, "reducing their interaction with other people in both work and leisure settings" (Danziger, 1985, p. 14). Yet our research indicates that people use computers to talk to people (Chapters 5 and 6) and people who use computers to talk to people talk to more people than do people who don't use computers (Chapter 9). If the distribution of social contact changes as a result of computerization, people will have the opportunity to talk with people they would not meet otherwise, and they will exchange information they would not exchange otherwise.

Various writers have claimed that computers will reduce the opportunities people have to exchange information. Computerization is said to increase the control of central authorities, increase monitoring of behavior, reduce privacy of individuals and of small groups, and serve the interests of those in power (Danziger, 1985, pp. 14–16). These claims have a basis in observations of mainframe computing in the 1960s and 1970s, when computer center administrators and technicians were the only people who had the knowledge and budget to operate computers. Today, the technology makes it possible for anyone to create a computer data base of information and to exchange information directly with others, and even to do "bottom up" monitoring (workers could keep track of their supervisors; people in an old age home could keep tabs on their caretakers). Thus the problem is one of policy, not technology. In centralized and authoritarian organizations, computers might be used to centralize authority further in those kinds of organizations. In decentralized organizations that foster autonomy, computers might work like the telephone, a technology whose application is controlled by all the people who use it, not just by the people who own it. This democratization of control is seen in the way administrators and secretaries can use computer information systems to obtain organizational data on personnel and student records that used to be impossible or difficult to acquire (Chapters 4, 9, 11). Social contact is becoming less controlled. Electronic discussions on the opinion BBoards read like an electronic cocktail party in progress, and anyone who has access to that network can participate.

Implications for Other Organizations

The fundamental conditions that contributed to major technological change at Carnegie Mellon University should contribute to technological change in other organizations. Two general characteristics of these conditions are energy and flexibility (see Perrow, 1970; Drabek & Haas, 1976). Organizations that have high energy and flexibility will be those in which organizational participants have the interest and ability to come up with new ideas, to take risks, to persevere in the face of routine and nonroutine demands on time and attention, to mobilize and to coordinate the behavior of many people, and to socialize and to select people so that competence increases. Energy and flexibility vary across time and units within organizations and across different organizations. Energy is high when demands on the organization are low or capacity for meeting demand is high. Hence energy depends on the larger environment and is not simply an organizational characteristic that can be changed at will. Small organizations, rich organizations, organizations with an educated work force, organizations that dominate market share, and prestigious organizations tend to have more energy than organizations with the opposite attributes. New organizations, nonbureaucratic organizations, democratic organizations, homogeneous organizations, and competitive organizations tend to have more flexibility than organizations with the opposite attributes.

An organization does not need to be a CMU or an educational institution to undergo a major technological change similar to what happened at CMU. For instance, during the time frame of this study, Manufacturers Hanover Trust Bank installed a computer network that now reaches thousands of employees all over the world (Nyce & Groppa, 1983). The network has over 50 different applications, including a computer mail system that many employees use several times daily. Tandem Computers is another company that revolutionized its technology in the period covered by this book. This company illustrates the energy and flexibility we have described in innovation-fostering organizations. Tandem was created in 1974 with only four employees. By 1984, it was a Fortune 500 firm, but still moderately sized (5,000 employees). The work force was educated, skilled, and relatively homogeneous. The organization had legitimacy and élan deriving from its niche in high technology. It operated in a highly competitive but growing market. It was fervently unstructured, non-bureaucratic, and self-managed. The president and founder said, "Change is the order of the day" (Trebig, 1985). To promote change, organizational policy followed the principles of fostering employees' competence and commitment to the company: "The goal is to make people part of the corporation while also allowing them to be individuals who grow and learn and enjoy working" (p. 7). One policy was to give every employee a computer terminal connecting him or her via electronic mail with every other employee in the company. The system was completely unstructured and self-policed. Employees also used computers to produce a real-time newspaper. People in the company from all over the world would submit their news on Thursday. It arrived in time for delivery to all sites by Friday. The company created a video conference system that allowed anyone to break in and to participate. The conference system was used for annual meetings, new employee orientations, special promotions, new product news, manufacturing seminars, customer briefings, and other many-to-many communications. Thus technological change at Tandem emerges from and changes the organization itself, just as we have claimed is true at Carnegie Mellon University.

Policy Making for Computing

Today we can do things that would have been considered fantasy just 20 years ago. A computer keeps track of the trees on campus and reminds the groundskeepers when they need pesticides, fertilization, and pruning. Computers tutor students in experimental design and computer programming. Computers make possible long-distance management, electronic project groups, and computer surveys of people's opinions. How does one design policies for technology that does things that have never been done? For example, if you have the potential for forming electronic project groups, you need policies to determine when they are permissible. Based on what criteria do you make this determination? You can anticipate and evaluate the intended technical effects of using the new technology, but not the transient and social effects. Because they are not prescient, managers should formulate policies according to general principles, and these must come from organizational goals. Thus in the case of electronic project groups, an important organizational goal is innovation; running a tight, centrally controlled ship is less important. Thus the principle is to encourage initiative and the policy is to allow electronic groups to develop freely.

The proper role of research in technology policy making is not to determine goals or principles, but to help policy makers learn from their own and others' experience. Research is a way of systematizing experience so people can learn. Because every organization has unique goals and experiences, we are reluctant to provide general advice on how to introduce computing into organizations. As an alternative, we demonstrate the practical implications of our research by reviewing some of the advice we have provided to CMU policy makers in the recent past.

At CMU computerization must fit with and promote four goals. One: computing should reinforce individuals' intellectual development and their sense of social responsibility. Two: computing should promote high-quality research. Three: computing should strengthen interactions as a community. Four: computing should exemplify values appropriate to education.

As an example of how research is relevant, our data indicate that electronic communication is a vehicle for social interaction (e.g., Chapter 5), hence it is relevant to the goal of promoting community. We have learned that when people use electronic communication, they receive work-related messages they would not have received otherwise. Consequently they feel dependent on the technology and connected with other people on the network. If policies permit (as they do at CMU), they also receive messages that have nothing to do with work. People like to be sociable and they will use a technology that makes it easy, whether it be a water cooler or a computer. Also, we find that computer-mediated communication loosens cultural constraints by reducing the reminders a person gets of norms, surveillance, and social feedback (Sproull & Kiesler, 1986). Reducing social context cues reduces people's embarrassment over being considered foolish and reduces their feelings of obligation to respond in a certain way. Hence even busy, shy, or obnoxious people can use electronic means to communicate comfortably in situations that would be more constrained if the communication occurred face-to-face. A policy of open computer communication to anyone on any subject promotes playfulness and a sense of neighborhood. A policy of limited access to computer communication promotes control, but also reduces playfulness and neighborhood. Hence, in order to encourage feelings of affiliation and commitment to the organization, you risk foolishness, extraneous information, and deviant behavior. Nonetheless, if fostering community is an important goal, it is a worthwhile risk. Notice that this choice is a question of values and goals, not one of technical and economic attributes of the technology.

One policy arena we have thought about at CMU is the area of computer resource allocation. More than most universities ours is driven by market mechanisms, so stronger departments tend to get better computers. Although the new computer network is simply too large a project to develop and deploy based on the diffuse, self-initiated processes typical of CMU, it is likely that decision makers will want to depend as much as possible on self-management and decentralized control of resources. However, this approach may foster undesirable inequality of computational resources. Inequality of computer resources can lead to inequality of computer access, which contravenes the goal of fostering individual development and a sense of community in all students and employees. Hence equity of computer access must be a guiding principle for policy. We have proposed policies like the following:

1. Provide free access to the university network. The network should be considered a universal, essential educational resource just as the library is.

2. Provide reasonable levels of text editing, printing, and communication applications free. Text editing, printing, and communication have been the most important uses of computers for all groups since we have studied them. Scholarship will always require almost everyone to produce, exchange, and read documents.
3. Provide free or discounted computers for education to all departments. This should include support for maintenance and repair.
4. Ensure that any CMU student who wants one can buy a personal computer and connect to the network. Our data show that a PC or terminal in one's living quarters contributes importantly to access and usage, and to students' participation in electronic forums. The ability to participate in electronically dependent education ought not to depend on one's financial wealth.
5. Provide portable computers that students and faculty can check out of the library, at no cost, for use in field work and classrooms.

Another important area of policy is computer services. Increasingly, as we noted in Chapter 4, CMU has moved toward decentralization of computer services. Many departments employ faculty or staff who have become local experts or "gurus" in some areas of computing. Department members go to them for advice and for help on small jobs such as PC installation and running statistical programs. Decentralization benefits CMU by increasing the distribution of computing expertise, increasing the ability of departments to handle their unique needs, and increasing local autonomy and speed of response.

Five kinds of data are relevant to computation services: (1) The most powerful computer service in the university is informal advice and help exchanged among electronic and physically proximate neighbors. (2) Face-to-face contact is an essential element of this informal system; that is, the electronic network does not function as a one-to-one substitute for face-to-face interaction. (3) Social networks are the way people find informal advice and help. (4) Experts and novices display similar help-seeking and help-giving behaviors. All experts are novices in some areas and in these areas they behave just like people who have never used a computer (Borenstein, 1986). (5) Secretaries and other support staff are significant participants in the informal service process. Many have developed considerable computing skill, which they use to help faculty and students.

In order to encourage the development of people's own competence and social responsibility while at the same time providing what is needed to conduct first-class research, two principles should guide computation service resource allocation and management, leverage and linking. Leverage means that computation center staff emphasize services that increase the broad distribution of expertise and make it possible for people to help each other learn and use new systems. Linking means that computation center staff provide easy ways for people to find other people who can help and give advice, that is, to build a self-service social network in informal computing services. These ideas lead to the following policy recommendations:

1. Provide an on-line directory or data base of staff and volunteers who have expertise in different areas, including their university position and computer address (and telephone numbers if they are Computation Center consultants). The directory should be designed for network or keyword searches. The directory should be accessible using functional and organizational categories (such as "teaching," and "preparing documents"), not just hardware and software categories (such as "Macintosh" or "Emacs").
2. Make it easy for groups to create and maintain bulletin boards for exchanging helpful information electronically. For example, there should be BBoards or distribution lists for secretaries and for teachers using computers in courses.
3. Assign computation center consultants to the field, that is, to work in close physical proximity to people in departments on campus. These field workers would serve as trainers and as ombudsmen in computation services.
4. Provide incentives and role models for developing and sharing expertise. Staff should be compensated for their computing skills, responsibilities, and contributions, not just for the traditional skills and requirements. Students, faculty, and staff who develop useful software and who help others should be recognized and rewarded with, for example, extra computing resources.
5. Make the computer store a complete service center for computers on campus. Make it easy for people to find experts who can repair their computers. Make it easy to meet and learn from repair and maintenance staff.
6. Provide detailed, deeper, more functionally job-related computer education for secretaries. The courses should be taught by secretaries or by secretarial consultants. Provide incentives for departments to provide released-time for staff to attend these courses.

As a final illustration of policy development, let's return to the issue of communication. We cannot legislate that computers will foster community, but we can design systems and make policy according to a general principle that says community is important. So we have proposed the following at CMU:

1. Make a commitment to develop and support group communication. We mean by this that easy distribution list mechanisms and versatile electronic bulletin board mechanisms need to be developed. Anyone should be able to create an electronic group easily.
2. Give people the ability to "talk" on-line. This is a capability that is useful to people working on group projects, to people giving and receiving tutoring, to people who need computing help, and to friends.
3. Acquire or develop computer conference facilities.
4. Support and develop extra-university communication through national and international networks. Support access to external on-line information sources.
5. Make it as easy to find people on the computer network as it is to find people in the telephone network. Make social locator programs (such as Finger, which is described in Chapter 5) completely machine independent. Install on-line directories of people's names, offices, telephone numbers and computer addresses, and of group communication names and addresses.
6. Make useful news and data available to everyone through the computer network. Examples of news: campus calendar, examination schedules, classroom and course changes, snow emergencies, intramural sports schedules. Examples of data: the library catalog, citation indices, requirements of each college major, course evaluations, varsity sports scores.

7. Actively encourage the creation of electronic forums. Provide technical assistance to establish an on-line counseling service and student advising. Experiment with electronic events, e.g., debates, teach-ins, discussion groups.

8. Offer strong incentives to departments to connect departmental networks to the university network. For example, connections and computing on the university network should be provided at no cost, and important university business should be conducted over the network.

We have argued that our networks will link us with thousands of people inside and outside CMU. Hence the social environment of computing will be important. Few people say it, but many act as though computing has nothing to do with the social environment. People are not alone when they use a computer network! Beneficial social behavior in the computer network includes timely advice or research suggestions offered through computer bulletin boards. Undesirable behavior includes infringements of privacy, junk mail, and file break-ins.

How does the design of a computer network affect the desirability of behavior? We have shown that when people use a computer network, they feel relatively self-centered, anonymous and less concerned with others, and act without inhibition (in comparison to their face-to-face behavior with others) (Kiesler, Siegel, & McGuire, 1984). When people are not identified by name or when they use an alias, these tendencies are reinforced (e.g., Diener, Fraser, Beaman, & Kelem, 1976). These tendencies can be mitigated by design and policy decisions.

1. Make computer IDs people's full names, not initials, integers, or aliases.

2. Make identified behavior the default. If people are identified, they will sanction one another and there will be little need for a computer "police force" to monitor users of the system. If individuals violate community standards, the normal channels for dealing with academic violations should be used. (Of course, some exceptions will be appropriate, as in confidential counseling services.) Another advantage of identified behavior is that a real crime can be punished by examining the electronic records.

3. Encourage disclosure to be the norm. A sense of community is increased if people can find out who other people are. Encourage use of plan files.

4. Provide role models and incentives for students to act responsibly. Faculty and staff should visibly conduct business within the computing environment. Students (and others) should be rewarded for developing software, finding bugs, and offering helpful suggestions to users. Students should be trained and employed as computer service representatives and consultants.

5. Actively encourage participation by all segments of the population.

There are many actions we can take to turn the technical capabilities of computer systems to the advantage of organizational goals. In discussing policy, our intentions are not to complain that these actions are not taking place, but to endorse their importance. Today we can perform more technical miracles with computers, but real organizational leverage will come from asking what social miracles we perform with them.

CMU, among other universities, has been gaining experience with all facets of computer technology for two decades and can claim increasing success. Presumably, institutions that have experimented less successfully in this direction directed their resources in other directions. Within CMU, the same process operates. People and subunits are rewarded for success in computer-oriented programs such as artificial intelligence; the best of these will increase their participation. Those who feel uncomfortable in this environment take other initiatives. For the present, CMU's affair with computers is successful, but more important is its attitude about experimentation. Inevitably, the environment of organizations changes and organizations need to adapt to this change. To guard against inflexibility, a mix of new solutions, independent of computing, should be fostered and vigorously protected. In ten years, perhaps we will write a book about CMU's revolution in the arts.

References

Abelson, R. P. (1982). Three modes of attitude-behavior consistency. In Zanna, Mark P., Higgins, E. Tory, and Herman, C. Peter (Eds.), *Consistency in social behavior: The Ontario symposium* (pp. 131–146). Hillsdale, NJ: Lawrence Erlbaum Associates.

Ajzen, I., & Fishbein, M. (1980). *Understanding attitudes and predicting behaviors.* Englewood Cliffs, NJ: Prentice-Hall.

Amick, B., & Damron, J. (1984). Considerations in defining office automation: A case study of the world bank–Eastern Africa region, Washington, D. C. Paper presented at the Symposium on Human–Computer Interaction meeting of the International Commission on Human Aspects in Computing, Honolulu, Hawaii.

Anderson, R. E., Hassen, T., Johnson, D. C., & Klassen, D. L. (1979). Instructional computing: Acceptance and rejection by secondary school teachers. *Sociology of Work and Occupations, 6,* 227–250.

Arndt, S., Feltes, J., & Hanak, J. (1983). Secretarial attitudes towards word processors as a function of familiarity and locus of control. *Behavior and Information Technology, 2*(1), 17–22.

Bandura, A. (1977). Self-efficacy: Toward a unifying theory of behavior change. *Psychological Bulletin, 84,* 191–215.

Bareff, M. L., and Galbraith, J. R. (1978). Interorganizational power considerations for designing information systems. *Accounting, Organizations and Society, 3,* 15–27.

Beniger, J. R. (1983). Does television enhance the shared symbolic environment? Trends in labeling of editorial cartoons, 1948–1980. *American Sociological Review, 48,* 103–111.

Bikson, T. K., & Gutek, B. A. (1983). *Advanced office systems: An empirical look at utilization and satisfaction.* Santa Monica, CA: The Rand Corp.

Bikson, T. K., Gutek, B. A., & Mankin, D. A. (1981). *Implementation of information technology in office settings: Review of relevant literature.* Santa Monica, CA: Rand Corporation.

Black, J., & Moran, T. (1982). Learning and remembering command names. Paper presented at the Human Factors in Computer Systems meeting of the Association for Computing Machinery, Washington, D. C.

Boguslaw, R. (1981). *The new utopians.* New York: Irvington Publishers.

237

Boli, J., Allen, M. L., & Payne, A. (1985). High-ability women and men in undergraduate mathematics and chemistry courses. *American Educational Research Journal,* *22*(4), 605–626.

Borenstein, N. (1986). *The design and evaluation of on-line help systems.* Pittsburgh, PA: Carnegie Mellon University.

Braverman, H. (1974). *Labor and monopoly capital: The degradation of work in the twentieth century.* New York: Monthly Review.

Brockner, J. (1979). The effects of self-esteem, success-failure, and self-consciousness on task performance. *Journal of Personality and Social Psychology, 37,* 1732–1741.

Burnham, D. (1983). *The rise of the computer state.* New York: Random House.

Bury, K., Boyle, J., Evey, J., & Neal, A. (1982). Windowing vs. scrolling on a visual display terminal. Paper presented at the Human Factors in Computer Systems meeting of the Association for Computing Machinery. Washington, D.C.

Byrnes, F. C. (1966). Role shock: An occupational hazard of American technical assistants abroad. *The Annals, 368,* 95–108.

Caporael, L. (1985). College students' computer use. *Journal of Higher Education, 56,* 172–188.

Carnegie Mellon University. (1984). *Undergraduate catalog 1984–86.*

Carnegie Mellon University. (1986). *Distributed personal computing environment.* University Relations. Pittsburgh, PA.

Carver, C. S., Blaney, P. H., & Scheier, M. F. (1979). Reassertion and giving up: The interactive role of self-directed attention and outcome expectancy. *Journal of Personality and Social Psychology, 37,* 1859–1870.

Carver, C. S., & Scheier, M. F. (1982). Control theory: A useful conceptual framework for personality – social, clinical, and health psychology. *Psychological Bulletin, 92,* 111–135.

Chen, M. (1985, October). Gender and computers: The beneficial effects of experience on attitudes. Paper presented at the conference on Computers & Children, University of Michigan.

Chen, M. (1986). Social equity and computers in education. Proceedings of the International Communication Association Conference, Chicago, IL.

Church, A. T. (1982). Sojourner adjustment. *Psychological Bulletin, 91,* 540–572.

Cohen, M., March. J., & Olsen, J. (1972). A garbage-can model of decision making. *Administrative Science Quarterly, 26,* 171–186.

Cohen, S., Sherrod, D. R., & Clark, M. S. (1985). *Personality and the stress-protective role of social support.* Carnegie Mellon University Department of Psychology, Pittsburgh, PA.

Crawford, A. B. (1982). Corporate electronic mail – A communication-intensive application of information technology. *Management Information Science Quarterly, 6,* 1–14.

Cyert, R. M. (1981). Charge to the Task Force. *Task Force for the Future of Computing at CMU*. Pittsburgh, PA: Carnegie Mellon University.

Cyert, R. M., & March, J. G. (1963). *A behavioral theory of the firm*. Englewood Cliffs, NJ: Prentice-Hall.

Daft, R. L., & Becker, S. W. (1978). *The innovative organization*. New York: Elsevier.

Danziger, J. N. (1985). Social science and the social impacts of computer technology. *Social Science Quarterly, 66*, 3–21.

Danziger, J. N., Dutton, W. H., Kling, R., & Kraemer, K. L. (1982). *Computers and politics*. New York: Columbia University Press.

David, K. H. (1971). Culture shock and the development of self-awareness. *Journal of Contemporary Psychotherapy, 4*, 44–48.

Dawes, R. M., & Smith, T. L. (1985). Attitude and opinion measurement. In Lindzey, G., & Aronson, E. (Eds.), *The handbook of social psychology* (pp. 509–566). New York: Random House.

DeYoung, G., Kampen, G., & Topolski, J. (1982). Analyzer-generated and human-judged predictors of computer program readability. Paper presented at the Human Factors in Computer Systems meeting of the Association for Computing Machinery. Washington, D.C.

Diener, E., Fraser, S., Beaman, A., & Kelem, R. (1976). Effects of deindividuating variables on stealing by Halloween trick-or-treaters. *Journal of Personality and Social Psychology, 33* (Bibliography B), 178–183.

Downs, A. (1967, September). A realistic look at the final payoffs from urban datasystems. *Public Administration Review*, pp. 204–210.

Drabek, T. E., & Haas, J. E. (1976). *Understanding complex organizations*. Dubuque, IA: Brown.

Dutton, W. H. (1981). The rejection of an innovation: The political environment of a computer-based model. *Systems, Objectives, Solutions, 1*, 179–201.

Ellul, J. (1964). *The technological society*. New York: Vintage Books.

Fazio, R. H., & Zanna, M. P. (1978). Attitudinal qualities relating to the strength of the attitude-behavior relationship. *Journal of Experimental Social Psychology, 14*, 398–407.

Feldberg, R., & Glenn, E. (1983). Technology and work degradation: Effects of office automation on women clerical workers. In J. Rothschild (Ed.), *Machina ex dea: Feminist perspectives on technology* (pp. 59–78). New York: Pergamon Press.

Feldman, K. A. (1972). Difficulties in measuring and interpreting change and stability during college. In K. A. Feldman (Ed.), *College and student* (pp. 127–142). New York: Pergamon Press.

Feldman, K. A., & Newcomb, T. (1969). *The impact of college on students*. San Francisco: Jossey-Bass.

Feldman, M., & March, J. G. (1981). Information in organizations as signal and symbol. *Administrative Science Quarterly, 26*, 171–186.

Felter, M. (1985). Sex differences on the California statewide assessment of computer literacy. *Sex Roles, 13* (3/4), 181–191.

Festinger, L. (1961). The psychological effects of insufficient reward. *American Psychologist, 16*, 1–12.

Franz, C. R., & Robey, D. (1984). An investigation of user-led system design: Rational and political perspectives. *Communications of the ACM, 17*, 1202–1209.

Gamst, F., & Horbeck, E. (Eds.) (1976). *Ideas of culture: Sources & uses.* New York: Holt, Rinehart & Winston.

Gans, H. J. (1980). *Deciding what's news.* New York: Random House.

Giovengo, A. (1983). *Office staffs and computers.* Unpublished manuscript. Pittsburgh, PA: Carnegie Mellon University.

Glenn, E., & Feldberg, R. (1977). Degraded and deskilled: The proletarianization of clerical work. *Social Problems, 25*, 52–64.

Goffman, E. (1961). *Asylums.* Garden City, NY: Anchor Books.

Goodenough, W. H. (1970). *Description and comparison in cultural anthropology.* Chicago: Aldine.

Gunnarsson, E. (1984). The impact of organizational factors on visual strain in clerical VDT work. In B. G. Cohen (Ed.), *Human aspects in office automation* (pp. 43–61). Amsterdam: Elsevier.

Hawkins, J., Sheingold, K., Gearhart, M., & Berger, C. (1982). Microcomputers in schools: Impact on the social life of elementary classrooms. *Journal of Applied Developmental Psychology, 3*, 361–373.

Hess, R. D., & Miura, I. (1985). Gender and socioeconomic differences in enrollment in computer camps and classes. *Sex Roles, 13*, (3/4), 193–203.

Higbee, H. (1969). Role shock – A new concept. *International Educational and Cultural Exchange, 4*, 71–81.

Kanfer, F. H., & Hagerman, S. (1981). The role of self-regulation. In L. P. Rehm (Ed.), *Behavior therapy for depression: Present status and future directions.* New York: Academic Press.

Kanter, R. (1977). *Men and women of the corporation.* New York: Basic Books.

Kerlinger, F. N., & Pedhazur, E. G. (1973). *Multiple regression in behavioral research.* New York: Holt, Rinehart & Winston.

Kidder, T. (1981). *The soul of a new machine.* New York: Avon Books.

Kiesler, S., Siegel, J., & McGuire, T. (1984). Social psychological aspects of computer-mediated communication. *American Psychologist, 39*, 1123–1134.

Kiesler, S., Sproull, L., & Eccles, J. (1985). Poolhalls, chips, and war games: Women in the culture of computing. *Psychology of Women Quarterly, 9*, 451–462.

King, J. L., & Kraemer, K. L. (1984). Evolution and organizational information systems: An assessment of Nolan's stage mode. *Communications of the ACM, 27*, 466–475.

Kling, R. (1980). Social analyses of computing: Theoretical perspectives in recent empirical research. *Computing Surveys, 12*, 61–110.

Kling, R., & Scacchi, W. (1979). Recurrent dilemmas of computer use in complex organizations. Paper presented at the National Computer conference meeting of the AFIPS.

Kling R., & Scacchi, W. (1980). *Computing as social action: The social dynamics of computing in complex organizations.* New York: Academic Press.

Kling, R., & Scacchi, W. (1982). The web of computing: Computer technology as social organization. *Advances in Computers, 21*, 1–90.

Kotlowitz, A. (September 16, 1985). The computer-generated gap. *Wall Street Journal*, p. 48.

Kraemer, K. L. (1982). Computer models in urban policy making. Paper presented at the Second Annual Symposium on Information Processing in Organizations, Carnegie Mellon University, Pittsburgh, PA.

Kraft, P. (1984). A review of empirical studies of the consequences of technological change on work and workers in the United States. Paper presented at the Committee on Women's Employment and Related Social Issues meeting of the National Research Council.

Lawler, E. (1971). *Pay and organizational effectiveness: A psychological view.* New York: McGraw-Hill.

Lepper, M. R. (1985). Microcomputers in education: Motivational and social issues. *American Psychologist, 40*, 1–18.

Levy, S. (1982, April). A beautiful obsession with the binary world. *Rolling Stone*, pp. 42–51.

Lindblom, C. E. (1958). The science of muddling through. *Public Administration Review, 19*, 79–88.

Linn, M. C. (1985). Gender equity in computer learning environments. *Computers and the Social Sciences, 1*, 19–27.

Lockheed, E. B., Nielsen, A., & Stone, M. (1983). Sex differences in microcomputer literacy. *Proceedings of the National Educational Computing Conference, 5*, 372–376.

Louis, M. (1980). Surprise and sense making: What newcomers experience in entering unfamiliar organizational settings. *Administrative Science Quarterly, 25*, 226–251.

Loyd, B. H., & Gressard, C. (1984). The effects of sex, age, and computer experience on computer attitudes. *AEDS Journal, 18*(2), 67–77.

Lucas, H. D., Jr. (1982). *Information systems concepts for management.* New York: McGraw-Hill.

McCorduck, P. (1979). *Machines who think.* San Francisco: N. H. Freeman.

McFarlan, F. W., & McKenney, J. C. (1983). *Corporate information systems management.* Homewood, IL: Richard D. Irwin.

Machung, A. (1983). Turning secretaries into word processors: Some fiction and a fact or two. In D. Marschall & J. Gregory (Eds.), *Office automation: Jekyll or Hyde?* (pp. 119–123). Cleveland, OH: Working Women Education Fund.

McLaren, R. I. (1982). *Organizational dilemmas.* New York: Wiley.

March, J. G. (1981). Footnotes to organizational change. *Administrative Science Quarterly, 26,* 563–577.

Markus, M. L. (1983). Power, politics and MIS implementation. *Communications of the ACM, 26,* 430–444.

Marvin, C., & Winther, M. (1983). Computer-ease: A twentieth century literary emergent. *Journal of Communications, 33,* 92–108.

Merton, R., & Rossi, A. (1968). Contributions to the theory of reference group behavior. In R. Merton (Ed.), *Social Theory and Social Structure* (pp. 279–334). New York: Free Press.

Meyer, J. N., & Rowan, B. (1977). Institutionalized organizations: Formal structure as myth and ceremony. *American Journal of Sociology, 83,* 340–363.

Mintzberg, H. (1979). *The structuring of organizations.* Englewood Cliffs, NJ: Prentice-Hall.

Mowshowitz, A. (1981). On approaches to the study of social issues in computing. *Communications of the ACM, 24,* 146–155.

Nelson, R. R., & Winter, S. G. (1974). Neoclassical vs. evolutionary theories of economic growth: Critique and prospectus. *Economic Journal, 84,* 886–905.

Novak, C. L. (1982, March). 1989 or half an hour in a small dorm room. *Focus,* Carnegie Mellon University.

Nyce, H. E., & Groppa, R. (1983, May). Electronic mail at MIT. *Management Technology,* 65–72.

Oberg, K. (1966). Cultural shock: Adjustment to new cultural environments. *Practical Anthropology, 7,* 177–182.

Ogdin, C. A. (1982, November). The software ergonomics. Software Technique, Inc., Alexandria, VA.

O'Reilly, C. A., & Pondy, L. R. (1979). Organizational communication. In Stephen Kerr (Ed.), *Organizational behavior* (pp. 119–150). Columbus, OH: Grid Publishing Company.

Papert, S. (1979). Computers and learning. In M. L. Dertouzos & J. Moses (Eds.), *The computer age: A twenty-year view* (pp. 73–86). Cambridge, MA: The MIT Press.

Perrow, C. (1970). *Organizational analysis: A sociological view.* Belmont, CA: Brooks/Cole.

Pfeffer, J. (1981). Management as symbolic action: The creation and maintenance of organizational paradigms. *Research in Organizational Behavior, 3*, 1–52.

Robey, D., & Markus, J. L. (1984, March). Rituals in information system design. *MIS Quarterly*, 5–15.

Rogers, E. M., & Shoemaker, F. F. (1971). *Communication of innovations.* New York: Free Press.

Rouvalis, C. (Jan 6, 1986). Software for girls. *Pittsburgh Post Gazette*, p. 26.

Schneider, M. L., Nudelman, S., & Hirsh-Pasek, K. (1982). An analysis of line numbering strategies in text editors. Paper presented at the of Human Factors in Computer Systems Meeting of the Association for Computing Machinery. Washington, D.C.

Sears, D. O., Hensler, C. P., & Speer, L. K. (1979). Whites' opposition to "busing": Self-interest or symbolic politics? *The American Political Review*, 73, 369-384.

Shapiro, N. Z., & Anderson, R. N. (1985). Toward an ethics and etiquette for electronic mail. Santa Monica, CA: The Rand Corporation.

Sheil, B. A. (1981). *Coping with complexity.* Palo Alto: Xerox PARC.

Sheposh, J. P., Hulton, V. N., Ramras-Berlin, S., & Trinh, T. (1985). *Implementation of multifunction information systems at three Navy facilities* (Report No. NPRDC TR 85-17). San Diego, CA: Navy Personnel Research and Development Center.

Shields, M. (1986). Computing at Brown – an ongoing study. *Perspectives in Computing, 6*(2), 57–62.

Simon, H. A. (1977). *The new science of management decision.* Englewood Cliffs, NJ: Prentice-Hall.

Smalley, W. A. (1963). Culture shock, language shock, and the shock of self-discovery. *Practical Anthropology, 10*, 49–56.

Snyder, M., & Swann. W., Jr. (1976). When actions reflect attitudes: The politics of impression management. *Journal of Personality and Social Psychology, 34*, 1034–1042.

Sproull, L. (1986). *Social aspects of computing at CMU.* Unpublished manuscript, Carnegie Mellon University, Pittsburgh.

Sproull, L., & Kiesler, S. (1986). Reducing social context cues: electronic mail in organizational communication. *Management Science, 32*, 1492–1512.

Sproull, L., & Sproull, R. (1982). Managing & analyzing behavioral records: Explorations in non-numeric data analysis. *Human Organization, 41*, 283–290.

Sproull, L., Kiesler, S., & Zubrow, D. (1984). Encountering an alien culture. *Journal of Social Issues, 40*(3), 31–48.

Sproull, L., Zubrow, D., & Kiesler, S. (1985). *Socialization to computing in college.* Carnegie Mellon University.

Steele, G. L., Jr., Woods, D. R., Finkel, R. A., Crispin, M. R., Stallman, R. M., & Goodfellow, G. S. (1983). *The hackers dictionary.* New York: Harper & Row.

Stilgoe, J. R. (1983). *Metropolitan corridor.* New Haven, CT: Yale University Press.

Sudman, S., & Bradburn, N. (1982). *Asking questions.* San Francisco: Jossey-Bass.

Taylor, R. P. (Ed.). (1980). *The computer in the school.* New York: Teachers College Press.

Thompson, S. C. (1981). Will it hurt less if I can control it? A complex answer to a simple question. *Psychological Bulletin, 90,* 89–101.

Times of London, December 27, 1905.

Trebig, J. G. (1985). The take-off company: Self-management and flexible structure. In Smilor, R. W., & Kuhn, R. L. (Eds.), *Managing take-off in fast growth companies* (pp. 3–18). New York: Praeger.

Turkle, S. (1980). Computer as Rorschach. *Society,* pp. 15–24.

University Libraries. (1982a). *An electronic information system for an academic library: A model.* Pittsburgh, PA: Carnegie Mellon University Libraries.

University Libraries. (1982b). *Annual report 1981–1982.* Pittsburgh, PA: Carnegie Mellon University.

Updegrove, D. A. (1986). Computer-intensive campuses: Strategies, plans, implications. *Educom Bulletin, 21,* 11–14.

Van de Ven, A. H. (1986). Central problems in the management of innovation. *Management Science, 32*(5), 590–607.

Van Horn, R. L. (1981, November 15). A day with a live–in computer. *New York Times.*

van Maanen, J., & Schein, E. (1979). Toward a theory of organizational socialization. In Barry Staw (Ed.), *Research in organizational behavior, 1,* (pp. 209–264). Greenwich, CT: JAI Press.

Wall Street Journal (January 12, 1983). Some chief executives bypass, and irk, staffs in getting information.

Wildavsky, A. (1983). Information as an organizational problem. *Journal of Management Studies, 20*(1), 29–40.

Wilder, G., Mackie, D., & Cooper, J. (1985). Gender and computers: Two surveys of computer-related attitudes. *Sex Roles, 13*(3/4), 215–228.

Winer, B. J. (1971). *Statistical principles in experimental design,* 2nd ed. New York: McGraw-Hill.

Zimbardo, P. G. (Ed.). (1980, August). The hacker papers. *Psychology Today*, pp. 62–74.

Zucker, L. G. (1977). The role of institutionalization in cultural persistence. *American Sociological Review*, *42*, 726–743.

Author Index

247

Subject Index

access to computing, 45–8, 51, 58, 60, 71, 82,
90–2, 96, 100, 126, 129, 136–7, 142, 166,
175, 209, 218–9, 231–2
  distribution of, 43, 60, 138–9
administrators, *see* managers
adolescent, 21, 175
ambition: of secretaries, 126–7
  of students, 214, 220
anxiety, 2, 11, 116, 174, 177–9, 181–2, 190–1,
213–4, 231
applications, 48, 72, 95, 97–9
  see also intended change; uses of computing
artifact(s), 12, 152–3, 175
artificial intelligence, 2, 5, 13–4, 26
  see also knowledge
attention, change in, 34, 104–7, 145, 227–8
  effect of railroad on, 34
  self-concept as, 14–5
attitude(s) about computing, 7, 11, 30, 38, 41,
90–1, 121–2, 140, 155–6, 162–5, 181–5,
191–3, 195–209, 214
  correlation with use, 155, 162–4, 199–206,
218
  discipline differences in, 96–8, 196,
199–200, 205–6
  effect of organization, 114
  of faculty, 91–4, 99
  gender differences in, 98, 100, 183–5,
195–6, 199–200, 203, 205–6, 207–8
  of library workers, 139–40
  of managers, 152, 156, 161–5, 167
  negative, 11, 109, 121–2, 157, 163, 168, 178,
181, 188, 213
  of secretaries, 121–2, 128
  of students, 91–4, 99, 181–5, 191–3,
195–209, 213–7
  see also zeal
attitudes, measurement of, 42, 155, 157–8,
179–80, 197–8, 213, 217

BBoards, 35–6, 51, 66, 228
  see also communication; uses of computing
budget (funds), 28, 31, 38, 39, 143, 227
  see also resources

Carnegie Mellon University, 10, 23, 37–40,
153–4, 158, 185, 194, 218–9
  as an experimenting organization, 227, 235
  importance of computing at, 37, 43, 44, 217,
226
centralization (decentralization), *see* reor-
ganization
change, forecasting, 4–7, 18
change, management of, 7, 21, 33, 38–9, 52–4,
60–1, 70, 139–40, 151, 153–4, 165, 177,
230
  attention to, 28, 101, 137, 143, 161–2, 174,
229
  hiring in, 139
  incentives in, 38, 59–60, 141, 161–2
  intentions in, 152
  support of change, 28–30, 132
  technical solutions in, 151
  see also managers; change, process of
change, process of, 28–33
  chaos in, 28, 132, 135, 137, 140, 167
  competence–multipliers, 32, 39, 59–60, 135,
137–8, 152
  as entrepreneurship, 38, 231
  as experimentation, 12–3, 28, 235
  mutual transformation, 32, 40, 132, 135–8,
226
  organizational conditions for, 28–30, 131–2,
229–30
  routine-driven change, 31–2, 39, 58,
197–208
  solution-driven, 32, 40, 60, 101, 132
  see also change, management of; managers
change (effect[s]), intended, 5, 16, 18, 20, 33,
43–4, 226
  in library, 133–5, 139, 143
  by managers, 20, 70, 161
  technical, 33, 133–5, 136–7, 147, 151, 229
change (effect[s]), unintended, xii, 18, 32,
33–4, 124, 133–4, 226
  and distribution of resources, 43
  as enduring effect, xiii, 148
  as indirect effect, 9–10, 18, 42
  as problem, 24, 33, 114, 135, 159, 167, 194
  as social effect, 28, 33–7, 43

250

Colophon

In keeping with the spirit of computing on campus (for better or for worse), this book was entirely, with the exception of the photographs, digitally typeset at CMU by Mike Blackwell and the Committee on Social Science Research in Computing.

The text and tables were set with the aid of the Scribe Document Production System running on a campus mainframe. Figures were created with Spoof, a Unix plotting program developed at CMU, and with Cricket Draw, a drawing program running on an Apple Macintosh. The figures were then automatically inserted into the text by Scribe. Scribe, Spoof, and Cricket Draw all produce output in the PostScript page description language.

The resulting PostScript files were first printed on an Apple LaserWriter, a 300 dot per inch laser printer, for proofing. The final copy was printed from the same PostScript files on a Linotype Linotron-300, a 2500 dot per inch digital photo typesetter. This output was delivered, camera ready, to Cambridge University Press.

Adobe's Times Roman typeface family was used throughout for all body type. The chapter titles and author names are in Adobe's New Century Schoolbook. Adobe's Symbol font was also used.